INCULTURATION OF CHRISTIAN WORSHIP

Inculturation – the creative and dynamic relationship between the Christian message and culture or cultures – is of interest to many churches throughout the world, particularly since the Second Vatican Council made it part of the Roman Catholic agenda.

This book looks at the question of the inculturation of Christian worship, particularly in the Eucharist. Looking at the relationship of worship and culture requires insights from both theology and anthropology; Tovey develops the tools to interconnect perspectives into an interdisciplinary exploration of different models of inculturation.

Inculturation of Christian Worship is both interdisciplinary and ecumenical in approach. Case studies are drawn from the Ethiopian Orthodox Church, African Independent Churches, The Roman Catholic Church and the Anglican Communion. While there is a focus on Africa for particular examples, the issues are discussed in a world wide context.

LITURGY, WORSHIP AND SOCIETY

SERIES EDITORS

Dave Leal, Brasenose College, Oxford, UK
Bryan Spinks, Yale Divinity School, USA
Paul Bradshaw, University of Notre Dame, UK and USA
Gregory W. Woolfenden, Ripon College, Cuddesdon, Oxford, UK
Phillip Tovey, Diocese of Oxford and Oxford Brookes University, UK

This new series comes at a time of great change in liturgy and much debate concerning traditional and new forms of worship, the suitability and use of places of worship, and wider issues concerning the interaction of liturgy, worship and contemporary society. Offering a thorough grounding in the historical and theological foundations of liturgy, books in the series explore and challenge many key issues of worship and liturgical theology which are currently in hot debate – issues set to make a significant impact on the place of the church in contemporary society. Presenting an ecumenical range of books, comparing and contrasting liturgical practices and concerns within various traditions and faiths, this series will appeal to those in university and theological colleges; adult education colleges; those on other ministry or lay ministry training courses; and practitioners and those involved in worship in churches across a broad ecumenical range.

Other titles in the series include

Death Liturgy and Ritual
Volume I: A Pastoral and Liturgical Theology
Volume II: A Commentary on Liturgical Texts
Paul P.J. Sheppy

West Syrian Liturgical Theology
Baby Varghese

Daily Liturgical Prayer
Origins and Theology
Gregory W. Woolfenden

Rituals and Theologies of Christian Baptism:
Beyond the Jordan
Bryan D. Spinks

Inculturation of Christian Worship

Exploring the Eucharist

PHILLIP TOVEY

LONDON AND NEW YORK

First published 2004 by Ashgate Publishing

Reissued 2019 by Routledge
2 Park Square, Milton Park, Abingdon, Oxon OX14 4RN
52 Vanderbilt Avenue, New York, NY 10017

Routledge is an imprint of the Taylor & Francis Group, an informa business

Copyright © Phillip Tovey 2004

The author has asserted his moral right under the Copyright, Design and Patents Act, 1988, to be identified as the author of this work.

All rights reserved. No part of this book may be reprinted or reproduced or utilised in any form or by any electronic, mechanical, or other means, now known or hereafter invented, including photocopying and recording, or in any information storage or retrieval system, without permission in writing from the publishers.

Notice:
Product or corporate names may be trademarks or registered trademarks, and are used only for identification and explanation without intent to infringe.

Publisher's Note
The publisher has gone to great lengths to ensure the quality of this reprint but points out that some imperfections in the original copies may be apparent.

Disclaimer
The publisher has made every effort to trace copyright holders and welcomes correspondence from those they have been unable to contact.

Typeset in Times New Roman by SetSystems Ltd, Saffron Walden, Essex

A Library of Congress record exists under LC control number:

ISBN 13: 978-0-8153-8970-5 (hbk)
ISBN 13: 978-1-138-35611-5 (pbk)
ISBN 13: 978-0-429-19941-7 (ebk)

My thanks go to the staff and students of Archbishop Janani
Luwum Theological College, Douglas Davies, Michael Vasey,
Geoff Morgan, members of the Ashgate editorial board,
other friends, and family who have been an encouragement
in the writing of this book.

Contents

List of Figures		ix
1	Introduction	1
	Definitions	1
	A Map	4
	The Next Steps	7
2	Theology of Symbol	8
	Paul Tillich	8
	Louis-Marie Chauvet	15
	Alexander Schmemann	22
	Theological Approaches to Symbol	29
3	Anthropology and Symbol	33
	Anthropological Approaches	33
	Orectic Issues	43
	Ideological Issues	47
	Anthropology and Inculturation	55
4	The Ethiopian Orthodox Church	56
	The Integration of Symbol Systems	56
	The Ethiopian Orthodox Eucharist: A Symbolic Analysis	61
	The Numinous and the Eucharist	75
5	African Independent Churches	79
	The Church of the Lord (Aladura)	81
	The Cherubim and Seraphim	89
	The Kimbanguist Church	96
	African Independent Churches: Adaptations to Africa	103
6	The Roman Catholic Church	107
	The Roman Catholic Church and African Culture	109
	The Second Vatican Council	112
	Post-Conciliar Policies	119
	Roman Catholic Inculturation	124
	The Roman Catholic Church's Struggle with Inculturation	129

7	Anglicanism	130
	Developing Policy	132
	Inculturated Rites	139
	Anglican Struggles with Inculturation	149
8	Inculturation and Liturgical Theology	150
	Liturgical Theology	151
	Learning from Experience	153
	Theological Reflection	156
	Inculturation	160
Works Cited		163
Name Index		173

Figures

1.1	Inculturation map	4
2.1	Market exchange	17
2.2	Symbolic exchange	18
2.3	The eucharistic process	19
2.4	The objectivist model	19
2.5	The subjectivist model	20
2.6	The Vatican 2 model	20
4.1	The ritual process	72
8.1	Kolb's learning cycle	154
8.2	Boud, Keogh & Walker's learning cycle	155
8.3	Green's model of theological reflection	158

CHAPTER 1

Introduction

This book has been a long time in writing. It began with two years of the teaching of liturgy in Uganda. Inculturation was on the syllabus and in the first year I refused to teach it. Uganda was a troubled land at that time (cf. The Minority Rights Group, 1989) and I felt too green to teach about cultural issues, particularly when I was going through my own culture shock. However, I began to look around and talk to other teachers, which led to a brief experiment in the college with an inculturated rite (Diocese of Northern Uganda, 1985). Unfortunately the college was burnt down soon after I left and this experiment was discontinued.

Returning to England, I spent two years reflecting on this experience and preparing for ordination, which led to an academic award (Tovey, 1988a) and the publication of a monograph (Tovey, 1988b). There is much that has happened since and while this book is based on the thesis of the award there is considerable rewriting in the light of further reflection, study and experience. Some of the case studies in the original research were literature based. Since that time I have been able to visit Ethiopia, and worship with the Ethiopian Orthodox Church at first hand. I have also been able to supplement this by visiting their congregation in London. Similarly, I was able to visit a congregation of the Cherubim and Seraphim in Birmingham and experience for myself what I had previously only read about. Visits to India have also widened my experience of culture and of inculturation. My story then is one of experience and reflection on experience. This is the methodology of the book and a subject that I will return to.

Definitions

'Inculturation' is a somewhat flexible term. It sits alongside 'adaptation', 'indigenization' and 'contextualization'. Some definitions might be of help at this point to clarify the meaning of the term. Chupungco (1989, p. 29) says:

> Liturgical inculturation may be described as the process whereby the texts and rites used in worship by the local church are so inserted in the framework of culture, that they absorb its thought, language, and ritual patterns. Liturgical inculturation operates according to the dynamics of insertion in a given culture and interior assimilation of cultural elements.

In processes of liturgical change Chupungco differentiates between 'revision', 'adaptation', 'inculturation' and 'creativity'. Arbuckle (1990, p. 17) quoting Azevedo, says: 'inculturation is the "dynamic relation between the Christian message and culture or cultures; an insertion of the Christian life into a culture; an ongoing process of reciprocal and critical interaction and assimilation between them"'.

Shorter (1988, p. 11) looks at it this way: 'A short definition of inculturation is: the on-going dialogue between faith and culture or cultures. More fully, it is the creative and dynamic relationship between the Christian message and a culture or cultures'.

Tovey (1988b, pp. 5–6) said: 'Inculturation is seen as the transformation of the worship of the African Church to make it a more authentic expression of African Christianity ... the process of change by which alienation is destroyed'.

From this can be seen a wider and a narrower focus. At one level inculturation is a part of the Church's missiological imperative. This is the level of the interaction of gospel and culture (Gallagher, 1997). On another level it is the interaction of worship and culture.

Bevans (1998) rejects the term because he thinks that 'contextualization' is better and more inclusive incorporating in it issues of justice. Pieris (1988) is even more critical. He sees the term as based on a culture–religion dichotomy of the Latins. He says it often means (p. 52): 'The insertion of "the Christian religion minus European culture" into an "Asian culture minus non-Christian religion".' Calling this conceptualization inconceivable, he uses other terms such as 'enreligionization'. One of his conclusions is devastating (p. 53): 'Inculturation-fever might appear to be a desperate last-minute bid to given an Asian façade to a church that fails to strike roots in Asian soil because no one dares to break the Greco-Roman pot in which it has been existing for four centuries like a stunted *bonsai*!' He criticizes the lack of social analysis in much inculturation discussion and commends instead a liberation theology approach. This is a forceful attack on the idea of inculturation. He is aware that he might be criticized for relying on a neo-Marxist philosophy in his model of liberation. This is a criticism that Nalunnakkal (1998) raises against Indian leftist analysis in a discussion of Dalit Theology. He points out that the use of class and proletariat has a historic base (in the west) but that in India the basic discrimination is caste based. However, returning to Peiris's metaphor, from a liturgical perspective the whole point is to break the Greco-Roman pot, not to create a façade. This has been done before with the Syrian tradition in China and India, and the Coptic tradition in Egypt and Ethiopia. It may well take experimentation and time, but this does not mean that it is unattainable.

Kavanagh (1990) is also critical of the term 'inculturation'. Taking a historical perspective, he seems to say that it is a truism that liturgy changes with historical cultural change. However, the point of discussion is methodological and in part about not only using historical analysis but also sociological and anthropological critique. Perhaps it is important to hear the testimony of some other people at this point. Leslie Brown said of the changes in Africa in the second half of the last century (Brown, 1965, p. 10):

> With the spread of education even tribal and local cultures in many parts of the world are losing much of their hold on people ... If Christian faith and worship could be indigenised in the new culture, then it might be seen once more as the message of the world ... if Christians accept the new world culture and, while being in it and part of it, try there to live out and think out the gospel, the Spirit, the Interpreter, will enable us to interpret the old images, and find the new ones we need.

Clarke (1985, p. 10) talks of the failure of the Church in India to inculturate:

> Today the Indian Church is sometimes thought of as the carry-over of British Colonialism. The image we have given to the non-Christian world around is the image of the Indian Church being a faithful and true replica of the Western Church and Western Christianity. Christianity in India to the average non-Christian is the religion of the white man and the Indian Christian are followers of the white man's religion.

Here are clear indications of a problem with the cultural form of some expressions of Christianity and Christian worship.

Moving on, there is also a more narrow focus in the use of the term 'inculturation', that of the relationship between culture and worship. In this context 'inculturation' is still a common term (Gitari, 1994; Lumbala, 1998; Francis, 2000). The danger is that any process of change gets included in the term 'inculturation' under the dynamic of the relationship of culture and worship. That would be too wide a focus and thus Chupungco uses a variety of other terms to name some of the other change mechanisms. e.g. 'reform', 'adaptation' and 'creativity'. I have tried to narrow the field by introducing an idea of 'overcoming cultural alienation'. Cleary there could be a long discussion of the precise meaning but at this point I want to use the term to relate to three things, which should be seen as standing together:

- cultural issues to do with worship
- processes of liturgical change
- issues of cultural alienation in worship

Thus the focus is on liturgy and culture (and not confining the word 'liturgy' to a written text).

Clearly the nature of the subject requires an interdisciplinary approach. It requires the identification of alienated and inculturated worship. This is a matter of judgement and debate. Much of this book will thus be taken up with two things:

- developing the conceptual tools to look at inculturation
- examining case studies of inculturation

This will then lead back to the wider debate.

A Map

Various models have been put forward to look at the relationship between gospel and culture. Perhaps the most famous of these is in the work of Niebuhr (1952), which is still useful and will be used later. Bevans (1998) develops five models of contextual theology. I want to adapt this and put forward a six-branched schema at this point to show the breadth of the issue. The models can be illustrated in the following diagram (Figure 1.1):

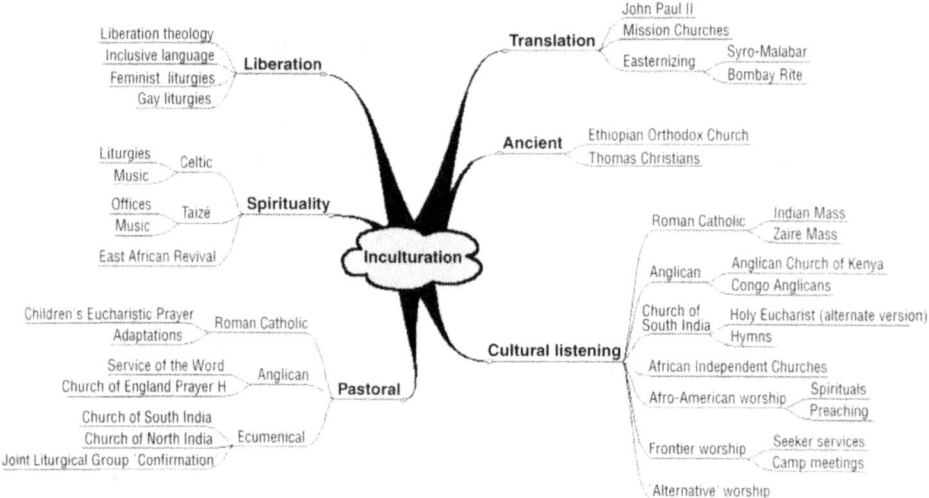

1.1   Inculturation map

This map has four main models: 'translation', 'cultural listening', 'liberation' and 'pastoral'. Two other models intersect with this grid: 'spirituality' and 'ancient'. The secondary arm of each model includes concrete examples of the models. They are not meant to be exhaustive lists; rather they are illustrative and based on my personal interests and experience. A glance at these secondary branches reveals that some aspects begin to connect with a different model, e.g. what I have called Afro-American worship under 'cultural listening' also connects to liberation theology under 'liberation'. Thus the secondary branches are not completely discrete and all bring out different aspects of inculturation. Sometimes a worship event or service book may combine a number of models.

'Translation' of a liturgy can be literally that, e.g. in the production of Books of Common Prayer in the Dioceses of Uganda. This can be done in a variety of ways, but most translators have been faced with critical issues of making services intelligible to a different culture. In the translation model the message or liturgy is the crucial point. There is something to be introduced, e.g. the eucharist, and there are elements of this that must be retained to keep it as a eucharist. Bevans sees the work of John Paul II on inculturation as a translation approach and he rightly points out that there are some good points to this approach, not least the notion of fidelity to the tradition. India has an example of another facet of the translation approach. The Oriental churches, particularly the Syro-Malabar Church have been decontextualized in a process of Romanization (Vellian, 1975). There is a strong group within the Church who are arguing that restoration of the Oriental rite is the most culturally appropriate way of worship for India. A similar argument was put forward by Winslow in 1920 when he adapted the West Syrian liturgy for Anglican use in *Christa Seva Sangha* to make the worship more Indian (Winslow, 1920; CIBC, 1923 in Wigan, 1962). Thus the core of this model is the translation of worship from one culture to another.

The other end of the pole to 'translation' is the model of 'cultural listening'. Here the focus is more on the local culture. As Mission Churches have in the past exported a European liturgy and introduced it to, say, Africa or India, so now these Churches are listening more carefully to local culture to inculturate their liturgy and produce something more appropriate. Here a number of examples can be introduced as they are more conscious attempts at inculturation, e.g. the Indian Mass and The Roman Missal for the Dioceses of Zaire in the Roman Catholic Church (Chupungco, 1989), the Alternate Eucharist in the Church of South India (Clarke, 1985), and the new orders of worship in the Anglican Church of Kenya (Kings & Morgan, 2001) and the new eucharist in the Anglican Province of Congo (Tarrant, 1999). Less conscious efforts of reform have occurred in some African Independent Churches (Turner, 1967, a & b). Likewise, this is a process that has occurred also in Black or Afro-American worship in the States (Pitts, 1993; Cone, 1972) and in the development of Frontier worship (White, 1989). In England the alternative worship movement has seen itself as a process of inculturation, in this case relating to youth culture (Roberts, 1999).

Another model of inculturation is the 'pastoral'. Here the focus is on change for the benefit of the Church itself. It may be that this cannot be separated from the mission emphasis in the other two models, but it was momentum within the Church that led to the revised worship. Thus the cultural change is here internal to the Church. Former patterns and symbols feel tired and a process of revision and renewal is needed. Examples of this are the allowed adaptations in baptismal, marriage and funeral rites in the Roman Catholic Church. The introduction of eucharistic prayers for use with children was another pastorally based change (Johnson, 2001). In the Church of England the Service of the Word was in part introduced in response to *Faith in the City*, which criticized the culture of much Anglican worship (Lloyd, 1990). Worship texts have also developed as a result of the ecumenical movement as in the Church of South India and the Church of North India (Garrett, 1961). In England the new cultural context of Local Ecumenical

Partnerships has required some new worship, e.g. Joint Confirmation (Joint Liturgical Group, 1992).

The last major model of inculturation, 'liberation', comes from the liberation theology movement. This has many excellent advocates, e.g. in Africa (Ela, 1986; Martey, 1993), or in Black Theology (Cone 1986, 1990; Kunnie, 1994), and in Asia (Pieris, 1988). It is not very clear how this has affected worship in much of the world. However, its feminist forms have undoubtedly driven the discussion on inclusive language and feminist communities have developed examples of new worship forms (Winter, 1987). The 'liberation' model has also led to the production of some rituals for gay and lesbian people (Stuart, 1992).

The other two models I include in Figure 1.1 run on a different axis. The first model is 'spirituality'. The British Isles have seen a great interest in Celtic spirituality with the production of service books and songs from places like the Iona Community (Iona Community, 1988) or Lindisfarne (Adam, 1996). Taizé has also been of interest, particularly in its work with young people producing both liturgies and distinct music (Taizé Community, 1998; Berthier, 1982). These two spiritual movements have changed worship in some churches. In East Africa the revival has influenced worship, not least in songs (Robins, 1983). Bevans (1978, p. 97) says that this model is not about producing a body of texts but about the affective and cognitive operations in the subject. A question here might be about the use of the term 'texts' by Bevans. If he is referring to liturgical texts in the narrow sense, then this might be true. If 'texts' are related to hymns, prayers, lives of saints and ethos of worship then the spirituality model can produce significant texts. In Africa the East African Revival has occurred alongside European liturgical texts, e.g. the 1662 *Book of Common Prayer*, but the Revival produced songs, prayer groups and a renewed ethos to the service. Spirituality flows through the issue of inculturation and can subtly alter the way texts – when fixed – feel and operate, and can generate new texts.

This other axis includes a model that I have called 'ancient'. In both African and India there exist ancient Oriental Churches. These are so distinctly different that I have put them as a separate model. In some ways they are inculturated Churches with a venerable history. We have, however, already seen that Romanization deeply infected the Syro-Malabar Church and later missionary work with the West Syrians was to result in a reformation producing the Mar Thoma Syrian Church (Mathew, 1991). The Ethiopian Orthodox Church is both African and unique. Even a Copt coming from Egypt might get lost in the Sunday eucharist in this church. Oriental Churches are distinct because they have a long tradition, they have had to deal with local culture, and have developed their own distinct ethos of worship and spirituality. Their presence raises questions about their place in the current debate over inculturation. Do they provide models to follow and indications of where other Churches might go?

This map was produced after a long process of study and reflection on inculturation. I have introduced it here to show something of the breadth of the subject and to give a wide setting for the debate. This book will not develop to look at all six models and discuss concrete examples. Most of the book will be case studies from the 'ancient' and 'cultural listening' models. It will focus on Africa, but the sub-branches on each model show that the issues relate just as much to western culture, even if in different ways. Indeed, each national Church or Conference is faced more than ever with a multi-cultural world, and with significant cultural subgroups that are asking for cultural consideration in their expression of worship. The schema is included to indicate some of the different processes of change and their motivations, and the complex scope of the issue. Inculturation is a wide-ranging issue with examples from the whole of the Church and Church's history. This is too much for one book. It also needs to be remembered that change itself is more complex and may employ a number of these models at the same time. There may also be other processes than inculturation going on at the same time in a period of liturgical change.

The Next Steps

The next section of the book begins to develop conceptual tools to look at the issue. When using the word 'inculturation' about worship and in particular about the eucharist, a most useful category to use is 'symbol', as this interconnects theology and anthropology. Thus the next two chapters will look at 'symbol' in these two disciplines as an interdisciplinary study. After that it will be possible to go on to examine some case studies from Africa. These are deliberately chosen from a wide selection. Many books on inculturation concentrate on one Church. This one will look at the Ethiopian Orthodox Church, three African Independent Churches, and two Mission Churches. The aim here is to spread the net wide to look at different models of inculturation. Finally conclusions will be arrived at relating the discussion to the debate about liturgical theology. This will be the journey in the next few chapters and through the book. I hope readers enjoy the trip.

CHAPTER 2

Theology of Symbol

Both earlier in the last century in academic circles and in much popular thinking today there is a conceptual opposition between reality and the symbolic. Bevan (1938, p. 296) said: 'We must always go on trying to make our conceptions less symbolic, more precisely correspondent with Reality'. This leads to the common statement 'It is only a symbol'. Symbol and reality are opposed. But this position is being challenged. The work of psychologists, such as Jung, anthropologists, such as Victor Turner and Mary Douglas, of philosophers, not least Susanne Langer, and of theologians such as Paul Tillich, Karl Rahner and Louis-Marie Chauvet has resulted in a re-evaluation of this approach to symbols. In many of the Protestant Churches there has been a rediscovery of the sacraments, and a reorientation towards a positive evaluation of the use of symbols.

The sacrament of the eucharist is a particular type of symbol, sharing the properties of symbols in general and of religious symbols in particular. Indeed, the concept of symbol is seen by some theologians to be central not only to sacramental theology but also to the whole of their theology. It is this concept that provides a link with the human sciences for it has been a central subject of investigation in anthropology, particularly in the examination of religious belief and ritual behaviour.

This chapter will examine the concept of symbol in relation to three theologians: Paul Tillich, Louis-Marie Chauvet and Alexander Schmemann. They have been chosen as an ecumenical cross-section of theologians who posit symbol as of central importance. They will also connect later to the case studies drawn from Roman Catholic, Anglican, Protestant and Orthodox traditions. This chapter is concerned not only with the doctrine of symbol *in esse*, but also of its relationship to the sacraments, to the Church and to the doctrine of humanity. It is on the basis of an examination of these doctrinal interests that an interrelationship of theology and anthropology can be developed.

Paul Tillich

Introduction

Paul Tillich (1883–1965) was a Protestant theologian who made the discussion of symbol central to his work. He attacked the reduction of the sacramental in Protestantism, resulting in only one sacrament – that of the Word – and called for the rediscovery of the sacramental level (1951). But symbol in his theology does not refer to sacraments alone but to almost all of the theological enterprise. Symbol is central to his thinking and the primary category of his theology; the sacraments are only a subsection of his work. Also, his doctrine of symbol starts at the point of a general doctrine of symbols, and religious symbols are then discussed as a subsection of this general theory. It is this broad base of approach to symbols that makes Tillich important. His theory opens out into a dialogue with other academic disciplines such as psychology and anthropology. Interface with the latter raises important questions on cross-cultural transference of symbol.

Tillich (1959) suggests two levels of religious symbols: the transcendent and the immanent. On the transcendent level the basic symbol is God himself. So he argues that 'God as being' is the only non-symbolic statement. All other propositions about God are symbolic and the first element of symbol is on the transcendent level. The second element embraces the attributes of God. The third element is the acts of God in relation to the world. This brings the discussion to the immanent level. The first element of this is the appearances of the divine in space and time, and here the incarnation is of particular importance, although this category is not claimed for Christianity alone. The second element is the sacramental. 'The sacramental is nothing else than some reality becoming the bearer of the Holy in a special way and under special circumstances' (p. 64). The third element is the material level. This is the sign-symbol; signs that have become symbols. In the study of eucharistic worship the latter two categories are of primary importance. However this typology of symbol is interlocking and these elements to some extent are related to the higher levels of symbol.

A symbol has a number of general characteristics. The basic characteristic is its figurative quality. The symbolic attitude (1966, p. 15) 'does not have the symbol itself in view but that which is symbolised in it'. This may lead to a chain of symbols each pointing to something of a higher rank. The second characteristic of a symbol is its perceptibility. 'Something which is intrinsically invisible, ideal or transcendent is made perceptible in the symbol and is in this way given objectivity' (1966, p. 15). The third characteristic is that the symbol has innate power. In this way Tillich can talk of the birth and death of symbols. A symbol is a living thing. In its encounter with another culture it can experience culture shock and that encounter can lead to isolation, integration, or death. The fourth characteristic is acceptability. A symbol is socially rooted and supported. The process of becoming a symbol and acceptance as a symbol belong together. These general characteristics also hold for religious symbols. The distinctive feature of the religious symbol is that it points to an object that can never become an object: ultimate reality.

Given this introduction to the theory of symbols in Tillich, particular aspects of his theory need to be examined with especial reference to the eucharist and the implications of its transference from one culture to another. These will be examined in terms of: sign and symbol; the two-edged nature of symbols; their birth and death; their truth and criticism; and, finally, sacramental symbols.

Sign and Symbol

The distinction between sign and symbol is fundamental for Tillich. It underlies the other parameters of a symbol, its two edged nature and vitality. Signs and symbols are not totally distinct. 'Symbols are similar to signs in one distinctive respect: both symbols and signs point beyond themselves to something else' (1959, p. 54). The common quality is then the 'pointing beyond'. But there is a fundamental distinction. 'Signs do not participate in any way in the reality and power of that to which they point. Symbols, although they are not the same as that which they symbolise, participate in its meaning and power' (p. 54). Thus the distinction is based on the notion of 'participation', or lack of it.

The sign–symbol dichotomy is a major distinction for others who are studying symbol, not least Victor Turner. In Turner's case (Turner & Turner, 1978) the difference rests in the monosemic sign and the polysemic symbol. So for Turner the difference is at the level of meaning, but for Tillich the difference is at the level of ontology. In his earlier work Tillich seemed to put the category of sign-symbol in an intermediate position between sign and symbol, 'a mixture of symbols and signs' (1955, p. 115). This would be inconsistent, if the definitions of sign and symbol were mutually exclusive. However, in later work the sign-symbol is clearly a subsection of the category symbol, an important one that will be returned to in the discussion of the vitality of symbols.

Rowe (1968) has criticized this definition on three grounds. Firstly, he raises the question of the meaning of 'pointing beyond'. Does it mean 'referring to', with the meaning identified with its referent? This would then be a primitive version of the reference theory of meaning. Therefore he assumes that for Tillich 'points beyond' means 'signifies', where meaning is not identified with its referent. The second criticism is that Tillich does not have a category of natural signs. For Tillich signs are always conventional. As clouds are not signs then they have to be symbols. Yet this is not the conclusion that is desired. This category of natural sign goes back to Aristotle, and it may be the antipathy of Tillich to Aristotelianism that caused him to avoid this category. Rowe's most important criticism relates to the meaning of 'participation in the reality'. The notion of participation is important to Tillich. It arises in his comments on early Franciscan theology (Dourley, 1975). It is central to his theology as 'every relation includes a kind of participation' (Tillich, 1953, p. 196). If this is so, then in what way are signs and symbols different? As the distinction between sign and symbol rests on 'participation', then special explanation of participation in the case of the symbol is necessary to support the distinction. Yet the question arises, given that, 'every relation includes a kind of participation', and that the fundamental distinction between sign and symbol is that the symbol participates in the reality it points to and the sign does not, in what way is the participation of the symbol distinctive from that of the sign (which presumably participates in a general sense)? Rowe (p. 119) concludes that all we are told is that 'there is *some relation* that symbols have to what they signify and signs do not have to what they signify', but that this relation is not clarified. Thus he says (p. 119): 'until some clarification is given it seems that Tillich's fundamental distinction between signs and symbols is quite uninformative'.

Dreisbach (1979) takes up the challenge of Rowe and comes to the defence of Tillich. He tries to restate the position of Tillich by making the meaning of participation clearer. Firstly, he comments that participation is a Platonic and Neoplatonic concept that was never clearly defined by Plato and is even more obscure in Tillich. He says (p. 329): 'Participation is simply a word which points to the relation of all beings to and their dependence on being itself'. The relationship between the symbol and the symbolizandum is 'some sort of ontological relationship between a being and being itself, a relation of dependency' (p. 329), but that Tillich does not elaborate the precise relationship. Dreisbach does not think that this relationship needs elaborating, yet this is the very point where Rowe is calling for clarification. Dreisbach points out that the word 'participation' is sometimes replaced by the other words, e.g. 'belonging to' and 'representation', but that the meaning of participation 'is indeed vague and will remain so, since it is more of a metaphor than an explanation' (p. 330). Thus he reinterprets Tillich's definition with the result that 'a sign merely stands for or indicates something else' (p. 330). The connection is one of cause and effect, or resemblance, or convention. At this point he has included the category of natural sign in Tillich's analysis. The connection between the religious symbol and the symbolizandum is said by Dreisbach to be of a different kind to that of the symbol but that the nature of this is not clear. The function of the religious symbol is to make present or to make manifest the symbolizandum, that it may become the centre of one's life, the object of ultimate concern. But there is no explanation on an ontological level. Dreisbach (p. 331) is forced to conclude: 'Tillich's use of the concept of participation is not sufficient to explain just what a symbol is or how it differs from a sign'. Thus, with Rowe, he is compelled to look at the other aspects of the symbol that Tillich elucidates.

The Two-Edged Nature of Symbols

This aspect of the nature of symbol is connected to the first. As Dreisbach (p. 326) correctly concludes, each of the three elements studied here are 'three elements of one doctrine'. Tillich (1957, p. 42) asserts that a symbol 'opens up levels of reality which otherwise are closed to us ... [and] ... also unlocks dimensions and elements of our soul which correspond to the dimensions and elements of reality'. The symbol is then two-edged in that it both opens up reality and it opens up the depths of human consciousness. The operation is in both directions. It is not just a question of human consciousness being opened up but also of reality itself being opened up. This then is an explanation of the vitality of a symbol.

This raises the discussion of symbols to include psychological dimensions. Symbols appeal, in Tillich's phrase, to the 'group consciousness'. This is one reason why they cannot be manufactured. A Church liturgical commission, for example, may decide to introduce a new symbol into a service but this will not be effective unless it finds acceptance in the 'group consciousness'. In the Church of England the peace is an example of a symbol that has gained acceptance in the churches, but not without a struggle. The taking of the bread is one that as yet has failed. There is an element of paradox here. To become a symbol there must be acceptance by the 'group consciousness'. But the symbol itself opens up dimensions of the 'group consciousness' that would otherwise be closed. So the process would seem to be one of positive feedback, of both reception by and disclosure to the 'group consciousness'. The cross-cultural dimensions of this are even more complex. The American flag may be a symbol to Americans and a sign to the non-American. But with a change of 'group consciousness', as in the Vietnam demonstrations in London in the 1960s, the flag becomes a symbol and so it is ritually burned in Grosvenor Square. Later it becomes a sign again as British perceptions of American foreign policy change.

With the use of terms such as 'group consciousness' and 'collective unconscious' Tillich is drawing on the work of the psychologists on symbol. What is this group unconscious? Perhaps it is helpful to view it as a matrix of attitudes and values within a culture, held collectively but not necessarily consciously, that makes the society open or closed to symbol and to the possibility of new symbols. In this way the concept becomes open to rational investigation.

The Vitality of Symbols

Part of the final parameters of Tillich's definition of symbols (1957b, p. 43) has already been touched on, 'symbols cannot be produced intentionally'. The implications of this in a cross-cultural context are vast, as the missionary intends to transplant particular symbols, both verbal and dramatic. The whole process is one that is intentional. But the previous point has been that symbols have an internal power to open up levels of reality. There is a dialogue here between the preunderstanding of the people and the power of the symbol to change that perception. This brings Tillich to perhaps the most fundamental of his assertions that symbols 'like living beings, they grow and die' (p. 43). This is perhaps ultimately more fundamental in Tillich than the concept of participation.

Symbols have a life of their own. They are born, live, and can cease to be. They are perhaps more resilient than human beings in that they can also grow and change and be reborn. Thus the peace was originally a greeting, it died out in the Reformation, was frozen in the Roman Catholic Church, and was reborn in the modern liturgical movement. Other symbols have undergone reinterpretation. Thus Augustine inherited a rite of baptism that included a number of exorcisms. As he did not believe that the candidate was literally possessed, this was reinterpreted in light of his doctrine of original sin. Kelly (1985) has called this process 'dramaturgical rationalization', and his work points out the power of symbols to continue, to live and to be reinterpreted. Tillich seems conscious that signs may be transformed into symbols, hence the category of sign-symbol, to describe signs that have begun to function as symbols. Thus part of the ground for the birth of symbols is the field of signs. Symbols also die and one of the reasons for the death of a symbol is demonization. This is where the reality and the symbol are integrated and thus the metaphor of participation no longer applies. This confusion of the symbol and the symbolizand is the death of the symbol not only in categorical terms, but also in existential terms, as the symbol no longer opens up consciousness to being itself.

In the discussion of the birth and death of symbols and the relationship to signs the concept of pastiche is important. Bridge (1958, p. 10) says: '*Pastiche* is the result of a slavish copying by one man of another's symbols for their own sake without understanding them or what they point to.' This concept taken from the history of art is an intermediate state, the transformation of a symbol into a sign. This copying may lead to the death of a symbol. It is hollow and does not open up levels of meaning. Thus the eucharist was celebrated within the Salvation Army for a few years, but the practice died out because the symbol was hollow. But it may be a phase prior to the rebirth of a symbol. The eucharist taken to an African culture might begin as a pastiche but then in the context of worship take on new meanings and open up new levels of reality.

The description of a symbol as being like a living being may prove to be the most important contribution of Tillich to the theology of symbols. Once again this is a metaphor, as is the concept of participation. The living nature of symbols leads to the difficult discussion of their truth and their criticism.

The Truth and Criticism of Symbols

Adequacy is Tillich's criterion for the truth of symbols. He says (1957b, p. 96): 'Faith has truth in so far as it adequately expresses an ultimate concern. "Adequacy" of expression means the power of expressing an ultimate concern in such a way that it creates reply, action, communication. Symbols which are able to do this are alive.' This criterion develops out of the second aspect of symbols, namely that they open up levels of reality. Mondin (1963) criticizes Tillich in his application of this concept of adequacy, saying that the applications that Tillich gives of this criterion look only at the subjective side of the symbol. Symbols both open up the depths of our being and they open up ultimate concern. Tillich concentrates on the subjective opening up of consciousness by the symbol. The objective side may explain the reason for the dormancy of the symbol. Primordial revelation may include some key symbols, which no longer speak to the people participating. However, they are retained as they are regarded as fundamental. The symbol is dormant, but there is the possibility that it will be revived if the primal experience is rekindled in the community. The revival of the eucharist in some Protestant Churches is one example of the awakening of a dormant symbol. The development of the eucharist in the Kimbanguist Church is an example of the resurrection of a symbol from the dead. The subjective side of adequacy is the power of the symbol to open up new levels of reality; the objective side of adequacy is the ability of the symbol to relate to revelation. Failure to do this is idolatry.

Symbols are born, in Tillich's terms, from the womb of the collective unconscious. They arise out of encounter with the holy. Thus symbols are independent of any empirical criticism and cannot be killed by science or history. There can, however, be prophetic criticism: the result of the interaction of the traditional symbols and the renewed religious experience within the tradition. Thus the result of the work of Luther is the death of the Papal symbol within Protestantism. There can also be the death of the symbol if the context of the community changes so much that the founding experience dies. Shifts in the collective unconscious lead to changes in the symbol system.

Sacraments

Sacraments are the fullness of symbolic principles: Any object or event is sacramental in which the transcendent is perceived to be present (Tillich, 1959, p. 65). Tillich (p. 120) begins his approach to sacraments with a critique of the reductionism of Protestant thinking: 'In the course of its history Protestantism has become so indifferent to sacramental thinking that even the two remaining sacraments have lost their significance, with the result that only the word has retained a genuinely sacramental character'. The result of this thinking would be the dissolution of the visible Church. Thus to rediscover the sacraments is the pressing need for Protestantism. The key question is: what is the relationship between the word of God and the sacramental material? Tillich outlines three approaches. Firstly, the symbolic-metaphoric, which sees the action as a visible representation, a pictorial action, but this makes the connection arbitrary. Going down into a cave could just as well represent death and resurrection as immersion in water. This approach reduces the sacraments to signs by Tillich's definition. Secondly, there is the ritualistic interpretation, which posits the relationship as merely arbitrary. The important factor is that Jesus performed the event or words. This is found in the Protestant claims that Christ must institute the sacrament. Tillich rejects this because of its nominalistic presupposition. The third interpretation is his own approach, which is realistic. He rejects any arbitrary link of the elements and the sacrament. The power of the element from its existence and the power of the sacrament interconnect. Putnam (1965, p. 112) does not see the alternatives that Tillich has posited as mutually exclusive, rather the 'realistic view is dependent, in part, upon' the other views. The contributions of depth psychology would strengthen the symbolic-metaphoric approach, and at the root of Tillich's rejection of this approach is the distinction between sign and symbol, fundamental to Tillich but itself having problems.

Yet for Tillich there is an intrinsic relationship between the element and the sacrament. The natural power in the element makes it suitable to become the sacrament. 'Sacraments originate when the intrinsic power of a natural object becomes for faith the bearer of sacramental power' (1951, p. 124). They are not arbitrary, nor are there such things as natural sacraments, for the origin of the sacrament is the history of salvation. Thus there is an ambiguity, for conceivably the elements could be changed in a cross-cultural encounter, provided this was acceptable to the collective unconscious, and that the new elements were intrinsically related to the sacrament. But as sacramental realities are dependent upon a tradition, which goes back to the roots of salvation history, changing the elements is potentially inadequate. The only way to change the tradition is by prophetic criticism.

Conclusions

The concept of symbol is central to the work of Paul Tillich. There is no systematic treatment of the subject, particularly with reference to the eucharist, nor is it related to concepts of the body. The definition of symbol rests on the fundamental distinction between sign and symbol based on the concept of participation. Rowe has forcefully argued that the meaning of this term is not clear. However, other aspects of Tillich's doctrine of symbol, particularly the way symbols are seen as living entities, are more illuminating. The defence of Tillich has been that his use of participation is itself a metaphor as is the idea of a symbol as living. Neo-Platonic presuppositions lie behind the definition of symbol, and their reception depends on the larger question of the validity of a Platonic doctrine of metaphor.

Louis-Marie Chauvet

Introduction

Louis-Marie Chauvet is professor of sacramental theology in the Institut Catholique in Paris. He has written a number of books and articles (e.g. 1992; 1995a; 1995b), the two most significant books for this study being *Symbol and Sacrament* (1987, ET 1995) and *The Sacraments* (1997, ET 2001). They cover much the same ground, the latter being in part a more popular version of the former. His position is clearly within a postmodernist world and he is multidisciplinary in his approach, drawing on philosophy, linguistics, anthropology and biblical theology to synthesize his sacramental theology. Zimmerman has described his writing as (1999, p. 91) 'the most influential work in the direction of post-critical methods'. He makes the symbolic order the key location of his approach to the sacraments, and while he talks about both baptism and the eucharist as 'paradigmatic expressions' his approach widens out to other sacraments and sacramentals. He begins to tackle cultural issues particularly in the second book but does not begin to deal with inculturation directly. This section will look at some of his key themes as related to symbol and draw out the discourse in the inter-cultural dimension.

Critique of the Metaphysical

Chauvet begins his work with a critique of onto-theology. Following the discussion of Heidegger on the nature of being, he wants to displace the traditional metaphysical roots of theology. This is necessarily an ambitious project and to some degree its success is not integral to his approach to the eucharist in relation to inculturation. McKenna (1999) tries to argue that Chauvet is not trying to do away with metaphysics but to recognize its limit, but this seems to underestimate the radical nature of the postmodern critique. Bracken (1998, p. 703) says: 'I am profoundly uneasy at the prospect of constructing a contemporary theological worldview without an underlying philosophical scheme to give it a stronger claim to objectivity and academic respectability'. He thus argues for a third way that will modify philosophical theology based on intersubjectivity. While this does recognize the radical departure of Chauvet, it tries instead to modify tradition. Chauvet, however, wants to move on from it.

Chauvet is also critical of the use of causality in onto-theology. He points to the materialistic use of causality in Aquinas based around the metaphor of the relationship of boat builder to boat. This is in contrast to Chauvet's preferred metaphor of lover and beloved. Power (1992) is unsympathetic of this distinction, saying that there are other elements in Aquinas's theology that would modify a literal interpretation of the boat building metaphor. However, Chauvet wants to discourse on sacramental theology in personalist terms rather than in material terms. Symbolic exchange is between persons.

An aspect of Chauvet's approach is the way concepts interact. In onto-theology concepts are defined. This can be seen as describing them like a box, looking at the edges and the way they build a wall with other concepts. Chauvet includes passages where the box approach is criticized. He looks not at this type of definition but at the interaction. It is not things 'in and of themselves' by definition that are important, but the interaction of the concepts with the focus on this interactivity. This is attractive when applied both to God and culture. Both of these are open-ended. He is rightly critical of onto-theology putting God in a box, of God becoming a subject. This ends up with the 'God of the philosophers' taking over the Christian God, hence the language of 'unmoved Mover' or 'Sovereign Good'. Thus Chauvet makes the paschal mystery the point of departure for his theology and his understanding of God. He also believes that language is a given rather than a subject, for we can only study language by language. This by extension could be said about culture.

The Symbolic Order

Chauvet talks about a symbolic order. This is more than a discussion of symbols, which in so doing become an object for study. Power (1994, p. 685) says: 'To speak of *symbolic* rather than simply of *symbol* avoids taking any symbol as adequate to the expression of the divine or fixing the gaze on symbols rather than on one who approaches humanity through the symbolic'. Thus Chauvet sees existence as in a symbolic order, which mediates grace, the interpersonal relationship with God. Following Rahner, grace is not a thing, like an inoculation, but is relational. We are a part of such an order not least because of being material bodies. The importance of the body is indicated in the subtitle of the second book: *The Word of God at the Mercy of the Body*.

Chauvet, like Ricoeur (1971, ET 1981), moves from language to symbolic action; both do this via the work of Austin (1962, 1975) and Ladrière (1973), which for Ricoeur enables discourse on meaningful acts and for Chauvet acts of grace. He notes a distinction between sign and symbol, symbol being a more complex sign – being polysemous, but this is not to become a major part of his discourse, more important are symbolic exchange and symbol and body.

In discussing symbolic exchange Chauvet begins with anthropological data and the great French anthropological tradition. In many societies, e.g. native Americans and Canadians of the Pacific Coast, a whole network of relations is set up by symbolic exchange. This is done where exchange is done outside the order of value and produces obligatory generosity. Thus goods are acquired not for the amassment of personal wealth or possessions. Rather they are given away as gifts in a feast or are ritually thrown away. This system entails obligatory generosity and mandatory gratuitousness. This is his starting-point for a discussion of symbolic exchange and of grace. Chauvet tries to create links with western culture suggesting that both societies have symbolic exchange and market exchange. He has to admit that the position of each system in the culture is different. While it was necessary to make this connection for the links in his argument, it seems stretched and he has implicitly rejected the possibility of the historical development of reciprocity into market economics. It does, however, help explain his position of grace being a symbolic exchange. He clarifies the two positions in his second book by the following diagrams:

Gift ⇌ Return gift

2.1 Market exchange

Market exchange is the barter system, or the market place, e.g. in the realm of purchase of food or manufactured goods. It is the order of economics. Symbolic exchange is different. It is about relationships and outside of direct market value:

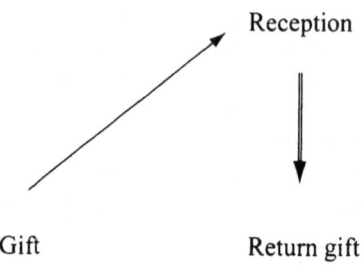

2.2 Symbolic exchange

In symbolic exchange there is no direct transaction. The giver is worse off than before, but the receiver is now left in a position of obligation. It is this approach that Chauvet applies to his sacramental theology. Indeed he goes on to analyse the discourse of eucharistic prayer, in this case that of the Roman Catholic Eucharistic Prayer 2, using this model in a most fruitful way. Chauvet's work at this point takes most seriously the vision of working from the liturgy, which will be picked up later in the discussion of liturgical theology. He does this in quite a text-bound way (cf. Hoffman, 1987), but is conscious of the interaction beyond the text at least in the interpersonal transaction between Christ and his body.

The Symbolic and the Body

In discussing the eucharist one of Chauvet's key patristic references is Augustine's comment: 'Because you are the body of Christ and his members, it is your own mystery that lies on the altar, it is your own mystery that you receive ... Be what you see, and receive what you are'. This and other considerations lead Chauvet to make the body central to the system. The symbolic system is mediated grace: God's presence and the presence of the absence of God. Grace is mediated through the body, in the symbolic system.

The body in the eucharist has a number of referents. Firstly, there is the bread, the body of Christ. Secondly, there is the body of Christ, as in the body of the person who was there on the night he was betrayed. Thirdly, there is the assembly the body of Christ, the mystery of the Church. Augustine uses the metaphor of the body to move from sacramental act, to assembly, to ethical exhortation. Chauvet wants to do the same thing. Thus he develops symbolic exchange into a rich scheme by putting the body in a vital position in his theology. While not quoting Mary Douglas (1970, 1973) on this point, he parallels her position, as we shall see

Theology of Symbol

later, in a discussion on anthropology of symbol. He also develops Rahner (1966), who also made the body significant in his theology. This schema is contained in the figure that follows:

2). RECEPTION
  a) Sacrament
  b) Sacramental body of Christ
  c) Reception under mode of oblation or thanksgiving
  d) Present

1). GIFT
  a) Scripture
  b) Historical and glorious body of Christ
  c) Gift from God: giving grace
  d) Past

3). RETURN GIFT
  a) Ethics
  b) Ecclesial body of Christ already now in the Kingdom
  c) Return gift of living in grace
  d) Eschatological future already not yet

2.3 The eucharistic process

The second referent b) in the above schema is the body of Christ. The figure connects this metaphor to other aspects of Chauvet's design, which we will now consider.

Models of Sacramental Theology

In his second book Chauvet develops more clearly his models of sacramental theology. He discerns two opposing models and sees his as medial. The first model he calls objectivist:

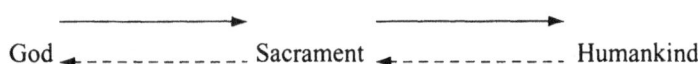

God ←----------- Sacrament ←----------- Humankind

2.4 The objectivist model

He finds this in some of the popular catechisms prior to Vatican 2. The images of the sacrament are of operative means, instrument, remedy, channel and germ. He questions the presentation such a model makes of *ex opere operato* in which the priest becomes a sacramental intermediary and piety is individualistic.

He contrasts this with the subjectivist model:

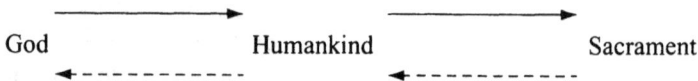

God   Humankind   Sacrament

2.5 The subjectivist model

This he sees in a variety of groups, those who talk of gospel without church, those who make certain values declared by the group as normative, e.g. freedom, and the baptismal theology of Karl Barth. While he does not say this, it could represent some Protestant traditions. The problem here is that sacraments are made an optional extra. This is impossible for Chauvet, for there never was a Church that was non-sacramental. Sacraments are part of the Church's matrix.

The third model he calls that of Vatican 2:

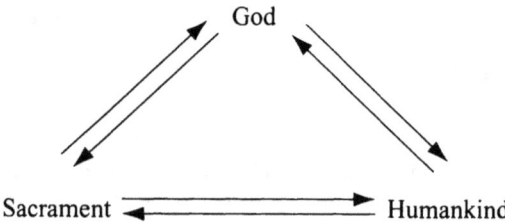

2.6 The Vatican 2 model

This model he sees as medial. Vatican 2 is seen as giving equilibrium to traditional sacramental models in the Roman Catholic Church. While Chauvet gives a persuasive exposition of this model, and it explains new aspects of his sacramental theology, not least the interrelationship of the three identified poles, my suspicions are aroused when two opposing views are presented and then knocked down to be supplanted by a reasonable median position. If this is the equilibrium required, why does he acknowledge that subjectivist models have been flourishing since the Council? To say that they are the result of other forces in the Church is perhaps to admit that the balance was not restored quite as much as is suggested.

That having been said, it is important to mention that his preferred model indicates the subtlety of his sacramental system. For Chauvet it is efficacious, mediating grace, that is a relationship between God and the body of Christ and thus to humankind. The body of Christ has thus a key role in human history. In the first book this is strongly identified with the institutional Church. This theme seems to be softened in the second book, which speaks less of this as an institution.

Culture and Symbol

Chauvet does not look systematically at culture and symbol. In his move from language to symbol he makes them both a part of the given of existence. It could be extrapolated that culture would occupy the same position (1987, ET 1995, p. 84):

> Reality is never present to us except in a mediated way, which is to say *constructed* out of the symbolic network of the culture which fashions us. This *symbolic order* designates the system of connections between the different elements and levels of a culture ... a system forming a coherent whole that allows the social group and individuals to orient themselves.

Chauvet subtitles the section this is quoted from 'No Speech, No Humankind'. It seems that he could also say 'No Culture, No Humankind'. Culture mediates reality. It is something we analyse from within, not from without.

In a discussion of traditional initiation, i.e. rites of passage from Burkina Faso, he relates African rites of passage to Christian initiation, something we will return to later in a discussion of Victor Turner. He comments (p. 363): 'Of course, since one cannot transfer an element of one symbolic system into another without producing completely different effects, there is no question of transposing the pedagogy of an African initiation into our own culture'. This is significant because had he reversed the direction of transference he might have modified his conclusion. Could this be used to argue for a *tabula rasa* approach to the eucharist in Africa? It is unlikely that Chauvet would argue for such a position, even if it might superficially look like it. Rather he is stressing the integral nature of a symbolic system within a culture. The effects of transposition can be seen in the African Church in the witness of cultural alienation mentioned in chapter 1, above.

In his second book (1997, ET 2001) Chauvet does mention the 'problems' of cultural differences (p. 109) as existing, while not beginning to look at solutions. His focus is more on the pastoral situation in France. In the enactment of a rite there must be pastoral negotiation. Factors such as the place, age, numbers attending and cultural sensibility have to be taken into account. He talks of the need to re-evangelize the Church from the inside and the capacity for faith to be supple enough to be 'resymbolized' with the culture of the present assembly. This book contains significant pastoral application of his theology. He is forced to discuss the approach of pastors to requests for baptism from those who seem to hold little explicit Christian faith. The whole tenor of the postmodernism that he has adopted is to suggest that there has been a cultural change and that modernism is dead: a new phase has begun. If so, the issue of resymbolization might well be the European counterpart to the question of inculturation in Africa and Asia.

Conclusions

Chauvet creates a sacramental theology in a postmodern world. As such he sees the symbolic order as the key mediation between humanity and God. In the sacramental exchange we experience God's gracious approach and within this is the ethical demand and promise of the eschaton. His implicit view that culture mediates reality is important within his sacramental theology. Chauvet struggles with the practical application of his approach; in which he seems to be a pastorally moderate person. Thus he can surprisingly argue for the acceptability of wafers while discoursing about the significance of bread. Alexander Schmemann, the next theologian to be examined, also struggled with his context. As an Orthodox theologian living in the very modern society of the United States of America he had to work out a theology in an unsympathetic culture.

Alexander Schmemann

Introduction

Symbol has been a central concept in the theology of the Protestant Paul Tillich and the Roman Catholic Louise-Marie Chauvet. There are few accessible Orthodox theologians writing in English who have systematically approached the theology of symbol. While it might have been appropriate to look at the exciting work of Zizioulas (1997), Alexander Schmemann's many works on liturgy and the eucharist complement much that has been already said. Indeed Schmemann's work is accepted within Orthodox circles in ways that others have yet to be. The chapters that follow will take examples from African Independent Churches, the Roman Catholic Church, the Anglican Churches and the Ethiopian Orthodox Church. There is not enough translated on which to base a detailed analysis of the latter's theological approach. Thus the work of Schmemann forms a general introduction to an Orthodox and Oriental approach to symbol.

Garrett (1984) says that Schmemann (1921–83) was a Russian Orthodox priest who wrote in Russian, French and English. He taught both in Paris and America, being for many years the Dean of St Vladimir's Theological Seminary. His interests were primarily liturgical and he argued strongly for the unity of prayer and doctrine. He maintained a lively interest in Russian theology (Schmemann, 1972b), but in his liturgical writings shows a great debt to the liturgical movement

(Schmemman, 1966a). He wrote in a non-systematic way and continued a number of themes throughout his life, not least the eschatological dimension of the eucharist and the need to develop a theological approach that has the *lex orandi* of the Church as its starting-point. As an émigré in America he experienced the problems of Orthodox worship in the secular world (Schmemman, 1972c) and its adaptation to the American context. Thus he discusses theology and symbol in the same context as Tillich, that of North America, and like Rahner he is concerned to relate tradition to the modern world. Yet he remains very critical of the western approach to both theology and liturgy. This weakness he perceives as the root of secularism. Thus he develops the notion of liturgical theology as the label that typifies his approach. It is with this that we must begin.

Liturgical Theology

Schmemann is very critical of the western approach to worship. This brings him into conflict with his own Church, as he sees that the Russian Church has undergone a 'western captivity' (1972, p. 89), particularly with reference to sacramental theology (1973b, p. 230). He states that there are two approaches in history to the relationship between theology and *leitourgia*. The first is the patristic approach. This forms an organic connection between the two. The axiom of this position is *lex orandi est lex credendi*. Theology is thus 'a "description" more than a "definition"' (1972a, p. 90). It is 'above all, a search for words and concepts adequate to and expressive of the living experience of the Church; for a *reality* and not "propositions"' (p. 90). The faith of the Church is 'not detachable from ... experience, but is indeed that experience itself' (p 90). 'The *experience* of the Church is primarily the experience given and received in the Church's *leitourgia* – in her *lex orandi*' (p. 90). But this does not mean that the liturgy is the primary source for theological data. 'The Fathers do not "reflect" on liturgy. For them it is not an *object* of theological inquiry and definition, but rather the living source and ultimate criterion of all christian thought' (1963, p. 167). Schmemann's definition here is not completely clear. He seems at first to argue that the worship of the Church, as expressed in the liturgy, is the primary source of theology. However he then goes on to categorically deny this. Perhaps above all he is setting before us a vision of the unity of theology and worship. In order to see what he is saying more clearly his second approach needs to be studied.

The second approach to the relationship between worship and theology he calls the scholastic type. This has been the predominant method in the western Church and has overtaken the east. In this approach the organic connection between worship and theology has been severed. Theology has independent rational status; it is a search for a system of consistent categories and concepts: *intellectus fidei*. Thus the position of the relationship between worship and theology is reversed. Worship is now no longer a source but an object, which has to be defined and evaluated within acceptable categories. Liturgy thus supplies theology with data, but the method of dealing with the data is free from any liturgical context. The categories for the selection and classification of the data are a product of the independent conceptual structure. This approach is typified by the medieval scholastics with their notions of causality, character and consecration with reference to the eucharist. The doctrinal categories then began to feed back into the liturgy with the development of ceremonies such as elevation, benediction, and feasts such as *Corpus Christi*. Thus the doctrinal has begun to influence the liturgy rather than vice versa. The Reformation did not alter this approach for it was, in the eyes of Schmemann, a doctrinal reform of worship. It used the newly developing Biblical theology of the day to reflect upon and criticize the worship of the Church. 'Theology remained independent of worship and claimed the right to control it, and to form it according to the *lex credendi*' (1963, p. 169).

However, it appears that Schmemann has not clearly defined the two approaches. It seems at first that he has delineated two starting-points, that of worship and that of formal theological categories, and argues that the first is the patristic way. However, he then continues to deny that the Fathers saw the liturgy as a datum for reflection. This may mean that reflection was not a process that incorporated analytic concepts derived from philosophy, or that reflection was not conceived as independent of the hermeneutical dialectic of theology and worship. Yet Schmemann comments, 'whatever a given object of theological scrutiny and investigation, the first and most important "datum" is its liturgical experience' (1972a, pp. 96–7). Thus he does not clarify how reflection on worship produces doctrine. He is happy with the patristic approach but not the scholastic. Certainly he does not want to let theology feed back and influence the liturgy. He calls for a rediscovery of the initial vision and wholeness of the relationship between worship and theology, which has been lost in methodological fragmentation. But is the choice of material selective in a way that favours the east? The west is accused of a wrong interrelationship of its *lex orandi* and *lex credendi*. Is the evidence of such a feedback in the east even among the Fathers ignored? Wiles (1967) has shown that there was an influence of doctrinal discussion on the form of the Gloria and the Gloria Patri. Feedback did occur in the patristic period from doctrine to worship, not least in the Arian controversy. Other factors underlie his categorization. But before a full evaluation of Schmemann's approach can be made, his position on the use of the concepts 'sacred' and 'secular' need be examined.

Schmemann (1965) challenges the dichotomy of the sacred and the profane, and (1985) the dichotomy of natural and supernatural. These are rejected for two reasons: firstly, because they are not biblical categories; and secondly, because they are false dichotomies. The primary biblical categories he sees as the contrast between the two aeons, the present age and the age to come. The liturgy is the actualization of the age to come in the life of the Church. Thus the biblical approach is primarily eschatological. In the Church the distinction of the sacred and the profane has been abolished, and so too has the cult. Here again we see the integrated approach of Schmemann. He desires to use biblical categories and hold various tensions together. It is in the destruction of these tensions that he sees the west as having strayed from the patristic tradition.

Lex orandi, lex credendi are in dialectical tension in the Church. The western approach, as typified by Wainwright (1980), would be to see this interaction as a hermeneutical circle, a part of the process of development. The Church under the guidance of the Spirit and the magisterium (in Rome or in the Bible) is led towards the fullness of truth. Underlying the work of Schmemann is the presupposition that the deposit was given to the Fathers and so truth is eternally the same. The deposit is contained not least in the unchanging liturgy. This may differ in expression but it is fundamentally a given. He starts from the *orandi* of the Church and although he is willing to open the liturgy to historical criticism, he is not willing to open it to doctrinal criticism. It is the experience of Christ in the liturgy that is the axiom of theology. Perhaps the best conclusion on this is that of Kenneth Stevenson (1986) who says that Schmemann gives us 'a pristine and quintessential expression of the classic Orthodox position . . . where everything comes together', but to the post-Enlightenment west the position seems foreign.

Before looking further at sacrament and symbol, it is worth examining briefly the work of Kavanagh (1984). As an American Catholic, he takes a similar viewpoint as Schmemann, but in a more westernized way. He distinguishes between primary theology and secondary theology. Primary theology is the worship experience as lived upon. Each service does not leave the person the same as when he came, but changed. Secondary theology is the reflection upon that experience as often done in the theological colleges, university departments or seminaries. Secondary theology has developed its own internal debate separate from the life of the first and yet the first is the source of theology. Again in the dialectic of worship and doctrine, primacy is give to the worship experience. In that he is similar to Schmemann. But Kavanagh is more consistent in grasping the worship experience as the starting-point in the hermeneutical circle, yet seeing the two as interacting with one another.

The Orthodox vision rests on a unity of cosmology, anthropology, ecclesiology and the sacraments. It is important, therefore, to look at symbol, humanity and the eucharist within this unified approach.

Sacrament and Symbol

Schmemann (1973a) continues his critique of the present Orthodox approach to sacrament, as being one of the more important examples of the ' "pseudomorphosis" suffered by Orthodox Theology', i.e., its western captivity. He rejects the distinction between the real and the symbolic and sees this as a shift in the doctrine of knowledge from an existential to an essential approach. The sacraments, then, are no longer studied in the context of the liturgical celebration of the Church, and thus the explanation of the sacrament is no longer an exegesis of the liturgy. The new scholastic approach is to study the sacraments in essence, by framing the question in terms of an opposition between the sacramental and the non-sacramental. Theology now takes the position of a 'rational and discursive knowledge *about*, rather than *of*, reality' (p. 142). The rational and the existential are dichotomized, or if not opposed at least ranked, such that the rational is given priority. This reduction is not the approach of the patristic way and is seen as the root of secularism.

To the Fathers 'symbolism is the essential dimension of the sacrament' (p. 139). The world, in being created by God, is fundamentally a symbolic structure. It is itself a sign of the sacred. Sacraments are then not exceptions to the natural order, but fulfilments of it. Like the heavens they proclaim the glory of God, but they do this because they manifest Christ and his kingdom. Jesus did not institute the communion *ex nihilo*, but in continuity with the natural sacramentality of the meal, for Christ came not to start afresh but to fulfil. The type of knowledge gained from the sacrament is knowledge that depends on participation. The symbol is a 'living encounter with and entrance into that "epiphany" of reality which the symbol is' (p. 141).

The patristic approach according to Schmemann (p. 141) rests on a different approach to symbol:

> In the early tradition ... the relationship between the sign in the symbol (A) and that which it 'signifies' (B) is neither a merely semantic one (A *means* B), nor causal (A *is the cause of* B), nor representative (A *represents* B). We called this relationship an *epiphany*. 'A *is* B' means that the whole of A expresses, communicates, reveals, manifests the 'reality' of B (although not necessarily the whole of it) without, however, losing its own ontological reality, without being dissolved in another 'res'.

As with Tillich, the manifestation of the reality is through the participation of the sign in the symbolized. The patristic approach is fundamentally an ontological one. But Schmemann does not posit any discontinuity between the world as a symbol and the symbolic nature of the sacraments. Thus the question posed to Tillich, of the difference between sign, symbol, and the religious symbol, is answered that there is no essential difference. For Schmemann there can be no ontological distinction between symbol and sign. The world and all in it points to God the creator of all things; the sacraments point to Christ the redeemer and the fulfilment of all things. Creation and redemption are not opposed but in harmony with one another. Symbols are signs of the reality and they are this because they 'point to' and 'participate in' that reality.

Christ is 'the Symbol of all symbols' (p. 148). It is the mystery of Christ that reveals and fulfils the ultimate meaning and destiny of the world itself. Indeed, symbol is the mode of presence and operation of the mystery. Christ instituted the sacraments in fulfilment of the natural sacramentality of the world and they point to the ultimate eschatological fulfilment of the world in Christ himself. This is the mystery of Christ, and this mystery is manifest in the Church and the sacraments.

The Church is then the symbol of the new creation and the sacrament of the world to come. It is through this intrinsic and participatory notion of symbol that Schmemann's Orthodox 'unity of vision' is held together.

The human as a priest

Starting from Feuerbach's dictum 'man is what he eats', Schmemann develops a doctrine of humanity as the hungry animal. 'Man is a hungry being. He is hungry for God' (1965, p. 15). This is because human beings were made for a unique role. They alone were made to bless God for creation, which Schmemann sees in the command that Adam should name the animals. 'To name a thing is to bless God for it' (p. 15). 'All . . . qualities of man . . . have their focus and ultimate fulfilment in this capacity to bless God' (p. 16). Thus the human being is (p. 16):

> first of all homo adorans . . . *the priest* . . . He stands in the centre of the world and unifies it in his act of blessing God, of both receiving the world from God and offering it to God . . . by fulfilling the world with this eucharist, he transforms his life . . . into the life of God.

Thus humans are the priests of a cosmic sacrament.

The fall also centres on food. The story is not primarily one of disobedience but of ceasing to be hungry for God alone. Humanity accepted a division between the sacred and the profane; the falling away from the vision that God is all in all. Thus humans lost the power to offer the world to God in blessing. The world had become an end in itself. The story of redemption is not one of a rescue so much as the restoration of the original intention, the completion of the original plan. Thus in Christ life is returned to humanity and in the sacraments, especially in the liturgy, the Church is renewed in that life. The Church is the sign of the new aeon. Thus the Orthodox vision unites the cosmological, the ecclesiological and the eschatological. The vision is of (1971, p. 235): 'the fundamental "sacramentality" of man, his total belonging to and dependence upon the world . . . and his power to transcend that dependence and to transform the world itself into communion with God'. This happens in Christ.

This united vision is destroyed by secularism. Secularism is 'above all a *negation of worship* . . . the negation of man as a worshipping being, as *homo adorans*' (1972c, p. 4). Secularism is a Christian heresy. It has its roots in denying the world its natural sacramentality and in radically opposing the natural and the supernatural. In so doing the world is defined independently of God and grace. The result of the rejection of the sacramentality of humanity and the world is the reduction of symbols to illustrations of ideas and concepts. This has happened through the collapse of the fundamental Christian mysterion, the antinomical holding together of the reality of the symbol and the symbolism of reality. The west has dichotomized reality and symbol and the fruit of this is the modern secular world. It is in Christ that the vision can be restored for he is the 'ultimate "epiphany" of man as worshipping being . . . the fulfilment of the world's essential "sacramentality"' (p. 7).

There are parallels here with the theology of Rahner. Christ as the fulfilment of humanity, humanity as a being open to God, and the unity of life in the mystery of God. This may be because of a common interest in the liturgical movement and of the primacy of the category of mystery in the Fathers, a doctrine that was revived in the west through the writing of Odo Casel. Perhaps the root of this doctrine of humanity is the concept of the human as *homo adorans*. The materialist reacts against this doctrine, but cannot escape the data of the history of religions that humanity has been fundamentally religious.

The Eucharist

The liturgy is the sacrament of the kingdom of God. It is the realization in the Church of the world to come. 'In reality the sacraments are to be seen as the *locus*, the very centre of the Church's eschatological understanding and experience' (1985, p. 10). In order to emphasize the eschatological dimension of the eucharist, Schmemann has to use historical criticism on the service. Three layers are seen to be the basis of the present rite. The first is the Jewish which is primarily eschatological. The mystagogical piety from the post Constantinian environment forms the second layer. The third comes from the monastic tradition, which was a reaction to false developments in the second and a reassertion of the eschatological. The second layer was the basis for the allegorizing of the liturgy. Thus it came to be seen as a recapitulation of the life of Christ. This tradition is rejected. The 'east lost sight of the meaning of the Liturgy through an absorption in fanciful symbolism, the west obscured its true meaning by making a sharp distinction between symbol and reality' (p. 10). The fanciful symbolism is found in the tradition of the eastern liturgical commentaries. But is not the approach now found in the texts themselves?

Rather than see the liturgy as a recapitulation of the life of Christ, Schmemann talks of the service as an ascension. In a way rather like Calvin, but talking about the Church rather than the believer, in the eucharist the Church is seen to be raised up to feast on Christ in the kingdom. It is a journey into the heavenlies. In the ascent humanity offers the bread and the wine to God. We were created as celebrants in the sacrifice of life. In Christ, the perfect human, the eucharist was restored to humanity. The eucharist is a sacrifice because 'man is a sacrificial being, because he finds his life in love, and love is sacrificial' (1965, p. 41). Humans offer the world and themselves to God but in so doing they find that all has been offered by Christ and they have nothing to give except for Christ himself. Thus they find that they are offering Christ, the life of the world. The ascension reaches its climax in the epiclesis, when a descent occurs. The Holy Spirit transforms the elements to manifest Christ to the Church. It has already been mentioned that Schmemann rejects the dichotomy between symbol and reality, thus the transformation is of the bread and wine into the body and blood of Christ. The Holy Spirit is the agent of change, revealing the eschatological dimension of the act. The descent of the Church is one of an empowered Church strengthened for the work of mission.

Thus the sacraments are not means of grace, but the living reality of the transformation of the Church. This is a transformation into the essential nature of the Church: in the eucharist the Church realizes her true identity. 'A sacrament... is not a "miracle" by which God breaks ... the "laws of nature", but the manifestation of the ultimate Truth about the world and life, humanity and nature, the Truth which is Christ' (p. 127). This is the way the integrationist position of holding together the natural and the supernatural, nature and grace, is worked out in Schmemann's sacramental theology.

Conclusions

Schmemann challenges the categories of western thinking, natural and supernatural, sacred and profane, and argues for the biblical eschatological dichotomy of the present age and the age to come. His strength is in questioning the dichotomization of these factors: he raises the question of the validity of such an opposition. But if an eschatological viewpoint is taken, does that mean that such dichotomies have to be rejected altogether? He is unusual for an Orthodox theologian in rejecting the allegorical tradition of the Church in interpreting the liturgy as the recapitulation of the life of Christ. But is this position not woven into the text of the liturgy itself, an eastern example of a doctrine altering the liturgical text? His doctrine of symbol is very close to that of Tillich, but the philosophical presuppositions of it are not developed. The great strength of his position is the integration of creation, anthropology, redemption, ecclesiology and the sacraments. The basis of his approach is to make the *lex orandi* of the Church the foundation of the *lex credendi*, but the way he formulates this relationship is not clear. As modified by Kavanagh, the position is one of emphasizing the worship experience as the basis for theological reflection, an issue we will return to in the last chapter. In so doing this opens the discussion of humanity and sacraments to scientific investigation of the nature of religious experience.

Theological Approaches to Symbol

These three theologians, Tillich, Chauvet and Schmemann, were chosen to represent modern and postmodern views from the three major branches of the Church: Protestant, Roman Catholic and Orthodox, and all have made symbol one of their most important categories. This chapter cannot pretend to be an exhaustive approach to their work, nor is it a full study of the different traditions that they represent, but it does give an indication of the contemporary position of thought from representatives of each tradition. This then gives some of the theological background for the examination of different Churches in the later chapters of this book. Prior to that there are some points of comparison that need to be made and a discussion of the relationship of theology and anthropology. This book is examining an existential problem in the world wide Church with case studies drawn primarily from Africa, i.e. the development of an authentic eucharist. It is adopting an interdisciplinary approach, in order to clarify the complex problem and give depth to the analysis.

All three theologians emphasize the reality of the symbol. For Tillich there is no 'mere symbol'; for Chauvet symbolic reality is central; for Schmemann the symbol is the reality, but not exhaustively so. Perhaps the most interesting of these positions is that of Tillich, for in Tillich there is a dynamic historical dimension, symbols are born and die, that would seem to be impossible in the more static theology of Schmemann and Chauvet. It will be suggested later in the book that the Reformation built a cultural suspicion of symbol into itself. There was an emphasis on the immediacy of the divine in the Word, and thus a symbol was the removal of that immediacy by one stage. Tillich has revolted against this and re-emphasizes the importance and reality of the symbolic. This may reflect an important paradigm shift within Protestantism. Tillich and Schmemann seem to have very much in common, not least their desire to say that a symbol participates in the thing symbolized. This is a problematic assertion, but the philosophical background for this is their assertion of the reality of the symbol. This would seem to rest upon Platonistic presuppositions. Chauvet accepts the postmodern critique of metaphysics but this makes the symbolic system more important not less important. Both Tillich and Chauvet want to distinguish between sign and symbol, but is Tillich able to do so and be consistent with the rest of his theology? This query points to the problematic nature of the category symbol. It would seem to be central to the nature of theology, but very difficult to explicate, hence the variety of theologies using symbol as central. It is not assumed that this book has solved the problem.

The nature of symbol is linked to the question of humans as symbol, and thus of the Man Jesus Christ as symbol. In both Modern Roman Catholic theology and Schmemann, Christ is the primordial sacrament, or the Symbol of symbols. Schmemann develops very clearly the position of Christ as the fulfilment of the creation and attacks much of the western approach to theology as dichotomizing nature and supernature. In so doing he points to the difference between symbol and sacrament not as one of ontology but suggests rather that sacraments are fulfilments of the sacramentality of the world. This may point to the resolution of some of the problems in Tillich and is a different approach to Chauvet's stress on the Paschal mystery. However, Schmemann's scheme was never fully developed and so the full implications of this neo-patristicism are not clear. His comment that a human being is *homo adorans* speaks of some deep desire in humanity and is reflected in the anthropological data.

In making Christ the central point of an approach to symbol, the question of approaching the subject 'from above', and 'from below' can be raised. This is a common methodological discussion in Christology, and it can also be applied in the doctrine of humanity. Christ is approached from above, by starting with God and God's revelation of the incarnation. He is approached from below, by starting with Christ as human being and asking questions about what this means in relation to humanness. With this starting-point particular attention has been given to a critical historical examination of the historical Jesus and the development of the early Church's doctrine of Christ. Likewise theology studies humanity from above with the doctrines of the image of God and original sin. There has also been extensive discussion of the nature of humanity in relation to concepts such as the soul and spirit. A more critical approach to the nature of humanity comes from anthropology and its empirical studies of particular societies, and theorizing on the nature of symbol, myth and rite. The two approaches are not necessarily in opposition to one another, but study humanity from the two different starting-points.

Schmemann was particularly scathing of the western approach to theology. In his reaction to the perceived scholastic approach, he asserted that the *lex orandi* should be the starting-point for theologizing. The discrepancies in his explanation of how this should happen have been examined, but the modifications as outlined by Kavanagh also open up the possibility of examining theology from below. The worship experience can be seen as the focus of primary theology. One qualification of the approach here is that the Christian worship experience is characterized by being profoundly Christological. Making this experience the primary data, there may be no clear distinction between knowledge from the experience empirically apprehended and knowledge that is revealed. The two are in a dialectical tension. It is within such a tension that this book operates.

Calvin commented at the beginning of the *Institutes* that there are two parts to knowledge: 'the knowledge of God and the knowledge of ourselves'. It is tempting to use this statement to contrast empirical knowledge (reason) and revealed truth (revelation). Schmemann would undoubtedly see this as a false dichotomy. He sees everything as related to the economy of Christ, both in creation and redemption. Such a holistic view raises the question whether empirical knowledge is not a part of the doctrine of creation. There is no clear answer to such a question. In that Christology has been enriched by the use of approaches from above and from below, it would seem that the same could be true of the theology of human beings.

Humanity and symbol are both of interest to the subjects of anthropology and theology. Both discuss the nature of these issues, if only implicitly at times. In the context of the discussion of the eucharist in the Church and particularly in Africa and the nature of indigenization, both anthropology and theology bring their particular insights to the problem. Indeed one of the central aspects of this problem, namely that of culture, is not directly accessible to theological investigation, but both Tillich and Niebuhr have written on the subject. Human beings as worshipping animals, or the *homo adorans* in the words of Schmemann, have fascinated anthropology and led to the development of ritual studies. There is also a growing study of Christian ritual in the flourishing of liturgical studies and Schmemann has pointed these studies in a doctrinal direction in his approach to liturgical theology. Thus there is a considerable overlap between the study of humanity in theology and the social science of anthropology.

Pannenberg (1985) has contributed considerably to the dialogue between the subjects. He comments that the use of theological concepts by anthropologists and anthropological concepts by theologians has often been very selective. For there to be a fruitful debate between the two subjects, what is required is not the incorporation of a few key anthropological ideas into theology, and vice versa, or the search for a point of contact, but a deep interaction between the two. Indeed, in a search for the truth about the issues to be studied, humans and their ritualization of religion, a dialectical approach is required. Anthropology and theology are in dialectical tension as thesis and antithesis. This book takes such a dialectical approach as the methodological tension for the examination of the eucharist in the Church and in particular in Africa.

The problems raised by the transfer of eucharistic worship from one culture to another will be discussed in relation to the concept of inculturation. Different examples will be taken from the great variety of Churches in Africa, including the Ethiopian Orthodox Church, African Independent Churches, the Anglican Churches, and the Roman Catholic Church. At the root of the discussion is the question: What is meant by authentically African and authentically Christian? The terms themselves reveal the tension of the African Church. Thus the next chapter will examine the eucharist from an anthropological perspective.

CHAPTER 3

Anthropology and Symbol

Symbol has been a central category to both anthropology and sociology from their very beginnings. Durkheim wrote about it, the great ethnologists were careful to record the symbols used in their fieldwork, and symbol remains an important category both for theoreticians and fieldworkers today. The use of symbols in religious ritual is also important, despite the anthropology of religion not being as influential as other aspects of the subject. One of the other primary concerns of anthropology is the subject of culture, and the related processes of culture change. The problem of inculturation is to be set in the wider context of the relationship between worship and culture, and of the cross-cultural transfer of symbol. Indeed, inculturation forms a part of the wider question of the processes of acceptance of a symbol by a particular culture and of the transformation of the symbol to fit that culture. Rather than try to review all the different anthropological approaches to symbol and culture change, a selection of writers has been taken, who have interests that encompass both traditional religion and Christian usages.

Anthropological Approaches

Introduction

Christianity came to Africa as a result of missionary activity: the message was planted by agents of another culture into a different soil. As the Churches have become independent of overseas control in terms of leadership, so there has been a growing independence of thought in the African theology movement, and in the movement towards African forms of worship. Sometimes it began by encouraging the use of local tunes, instruments, and song (e.g. Hodgson, 1990). This has developed into a discussion of the development of African principles of liturgy and the role of African categories in the development of a liturgical text.

The rise of contextual liturgy as a factor in the life of the Churches in Africa has not only a historical dimension but also an anthropological dimension. Indeed, the production of indigenous ritual requires an anthropological framework that can assess both local culture and Christian ritual, if an evaluation of the authenticity of the proposed rites is to be made. Dialogue with traditional religion and comparative ritual analysis often forms the basis of an attempt to produce contextual liturgy. Anthropological theory provides some of the tools to approach the problem. Thus this chapter will look at anthropological approaches to symbol, and the eucharist as symbol. The writings of Mary Douglas and Victor Turner in particular, and also those of Dan Sperber, help provide models of analysis and have done so for a number of decades (Bell, 2002). Having used them to consider some of the roots of the problem, it is then possible to look at various case studies of inculturation of the eucharist in Africa.

Mary Douglas

Mary Douglas (1970, 1973) has argued strongly for the link between social structure and cosmology. Social action and choice contain implicit meanings. Thus a link exists between action, belief and social structure. Douglas isolates two key factors in the social matrix, grid and group. These parameters have been difficult to formulate clearly and this led her to change considerably the definitions in the second edition of her book. However these two factors, clearly defined, will throw light on the inculturation issue (cf. Arbuckle, 1990).

From the work of Basil Bernstein, Mary Douglas adapts the concepts of 'restricted' and 'elaborated' codes as clues to the nature of group dynamics and interaction and thus to symbols in the group. Restricted codes are found in groups where roles, values and assumptions are clearly defined and regulated. Using the analogy of symbols as language, the concept is developed that symbols condense the values of society. They share and control the values of the group and this enables them to operate powerfully. Thus in a restricted code there are two elements, the communication and the control. It is therefore not only an issue of a particular group having its own jargon, but also of the control of the individual by the use of the code. When symbols are able to express and enforce a particular group interpretation, then they are said to be highly condensed. If the control is weak, then ritual is open to personal interpretation, and so the symbols are diffuse, which implies that the meaning of the symbol may differ from one individual to another. Symbols are seen as a form of restricted code. Elaborated codes are used in the context of a lack of common interpretation and control. This would happen in the case of people from different cultures conversing and in contexts where particular emphasis had been put on the freedom of the individual to express interpretations differing from the group consensus.

Group is not so much about the boundaries that delineate a particular tribe but the experience of social bonding that enables the existence of shared values. It has various parameters: temporary/permanent, inclusive/exclusive, hierarchical/decentralized. As these factors vary, so group forces can be either weak or strong. There are different groups in which people participate which include family, clan, tribe, nation, hunting party, football crowd, school, church congregation, prayer group. In all these, group can be in differing degrees strong or weak. Weak group means that the bonding is weak and individuals are able to assert their ego; strong group means that the bonding is such that the concerns of the many dominate the concerns of the individual.

Grid is the control of the system of classification of the group, and thus implicit cosmology. This too has various aspects, sexual roles, age roles, and charismatic leadership. Grid varies from strong to weak, contrast for example a monastic order with a tribal village, and with pluralist post-modern society. Weak grid means that there is the possibility of a private system of classification. Strong grid means that the shared classification of the group prevails over any individual freedom.

Strong grid and strong group tends to lead to ritualism. Weak grid and weak group favours effervescence. Douglas develops this further, in her earlier edition, to a 'crude typology' of social structure and the corresponding ideas about ritual, sin and self. Thus strong grid/group has a complex regulative cosmos and is ritualist. Weak grid/group has an unstructured cosmos and weakly condensed symbols. Strong grid/weak group has a success cosmology, syncretism, and ritualism. It is potentially millennial and contains private magic. Weak grid/strong group has a dual philosophy with the warring of good and evil, and a tendency to irrationalism. It is dominated by witches using magical objects, and is ritualist in that it is open to counter-witchcraft.

All this may seem a little speculative but the comparison of the Dinka, Nuer and Mandari demonstrates some of the evaluative power of the model. The relationship between grid and group is therefore connected to the different types of cosmology and the way that symbols operate in that society. This may seem a simple theory but it has important implications for localization of theology and worship.

The differences between the first edition of *Natural Symbols* and later editions have led to different interpretations of the theory. Walsh (1980) sees group as the boundary specifying common membership and belonging, and grid as the network of culturally defined roles. Thus in the first edition group was defined as a bounded social unit, and grid as the rules that relate one person to another. However, the later edition clarifies that grid is the control of the system of classification, and group is about the strength of bonding of a society. Mary Douglas became more cautious about the relationship of grid/group to cosmological systems in the later edition and cut out some of the important diagrams that linked grid/group with cosmology. Nevertheless the typology from the first edition (used above) underlies much of the discussion in the second edition.

Based on the typology of Mary Douglas the following question can be raised: What happens to a symbol system (such as a liturgy) as it is transported from one society to another? Let us take for example the 1662 *Book of Common Prayer*, which is widely used in the African Provinces of the Anglican Communion. The Reformation occurred as late medieval Europe was undergoing change. The strong grid power of the Papacy was weakening to the different grid power of nationalism. It was also a period of weakening group. There was new learning associated with the humanists and the beginnings of the age of exploration. The printing press was an important factor in change, ideas could now be published more quickly than ever before and the grid controls were less able to cope than had been the case when books had to be copied by hand. The Prayer Book contains features that are concomitant with this situation. There is a more cautious use of symbol as compared with the medieval Mass (or even if you compare the 1559 book which Cranmer produced with the 1552 book). The eucharistic interpretation steps away from the concrete to the more abstract. There is a tendency to explain the symbolic (e.g. the black rubric), a sign of a move away from strongly condensed to more weakly condensed symbols, for symbols no longer speak for themselves but have to be explained. This may indicate a shift in the capacity to appreciate the symbolic and a movement towards an emphasis on the rational.

This book was then transported to Africa by missionaries who themselves were from a different social context to the book. Their society was very different from that of the sixteenth century. It was not only exploring the world but also now civilizing and colonizing it. They were outside the constraints of the controls imposed at home (a position that was exploited by those who rejected the ideology of the Prayer Book, hence the Zanzibar rite of 1918 in Southern Tanzania). They came from a society that was increasingly questioning the basis of the message they were propagating, and they were either reacting defensively against that or were opening up to the new possibilities.

The Prayer Book is then taken to a different social context. There is a great variety of cultures in Africa but in general the societies are more strongly bounded and with tighter grid control than Europe, the exceptions being in the cases of the hunters and gatherers and the nomadic tribes. Societies with strong grid/group (e.g. the Baganda in Uganda) were among the first to be evangelized and to receive the message. Societies with weak group and strong grid (e.g. the Karamajong in Uganda or the Maasai in Kenya) have been more resistant. Nevertheless the grid and group strength in Africa was still greater than in late medieval Europe. African cosmology reflected this, e.g. the strong grid and group of African culture which transverses the boundary of death. Thus the ancestors are a central element in traditional spirituality.

The effect of translating Bible and Prayer Book together at the onset of evangelization has produced the attitude that they are both a received part of truth, the essence of Christianity. However, notwithstanding the conservatism of liturgy in the face of cultural change, the rise of discussion about the inculturation of rites and the exodus of people into the Independent Churches have both put contextualization onto the agenda of the Mission Churches. The tensions produced by a rite adopted from one social context and transferred to another were felt in England with the debates about the production of the *Alternative Service Book* and *Common Worship*. Similar tensions are found in Africa but many have felt the power of tradition, the Prayer Book being one of the aspects of Christianity received from the missionaries. At the moment it is sufficient to note that the framework of Mary Douglas has provided a structure that illuminates some of the anthropological reasons for the rise of the contextualization debate with regard both to theology and to liturgy. We move now to the work of Victor Turner who provides a framework that reveals other problems in the reception of the symbol of the eucharist in an African context.

Victor Turner

Turner (1968, p. 15) defines ritual as 'prescribed formal behaviour for occasions not given over to technological routine, having reference to beliefs in mystical (or non empirical) beings or powers'. The smallest unit of ritual behaviour is the symbol. It may be associated with any object, activity, relationship, word, gesture, or spatial arrangement in a ritual situation. Symbols are polysemic for they condense many values, ideas, concepts of a society, as in the use of bread and wine in the *Book of Common Prayer*. This speaks not only of the body and blood of Christ, but also of the giving of communion in both kinds, which was a symbol of being Protestant in pre-Vatican 2 days. The multivocality of the symbol distinguishes it from signs 'which by convention are restricted to a single referant' (p. 5).

Symbols are (p. 1), 'storage units, into which are packed the maximum amount of information ... they can ... be regarded as multi-faceted mnemonics, each facet corresponding to a specific cluster of values, norms, beliefs, sentiments, social roles, and relationships'. Put into the terms of Sperber (1974, 1975) they are objects that society uses to evoke a particular network of interpretations. The evocational nature of symbols makes the transference of symbol a more difficult procedure than the translation of words. The Bible may provide one set of symbolic interpretations, and the teaching of the missionaries another, but these cannot be isolated from evocations linked to traditional religion. Indeed Sperber maintains that there is a tendency towards integration of symbolic data. Thus traditional religion will provide some of the evocations as much as Christian sources. In other words the interpretation put on the symbol by the individual or group partially depends upon their pre-understanding and, in an African context, this includes concepts from the pre-Christian era.

The perceptions of the missionaries as agents of cross-cultural transference of symbol now become important. 'Far, far away in heathen darkness dwelling, millions of soul for ever may be lost'. This is still a popular hymn in Uganda today and expresses many of the attitudes of missionaries. The Africans live in heathen darkness, so there is nothing to learn from traditional culture, what is needed is a *tabula rasa*, the destruction of traditional culture in order to bring civilization (cf. Okot, 1980a). All power may have been given to Christ but at the time all power had also been given to the colonial nations. Thus two symbolic systems found an affinity: the preaching of the gospel and the civilizing of the heathen. The emphasis was on preaching rather than listening, on the Christ who came to bring the new, rather than to fulfil the old, on discontinuity rather than on continuity. Thus the major method of evangelism became the school. The older generation were only mildly evangelized, boarding schools were built to remove children from their culture in order to civilize and convert them.

As the missionaries were not able to keep the symbolic systems of Church and state divided in their own consciousness, neither were the Africans able to divide the two in theirs. Hansen (1985) has shown that the CMS mission in Uganda was relating to the state as if it were established. The mission tried to influence the state by introducing laws on marriage, and by trying to set up a Christian nation. The mission saw that the role of the state was to provide a setting for the advancement of Christian civilization. This process was encouraged by the fact that the missionaries and the colonialists were from the same country and often the same social background. But the mission could also exercise power over the state through supporters at home. Bishop Tucker at one point raised money from mission supporters to keep the East Africa Company solvent so that he could organize a lobby of parliament to have the nation taken over as a Protectorate. He was successful on both counts. The mission had great power in the colonial state, as it was the only organization, besides the government, that was nationally based. It had its own schools and its own newspaper. Thus the mission could put great pressure on the state to Christianize the nation. Perhaps the symbolic triumph of this is that the coronation of the Kabaka of Buganda became a Christian ceremony performed at the Anglican cathedral.

The mission may have arrived before the colonialists in some areas but the link between Christianity and colonialism was clear in the mind of the African. Colonial rule took away the power from the chief and a new world was opened. Taxes were required each year and the use of money, a new substance, was necessary. The missionary was one who could be turned to, as he had the advantage of being white like the colonial administrator. To understand these new ways education was required, and the mission provided this. The power of the white man was also seen in the ability to cure disease and again this came from the mission. Russell (1966) says people flocked to the church because it provided the route to understanding the new society that had been formed. He says that in Acholi, perhaps more than in any other part of Uganda, *dini* [religion, in this case Christianity] was welcomed for what it could give: entry to the new world. That part of *dini* which was connected with arithmetic and learning to speak English was of obvious and immediate value. That part of it connected with saying your prayers and singing hymns – and not marrying more than one wife – was of doubtful value but accepted as part of the whole. Thus Christianity came as a part of the whole of the new social order.

The attitude of the missions was of *tabula rasa*, the role of the missionary was seen as to bring Christianity and civilization. The assumption is that civilization is something that the African does not have, that his culture is primitive. The same attitude was common in the anthropological books of the colonial era. This has resulted in the destruction of much traditional society but also the production of a dual religious system of Christianity and traditional religion, not mixed together but held in tension at the same time, through partial assimilation but mostly by making the new order a superstructure to the old. The adoption of a package of both Christianity and the new order by the African has compounded the development of such a system.

As noted above, Turner commented that symbols are multifaceted mnemonics, which include specific values, beliefs and relationships. In their interpretation the pre-understanding of African religion is important for the eucharist. Mbiti (1971) raises a number of issues connected to the eucharist concerning the magical conception of the world. Firstly (p. 120), 'the Akamba think more in concrete than abstract forms'. Thus the use of the material to denote the spiritual is easily understood. However in Protestantism there is an ambiguity about this. The *Book of Common Prayer*, for example, is happy to call the elements the body and blood of Christ, yet at the same time the black rubric says that 'the sacramental bread and wine remain still in their very natural substances'. A whole set of philosophic issues is raised by such a comment that relate to European history but not to Africa. Yet these issues were seen as a part of the civilization that was to be brought there. African theology might well question the helpfulness of the philosophical category of substance, and the ambiguity of the position that the bread and wine are both the body and blood and are not the body and the blood. But it could also assert that there is little difficulty in an African context of understanding that bread labelled 'body' is symbolic cognition, rite and symbol being a familiar mode to traditional society. Indeed the problem in understanding the elements is more a European one where the status of symbolic cognition has been downgraded compared with the rational.

A second problem that Mbiti raises is also to do with a magical world-view. The tradition of the Africa Inland Mission (AIM) (p. 113) was that:

> at every celebration the minister reads the portion 1 Cor 11:23–34. The middle portion of this passage (especially verses 27–34) conveys what to the Akamba sounds like threats of magic and curse, to both of which the people are extremely sensitive. Perhaps unconsciously they transpose associations of magic and witchcraft with food and drink onto the elements at the eucharist.

Lack of dialogue on the part of the missionary with traditional culture gives this impression to the Akamba. As Turner has pointed out, ritual condenses cultural values and the field of evocation that a symbol raises will differ from one society to another. This is a particular example where a lack of a theology of listening has resulted in the exact opposite to what the missionary wanted to preach. AIM missionaries rejected any magical view of the eucharist and yet because they have had a *tabula rasa* approach they have ended up producing the very thing they wanted to avoid.

Thus Turner's comments on symbols condensing many values combined with Sperber's comments on fields of evocation raise important issues in the understanding of the eucharist and in the role of traditional religion within that understanding. But there are other matters that affect the eucharist and one is to do with its contrasting role in the sum total of Christian ritual compared with the system of traditional religion.

Turner discerns two types of ritual among the Ndembu: life-crisis rites and cults of affliction. The first group includes rites of passage, circumcision and funerals, which are to do with a passage from one state in society to another; for example, circumcision as a passage from infancy to adulthood. Rites of affliction respond to specific crises in society such as possession, sickness and infertility. These two categories cover all rites. The feature connecting them is that in these rites there is liminality and communitas.

In later life Turner (Turner & Turner, 1978) began to study Christian religion. In the work done among the Ndembu one of the paradigms of interpretation of rituals had been 'rites of passage' as developed from the work of van Gennep (1908, 1960). Much African ritual is a variation on the rite of passage model. Turner interpreted even the rituals of affliction within this framework. Turning to Catholic ritual he comments (pp. 31–2):

> the system does have something of the irreversible character of tribal rites of passage, giving direction to social and personal life . . . Baptism, confirmation, ordination to the priesthood, are all irreversible, once-only rites of passage which are declared dogmatically to 'imprint an indelible character on the soul' . . . the Eucharist and penance . . . neither of these is a rite of passage.

The relationship of the eucharist to the rite of passage model will be discussed in the next chapter. Yet it is possible to discern in all the sacraments (pp. 3–4) a 'somewhat truncated liminal phase'. Thus he develops the important category of liminoid or quasi-liminal.

The liminoid is akin to the liminal (p. 253) 'but not identical with it . . . [it] often represents the dismembering of the liminal, for various components that are joined in liminal situations split off to pursue separate destinies as specialized genres'. This splitting off can be seen in the history of Christian initiation. The complex rite of making a catechumen, preparation, baptism, confirmation, and first communion, which was one ritual complex in the early Church, was full of liminality and communitas, but it broke down into its component parts, each being liminoid (Maxwell, 1999). This divided pattern was incorporated into the service books and eventually transported to Africa. The Roman Catholic Church has potentially brought all the components back together with the Rite of Christian Initiation of Adults. There is, then, a major contrast between the total ritual complex of Traditional Religion and Christianity. Traditional Religion has as its central ritual paradigm rites of passage that exhibit liminality and communitas. Christianity has liminoid rites of passage but the central rite, the eucharist, is not a rite of passage or a rite of affliction.

Also important is the role of the ritual specialist. In Africa there has been a shortage of priests. Anglicans restrict the leading of the eucharist to a priest. These were few in number in the missionary-dominated Church and they have continued to be relatively few in number in the African-led Church. R. Bowen (in Buchanan, 1975, p. 239) comments:

> there is one 'disgrace' ... which sits upon the Anglican Church throughout the Third World: that, for the great majority of Christians, Holy Communion is nothing more than an occasional service, neither regular nor frequent. Thousands of Christians are waiting for the time when the Church will take appropriate steps to set apart *in every congregation* those who are given authority to preside at the eucharist.

The same problem exists in the Roman Catholic Church, e.g. in 1997 the Vatican published the statistic that there were 25,279 priests in Africa, a ratio of priest to faithful of less than 1: 4 500. The situation has not improved significantly since then. This contrasts with the abundance of ritual specialists in Traditional Religion who are indigenous and readily available.

Thus there are important differences in the ritual paradigms of Traditional Religion and Christianity. Christian worship is often liminoid and a combination of rites of passage and other forms of rite. There are a smaller number of ritual specialists and this leads to infrequent celebration of some rites. This compounds the problems in understanding the eucharist for the African Church. But before particular problems will be examined, not least the issue of what material to use for the elements, the work of Dan Sperber on symbol will be explored, in order to refine the understanding of symbols.

Dan Sperber

The work of Victor Turner has received criticism from Dan Sperber. Turner (1968) raises the problem of the meaning of a ritual symbol. He postulates two poles of meaning, the orectic pole, which relates to the particular matter used in the symbol, and the ideological pole, which relates to the more abstract meanings of the symbol. Turner then identifies three components or aspects of meaning: the exegetic/interpretative, the operational, and the positional. The exegetic meaning is that given by those inside the ritual system; the operational is derived from the use made of the symbol; the positional meaning is the relationship of the symbol in the total ritual system. It is over the nature of meaning that Sperber criticizes Turner.

Sperber (1974, 1975) rejects the idea that symbols are a language. This has been one theoretical approach to symbols used not least by Mary Douglas. Treated as a language, the symbolic code can be interpreted and rational statements can be made about any particular ritual. The assumption is that a move is made from the irrational to the rational, from the symbolical to the logical. But Sperber notes that exegesis is not as simple as that. People often do not know what a particular symbol means (compare, for example, the use of paper hats at a Christmas dinner). A code is expected to furnish exhaustive definition. Symbols do not. Even if a symbol is given an interpretation, the interpretation never enters analytic relationships proper to semantics. He continues (p. 34): 'Exegesis is not an interpretation, rather an extension of the symbol and must itself be interpreted'. To say that the bread represents Jesus as the Lamb of God is to continue in the same sphere of discourse and not to escape from it. Sperber also criticizes Turner for using the word meaning 'laxly'. He even suggests that the Ndembu concept of symbol is closer to his approach than to a semiotic one. The Ndembu see a symbol as a 'landmark', not a metaphor but a clue. Sperber proposes, instead of a semiotic approach, a cognitive approach.

The cognitive theory approaches symbols by the way the mind processes data. The mind classifies data in an encyclopaedic way. Facts are stored in various categories. The information is recorded in language following the rules of semantics. But some facts are 'facts'. They are not statements about the real world but are statements about beliefs. It is in the mechanism of distinguishing between facts and 'facts' that symbolic cognition is perceived. Data are received that are recognized to be a 'fact'. The mind now moves to looking at the problem rather than the data. This is the process of focalization, which continues into a process of evocation. Memory is searched for similar concepts that seem to relate to the data (now perceived to be symbolic). The process is not that of a computer but of a person browsing a library. Thus the connections are made for the symbolic interpretation of the 'fact'.

Holmes (1977) has attacked Sperber's criticisms of Turner and Sperber's notion of the existential order. He perceives behind Sperber's criticisms a commitment to 'Cartesian reduction'. He continues (p. 199), 'meaning to Sperber is rational and, consequently, related to technology and its values of control and prediction. Meaning is what can be reduced to a syllogism, fed into a computer, in order to predict the future'. Thus Holmes sees this rationalism as the basis for Sperber's disagreement with Turner over the meaning of meaning. Holmes regards the consequences of Sperber to be that symbols and rituals are meaningless, the symbolic mechanism is merely psychological, and that such reduction closes the possibility that symbols open to its ultimate meaning. But Holmes seems to have misunderstood Sperber. Sperber is not trying to be reductionist, but rather to change the paradigm through which we approach symbols from language to cognition. It is because the language paradigm produces difficulties at the level of meaning that Sperber proposes a paradigmatic shift. He clearly does not reduce meaning to the syllogism, rather he points to different mental processes that operate in different ways. Encyclopaedic knowledge is not rational compared with merely psychological symbolic knowledge. They are different levels of knowledge, different cognitive mechanisms. It is impossible to say from Sperber's premises that one is merely psychological and the other rational. Both are psychological and both are rational, but the processes of cognition are different in each. Thus symbols are not meaningless, but the mechanism of cognition is different from encyclopaedic knowledge. Sperber does not address the question of symbols and ultimate meaning but there is no inherent reason why a cognitive approach should close the relationship of a symbol to ultimate concerns.

Holmes's criticisms reflect a common problem as to the status of symbolic discourse. The rational and the symbolic are often opposed. Myth is by nature false. This opposition leads to the downgrading of the symbolic and the desire to move from the symbolic to the rational in discussion. Sperber's strength is in showing that this is an impossibility based on a false dichotomy. Symbolic discourse is an innate function of the mind. Thus it should be accepted together with the rational. It is worth while noting at this point that Sperber's category of symbol is very wide ranging. Not only does it cover myth and ritual but also most of theology, much of philosophy, world-views based on 'science', and contemporary ideologies such as 'the American dream', advertising and play.

It is at the level of the nature of the operation of the symbolic mechanism that Sperber can be criticized. Ornstein's (1972) theory of 'split brain' would require a modification of the explanation of Sperber. The different functions of the two halves of the brain suggest that logical and symbolic interpretations are occurring at the same time, rather than one after the other. Sperber's criticisms of Turner do not alter the value of much of Turner's analytical framework but may alter the status attributed to some of its interpretations. However, in Turner's complex and subtle approach there is not always the assumption that there is an opposition between symbol and meaning. In his discussion of the orectic pole we see that a close relationship is postulated between the physiological phenomena and meaning, which is regarded as a corollary of the physical matter. Sperber brings important qualifications to the work of Turner, but much of the work of both anthropologists is complementary.

Turner isolated two poles of meaning of a symbol: the orectic and the ideological. Having examined Sperber's approach to symbol, these two poles of meaning will be examined in relation to the eucharist in Africa. There is the difficult orectic issue of the nature of the material to be used for the elements. This will be examined first. Then there are various ideological issues, which will be investigated later.

Orectic Issues

Turner analyses symbols as being both multivocal and also as unifying disparate *significata*. They do the latter because they have two poles of meaning, the ideological pole and the sensory pole. The ideological pole relates to the moral and social orders, principles of social organization, and to norms and values inherent in structured relationships. The sensory (or orectic) pole relates to physiological phenomena and processes, where (Turner & Turner, 1978, p. 247) 'meaning is closely related to the outward form of the symbol'. This pole of meaning raises particular problems in the African context.

Bread and Wine

It may seem that the material to be used in the eucharist was defined by Jesus at the Last Supper, bread and wine. However, there have been a series of disputes in church history as to what sort of bread and what sort of wine. These early debates provide a framework to determine the appropriate elements, but also show that there has been diversity in the history of the sending Churches. It may seem that the issue of 'matter' had been decided by the time of the missionary era, but there were in fact a variety of traditions that were transplanted. Some were tied to a concept of 'validity' as the result of the historic debates, while others were more flexible in their approach. However, the situation is now compounded with the diversity of material used in the Independent Churches.

One of the first debates about the elements to be used began on African soil between Cyprian and the Aquarians who celebrated with water instead of wine. Cyprian (Roberts & Donaldson, 1957, pp. 358–64) argues against the Aquarians on a number of grounds. Firstly, the example of Jesus is held to be binding. 'Nothing must be done by us but what the Lord first did on our behalf . . . we must observe what he taught; that we do what he did'. Secondly, wine is essential as it was used by Jesus to fulfil prophecy. The bread and wine brought forth by Melchizedek are seen as types of the eucharist: Likewise the bread and wine in Proverbs 9. Thirdly, he argues that 'water by itself cannot express the blood of Christ'. Thus 'the blood of Christ is not offered if there be no wine in the cup, nor the Lord's sacrifice celebrated with a legitimate consecration unless our oblation and sacrifice respond to his passion'. For Cyprian wine is essential for a valid eucharist, an argument based partially on the property of water being deficient to symbolize the blood of Christ.

Cyprian also argues that the cup must be mixed. This partially goes back to Proverbs 9 'drink of the wine I have mingled for you'. He further argues for this by pointing to the blood and water flowing from Jesus' side. Therefore 'the cup should be mingled with a union of wine and water'. This is then interpreted allegorically: 'We see that in the water is understood the people, but in the wine is showed the blood of Christ. But when the water is mingled in the cup with wine, the people is made one with Christ, and the assembly of believers is associated and cojoined with him'. To offer water alone is only to offer ourselves and not to offer Christ. The mixing of water and wine in the cup speaks of the inseparability of Christ and his people 'that mixture [of water and wine] cannot any more be separated . . . nothing can separate the Church . . . from Christ'. Thus there is the close connection in Cyprian of water–wine and mixture–unity (of Christ and the Church). Wine and mixing are essential.

Erickson (1970) say that a more serious dispute arose in the eleventh century. Jesus probably used unleavened bread assuming that the Last Supper was a Passover meal. However, Woolley (1913) argues that by the time of the apostles the switch had been made to leavened bread. He bases this on the use of the word *artos* in the narratives of institution, since this word is always qualified if it means unleavened bread. Thus the tradition up to the eleventh century was to use leavened bread. As doctrine developed, emphasis grew on the presence of Christ in the bread. Thus the west changed to unleavened bread (wafers), as they do not produce so many crumbs, a change that was condemned by the east. They saw this as Judaizing. Jesus had brought a new covenant and so we do not need to follow the Passover pattern of unleavened bread. In fact the east used the contradiction in the gospels about the date of the Last Supper to deny that it was a Passover meal. Leavened bread must be used because Jesus is the living bread. Unleavened bread is lifeless. Thus the two traditions parted.

The Reformation led to another change in the west and the reintroduction of leavened bread but the arguments were not directly related to doctrinal issues. Later the elements used came to represent the party position, so that in the Church of England, the more Catholic used wafers and the Evangelicals used bread. Thus western missionaries brought to Africa a complex of issues relating to the material used.

Maize and Banana Wine?

Uzukwu (1980) points out that Africa has an independent tradition of agriculture and that different plants and animals were used in African religion. He concludes that the Israelites brought the fruit of their labour into the cult of *Yhwh* and that if they had lived in Africa they would have offered millet, maize, yam or cassava. Jesus was conditioned by space and time. Therefore the African Christian is (pp. 380–1) 'bound to celebrate the eucharistic memorial with food and drink, but this food and drink do not necessarily have to be wheat or barley bread and grape wine'. He suggests that the use of imported material undermines the 'natural parable' of spiritual nourishment and that material that has been used in traditional religion could be used, as it would then show the 'recapitulation of all sacrifices of the past in Christ'. Thus he recommends the use of maize or preferably millet and the use of palm or banana wine. This private view has not been taken by the Roman Catholic Church. Bishop Dupont (diocese of Pala, Chad, 1973–75) celebrated the eucharist using millet bread and millet beer due to difficulties of importing the wine and was subsequently relieved of his office. How have other Churches adapted to the African situation?

The Anglican Church arrived in Uganda in 1877. The Church Missionary Society began by translating the Bible and the 1662 *Book of Common Prayer* into the vernacular. Bishop Tucker aimed for an African church. He ruled that pastors and evangelists should wear the *kanzu* (a long white robe). Ward (personal communication, 1985) said that in a society where the basic food is the banana (the word *matoke* is used both for the banana and to mean food) he allowed *gonja* (banana) and *mubisi* (banana juice) to be used as the elements. This practice died out in the 1920s when wheat and wine were imported. The war of 1977 and the subsequent collapse of the economy resulted in a great variety of usage. For bread, wafers may be purchased from the Roman Catholics or *Malaika* biscuits (Swahili for angel) from the shops. As a bottle of wine may have cost the equivalent of three months' collection, the following have been used instead, Tree Top orange juice, Ribena, Blackcurrant Rise and Shine, Martini Rosso, or local wines from bananas. Economics determined the choice of the material (except in the case of the Martini). The ritual follows the 1662 order. The word used for bread in the Acholi book is *mugati*, a Swahili loan word that means European bread (i.e. made of wheat and risen with yeast, the use of both being unknown to traditional diet). The word used for wine is *vino*, an Italian loan word introduced by the Roman Catholic missionaries. The service is conducted on a *major maleng* (a holy table), *major* being another loan word, and it is conducted by a *ladit* (a local word meaning originally village elder). The language used illustrates some of the problems and the use of loan words and imported material helps foster the foreignness of Holy Communion. Foreignness inhibits the incarnation of the eucharist in the African consciousness. It is a factor that restricts embodiment of sacramental experience.

African Independent Churches broke away from the Mission Churches often over indigenization of leadership and worship. They desired to have Churches which followed the slogan 'Africa for the Africans'. Mbiti reports (1971) about The Friends of the Holy Spirit in Machakos who separated from the AIM. In Machakos town they did not celebrate the eucharist at all. In Kitui they met at night in a member's house and eat a meal together. At the end of the meal one *kyavati* (a sort of thin local bread) was consecrated and shared among the members. Then brown coffee with sugar was prepared, consecrated and distributed using only one cup. Communion is at night to prevent the participation of non-members. Mbiti comments that in their reaction against AIM they have recaptured the practice of the early Church, for they have unconsciously revived the agape, the fellowship meal of the church community.

In the Churches of Africa a great variety of material is used for the eucharistic elements. The Roman Catholic Church has continued in the line of Cyprian and argues that the elements should be those of the Last Supper, wheat bread and grape wine. The Ethiopian Orthodox (as we shall see in the next chapter) keeps to the spirit of Cyprian, if not quite the letter. Practicality of transport would seem to be one factor why at times they used steeped raisins for wine. In the previous chapter it was seen that Tillich argued that there was an intimate relationship between the element and the sacrament. He posited a natural power in the element that makes it suitable to become the sacrament. Likewise Turner did not see the choice of matter as purely arbitrary. The variety of material used does not suggest that there is a strict relationship between the symbol and the particular matter, but the comments of these two scholars suggest that there are some limits. These may be defined if not by Cyprian's dictum that we must use what Jesus used at the Last Supper, then by the limitation that it must be as close to that as possible, or that it must reflect the fact that Jesus used what was common food for his day. These issues continue to be points of debate, e.g. Uzukwu (1991), Lumbala (1998), Quevedo-Bosch (1994), Meyers (1998) and Gibson (2001).

At the Last Supper Jesus took bread, his followers use qurban, *gonja*, biscuits, bread, *kyavati* and wafers. Jesus took wine, his followers use the juice of steeped raisins, *musibi*, wine, Tree Top, Ribena, coffee, Fanta, honey and water. With a diversity of elements comes a diversity of interpretation associated with the material. Concepts include ordinary food, spotless lamb and fellowship meal. At one pole matter and interpretation are closely related but there is also an ideological pole, which influences the interpretation of the eucharist and may feed back to the particular elements used.

Ideological Issues

Turner identified two poles of meaning for a symbol. The previous section has examined the orectic pole and the issues related to the elements of the eucharist. This will be returned to in the case studies. The other pole of meaning in Turner's analysis is ideological. There has been a long debate through the history of the Church as to the meaning of the eucharist. The approach here is not to repeat that discussion but to raise those issues that are particularly contextually relevant. The starting-point for discussion of the eucharist is the *lex orandi*, the eucharistic service, for the ideological meaning is embedded in the ritual process, the service itself, rather than in abstract discussion.

Idowu (1965, p. 29) commenting on the existing situation said, the 'basic reason for the frustrating inadequacy of the existing liturgies in the Nigerian context is that they did not spring from the cultic needs and spiritual temperament of the Nigerians'. He continued (p. 30) the 'church has to put up with liturgies imported, ready-made from abroad with the prescription they must be used intact'. Each Church comes in for criticism; of the Free Churches he says (p. 28) 'those orders are planless and chaotic', of the Anglican he says (p. 27) 'the main reason for its unsuitability in this climate is purely and simply that it is Anglican; that is, it is for the English to be used by English worshippers', and of the Roman Catholics he comments (p. 28) 'what seems to cover up the liturgical unsuitability in their own set-up is the fact that it is heavily compensated for by the impressive paraphernalia of a dramatic, ritualistic worship ... it strongly appeals ... as a European system of incantation and magic'. These comments illustrate the tensions arising from the cross-cultural transplantation of symbol. If indigenous or contextual liturgy is to appear then it will come only as it engages in dialogue with African culture and this includes traditional religion. What are the issues posed by Africa for Christian ritual?

Hearne (1980) identified two focuses around which clusters of issues revolve: community and sacrifice. Firstly, community; this includes the role of ancestors in traditional rites and its relationship to the doctrine of the communion of the saints, the practice of public confession, and the incorporation of the individual into the community (which pertains more to initiation than to the eucharist). Secondly, sacrifice; this includes the practice of sacrifice and its relationship to the eucharist, the doctrine of the atonement and concepts of memorial. Though not exhaustive these provide a useful framework on which to examine specific issues.

Community and Ancestors

The African concept of community is very strong. Not only is it expressed in the extended family but also in religious convictions. In the west the dead are 'dead and gone' in Africa they are 'dead and still with us'. The Reformation contained a strong reaction against the cult of the dead and this has been strengthened by the age of reason, which influenced so much of western thinking. Thus Protestant missionaries were suspicious of the ancestor cult of African religions, and Roman Catholics came with a pre-packaged answer. It has only been as the African Church has come of age that the issue has come onto the agenda.

Shorter (1975a) develops a typology of six different approaches to ancestors:

1 Strict theism. Here both formal and experiential prayers are addressed directly to the supreme being. He gives the Galla, Kikuyu, Karamajong and Pigmies as examples of this.
2 Relative theism. Here both formal and experiential prayers are mediated through a mode of existence. These modes of existence are spirits, divinities or heavenly bodies that are conceived as modes of existence of god and not as distinct from him. The Nuer, Dinka and Bushmen are examples here.
3 Symmetrical mediation. Divinities or spirits, usually ancestral, are distinct intermediaries. They mediate man's worship to the supreme being and the gift of life itself. Examples include the Edo, Kongo, Tumbuka and Nyamwezi.
4 Asymmetrical mediation. The mediators are principally channels of formal prayer; the supreme being can be approached directly in experiential prayer. The Shona, Luba, Kamba and Zande are included here.
5 Strict deism. The religious reality of a supreme being is problematical. There is a bond of worship to spirits and divinities but it is unclear how far a supreme being underlies such phenomena. The Acholi and the Hazda seem to be the only examples of this and both of these are disputed.
6 Relative deism. Life is seen as controlled by guardian divinities, spirits and heroes of eminent ancestors to whom formal prayer is directed. This does not exclude direct experience and formal prayer to the supreme being whose relationship to the divinities is equivocal or at least tense. In fact it is not clear how far the supreme being is supreme as the divinities may be in revolt. Examples include the Nyoro, Soga, Shilluk, Ovambo, Akan and even the ancient Egyptians.

This analysis shows the variety of approaches to the role of ancestors in Traditional Religion. Protestantism takes the position of strict theism. Roman Catholicism does not quite correspond to any of the forms above but is a modified variety of asymmetrical mediation in that both formal and informal prayer is addressed to God and may be sought through the saints.

Sawyerr (1968, p. 128) concluded his discussion of ancestor worship by saying: 'Africans do worship their ancestors and divinities'. The typology of Shorter may be used to question this conclusion. In the deistic models this may be so but it is not a necessary conclusion in the theistic categories. Nevertheless the comment of Sawyerr (p. 129) that 'ancestor worship ... falls far short of Christian worship', illuminates the need for greater study of the issue.

Mbiti (1971) distinguishes three modes of existence for human life. Firstly, there is man in his living state. Secondly, at death a person becomes a living-dead. Such a person is remembered by name and communicated with. Their presence is not as strong as when living and there is a sense of separation. The living-dead appear only to the close relatives. After a few generations the living-dead can no longer be recognized by name and then, thirdly, they become spirits (*iimu*). In all this there is a continuing, if fading, sense of community.

Thus the bond of community fades as the name is lost, but the feeling of community beyond the grave is strong. This has obvious parallels to the communion of the saints, a fact which is implicit in some Protestant liturgy, 'therefore with angels and archangels and all the company of heaven'. It would seem that it would be possible to stress that we pray with all the company of heaven in a eucharistic prayer or in the intercessions without going beyond the bounds of the Reformation. Also various persons could be named in the rite in that the naming of an individual is one of the expressions of the continuing relationship. There is certainly much precedent in liturgical history for the naming of saints in the liturgy. The African Church could ask the west if its attitudes to death are particularly helpful and if its ritual expression of that is biblically deficient. It would seem that, rather than condemning the feeling of unity with ancestors, the approach could be of clarifying and amplifying. The New Testament stresses the unity of believers in Christ. Death is no longer a power over men because of the resurrection of Christ. Christians continue to be in Christ after death and therefore remain in unity with the living. The dead do not fade into a different existence but remain with Christ who knows them by name. There are sufficient areas in common with Traditional Religion to begin a fruitful dialogue and develop an African theology with a positive attitude to African culture.

The issue of praying for the dead is a controversial one in the western Church. Fasholé-Luke (1974, pp. 209–21) sees it as a Christian duty. 'African theologians must therefore recover the practice of the ancient North African church and pray in faith for the departed.' He considers that the traditional distinction between *dulia* and *latria* are sufficient grounds for an African veneration of the saints and proposes that this is the approach that the Church should take to the phenomenon of ancestor veneration. Taylor (1963, p. 165) concludes:

> is it not time for the church to learn to give the Communion of the Saints the centrality which the soul of Africa craves? Neither the inhibited silence of the Protestants nor the too-presumptuous schema of Rome allows African Christians to live *with* their dead in the way which they feel profoundly true to Man's nature.

The situation becomes more complex when dealing with non-Christian ancestors, but is a real problem in the many areas of first or second generation Christianity. Taylor (p. 171) links the question to the solidarity of mankind and suggests that 'the Christian's link with his pagan ancestors, in remembrance and unceasing intercession, may be part of . . . ultimate redemption', though he deferred the issue to the next generation of African theologians. Fasholé-Luke (p. 217) suggests 'African ancestors could be included in the communion of saints . . . since they had a faith which was not perfect'. In Roman Catholic circles the approach to the pagan ancestors is now much influenced by Rahner's doctrine of the anonymous Christian. In all Churches the question is compounded by the strong teaching on hell, which was a part of the gospel as preached. In the heathen darkness millions of souls were *forever* to be lost.

Liturgically there has been little development of an approach to ancestors (Vundla, 1990; Kings & Morgan, 2001). *The Roman Missal for the Dioceses of Zaire* includes an invocation of the saints and includes ancestors (Lumbala, 1998). Other invocations follow western patterns, e.g. the angelus or the litany of the saints. The Ethiopian Orthodox remembers the saints in the eucharistic prayers in an eastern way. The issue is one that is still debated and many Protestant Churches either follow the inherited patterns or have adopted the new patterns from the west. However Sawyerr (in Pobee, 1976, p. 95) gives a personal example of one invocation, which may be the route that will be followed. 'May the Shades of William Vincent Lucas, that devout Servant of God and bishop of Masasi (1926–44), our Christian ancestor, who strove to find a Christian approach to non Christian Customs, offer this experiment to the God he served as an offering in spite of its imperfections.'

Community and Confession

Turner (1968) reports the importance of public confession in a ritual of affliction. The ritual specialist carefully brings out the tensions in society and the breaches in society may be healed, though this is not automatic. Confession may also be required in cases of witchcraft, another period of affliction. In these cases the offender may not be conscious that he is the culprit. But confession brings about the restoration of social harmony. There are also examples of confession in rites of passage. Girls may be expected to confess if they are virgin at their initiation.

Confession is one symbol in a rite, which has as an object the reuniting of division; hence community is the dominant symbol. There are interesting links to the rite of penance.

The rite of penance emerged in the third century as a public system to deal with major post-baptismal sin (Dallen, 1986). It was regarded as a second baptism and was very severe. The breach in the community was healed by the public confession of the penitent and after repentance, a reincorporation of the person into the fellowship. The practice of public confession gradually died out and was replaced by private penance, which was made compulsory by the fourth Lateran council. It was then rejected by most of the Reformers who particularly objected to the conception of a priesthood who could remit sins. So the Roman Catholics brought the system of private sacramental confession, and the Protestants brought their suspicions of this but some have a practice of general confession.

The East African revival is significant in its resurrection of public confession of sin. J.E. Church (1981) documents the early history of the revival from the inside and comments that the 'time of light' is one of the features of the movement. In the Rwanda Mission there was a strong anti-Catholic attitude, which objected to any concept of priestly absolution even in the *Book of Common Prayer*, yet this feature of open confession in the prayer meeting, which was a spontaneous development at first, was encouraged. Stott (1964) says that this caused some debate 'at home' and has parallels to other revivals, but it is one of the distinguishing features of a movement, which has great impact on the East African Church. Max Warren (1954) drew attention to the public confession of sin in the Independent Churches in South Africa. In the Zionist Churches it is common for it to take place at baptism – a declaration of particular sins from which the candidate is being cleansed. Indeed one objection to infant baptism in these Churches is that infants cannot confess their sins.

In both these Christian rites, baptism (the rite of passage) and the prayer meeting (which has affinity to a rite of affliction), confession has become an integral part in some Churches. Discussion on confession has just begun to influence the eucharistic rite, e.g. The Tanzanian Liturgy of 1973/4 included these words in its general confession, 'I am very sorry, I repent of my sins and I desire to forsake them'. Bowen says that these words were deliberately included as an explicit expression of repentance, which is an important feature of East African spirituality and at the heart of the Revival movement.

Community and Space

One of the criteria that caused Turner (1978, p. 4) to differentiate between tribal rites and the sacraments of the Roman Catholic Church was the 'spatial location of liminality'. The use of space is also a symbolic factor. Mbiti (1971, pp. 123–4) comments:

> It would also be meaningful for the congregation to sit in a semicircle or a full circle, with the Eucharistic Table at the centre. The people have lived for years in circular houses, and obviously a circular or oval church building may give a more familiar atmosphere of community and fellowship than do the now common rectangular church.

This seems to be a point of contact with the liturgical movement, however there are limitations. Although the round hut is extremely common in Africa it is by no means universal. Donovan (1978, pp. 124–5) among the Masai reports that a more indigenous approach was for the Mass to be celebrated in different parts of the village:

> It was a strange kind of Mass. No church building, not even any special fixed spot where it took place. As a matter of fact it moved around the village. It started in the spot where several elders had lighted a fire ... As the Mass began, I picked up a tuft of grass and passed it on to the first elder ... 'the peace of Christ'. He accepted it and passed it on to his family ... The Mass moved from the place of the fire lighting to the place of the passing of the grass to the dancing area.

So far space has been used to emphasize a place as *domus ecclesiae*. There is, however, another tradition in the Christian Church, that of *domus dei*, and this is found in the Ethiopian Orthodox Church. Churches there are either square, hexagonal or, most commonly, round. The building is divided into three concentric circles. Ullendorff (1968) says that the centre is 'the holy of holies', the next circle is 'the place of miracles' and the outer circle is 'the place where the hymns are sung'. The inner circle is where the eucharist is consecrated, the middle circle is where the laity come to receive communion, the outer circle is where the laity stand throughout most of the service. This pattern is modelled on the temple of Solomon (an important figure in Ethiopian mythology) but there are important differences. Even in the square churches 'the holy of holies' is in the centre and not to one end. Men and women stand in different places in 'the place where the hymns are sung' but there is no separate court of women. The middle circle is not the domain of a particular group (cf. the Levites in the temple) but used only to receive communion. The Ethiopian Church received the gospel in the fourth century when the *domus dei* tradition was developing and has never received the *domus ecclesiae* conception. Nevertheless it has adapted its model to fit both a Christian interpretation and the African architecture of the round hut. Thus roundness need not represent community but is certainly more indigenous in style in those areas where round huts are most common.

Sacrifice

Pobee (1983, p. 5) says that 'African spirituality is very much Old Testament in texture and orientation'. Part of the reason for this is the fact that animal sacrifice plays an important part in both. To Christians in the west the concept of sacrifice is refined and abstract. To the African it is an everyday occurrence. In some Christian Churches sacrifices still have a part to play: the Ethiopian Orthodox sacrifice at the consecration of a new church, and Naussbaum (1984) reports that some Independent Churches accept the offering of sacrifices.

Sawyerr argued that the sacrificial practices of African peoples are a reliable bridge leading from traditional religious practice to the heart of the Christian message. Hearne (1980) also sees sacrifice as a link with Christianity, as does Amusan (1998). Thompson (1974), however, argued the essential difference between the two sacrificial systems. Most African rites have a forward-looking reference; those in the Old Testament are retrospective. The purpose of sacrifice in the Old Testament is to give thanks or to atone for sins, and it is directed to God. African sacrifice is offered to ancestors to secure some desired favour.

Anthropological study of sacrifice reveals a number of similarities and differences between traditional sacrifices and the eucharist. Bourdillon (1980) views sacrifice as a natural symbol due to its almost universal use in religious ritual. It is often used in the rites of passage where it may have a prophylactic function (to drive away evil spirits or enlist good spirits). But there are many other contexts in which sacrifice may occur and there is a close connection between sacrifice and power. There are contrasts between the eucharist and traditional sacrifice. The most obvious one is that in the eucharist there is no slaying of a victim. Eucharistic sacrifice is a metaphor; traditional sacrifice includes the death of an animal.

Sacrifices are used on a variety of occasions in traditional religion, not least those associated with the rites of passage. In Christianity rites of passage and sacrifice have been divided. Thus catechumens do not receive communion at baptism (because most of them are infants) or at confirmation. Passage and sacrifice are more likely to be connected with marriage in the Church in Africa, and with ordination. Perhaps the division of sacrifice and passage is another factor in making Christian rites liminoid.

The theology of sacrifice and its relation to the eucharist is a tendentious one. This has been an issue of debate since the Reformation. Those with a more Protestant theology may feel that Sawyerr has a hidden agenda in his work, but perhaps his background makes him more open to the concept of sacrifice. Yet the perceived relation between the Old Testament and traditional religion puts the sacrificial nature of the eucharist on the agenda.

Naussbaum (p. 50) makes an important observation about the western approach to sacrifice:

> Some ... have so lost touch with the world in which bonds are conceivable between people and their livestock that to them the Old Testament sacrificial cult is an embarrassment and even the New Testament talk of the sacrificial blood of Jesus is an empty message. They search for other ways to speak of the meaning of the cross.

Certainly there is no such embarrassment in the East African Revival. 'The blood' is an important part of the message and the theme tune of the Balokole is *Tukutendereza Yesu* which when translated, says: 'We praise you Jesus, Jesus lamb of God, Your blood cleanses me, I praise you Saviour'. The words have found an affinity with the African consciousness. They are not dogmatically tied to the eucharist but are often sung in the Holy Communion and at other services.

Sacrifice and Memorial

The concept of memorial is central to the eucharist, 'Do this in remembrance of me'. The analysis of time is thus an important issue in pre-understanding. Mbiti (1969) uses an African concept of time as the paradigm to analyse traditional religion. Time in Africa is a two-dimensional phenomenon and moves backwards rather than forwards. It is two-dimensional in that there is a long past, a present and virtually no future. The future extends to the next harvest only, beyond that there is nothing. Even the next harvest is uncertain. The present is influenced by the past. The past is the realm that has most influence. It is from there that the ancestors influence the present life. It is the myths of the past that explain the present. There are no myths about the future. There is no conception of the end of the world. Immortality is becoming one of the living-dead not joining some eschatological realm. The future dimension is only developing as a result of the introduction of Christianity. The result is that belief in the second coming of Jesus is strong and the event is expected soon. Mbiti (1971) goes so far as to suggest that there is a growing crisis because of the delay of the parousia in Africa today. This can only distort the eschatological aspects of the eucharist, however; the backward vision may enhance the concept of anamnesis.

The sense of continuity with the past is important but less so is historicity. Hearne (1980, p. 57) comments that 'traditional religion ... seems more centred on nature and the seasonal rhythms, it may seem that there is no real sense of memorial in it'. However, there are stories of the migrations of the different groups such as the Luo tribes who have an oral history of their migration through Sudan, Uganda and on into Kenya. The stories also relate why different groups settled and thus how the various tribal differences occurred. This is not a very explicit concept of memorial but Hearne links it to the prayers that express a link with the past. An example of this is this Dinka prayer at the sacrifice for a sick man:

> And you my father, if you are called, then you will help me. And join yourself with my words ... And you, my prayer, and you prayer of the long distant past, prayer of my ancestors, you are spoken now. Meet together, ee! It is that

of my ancestor Guejok. It is not of the tongue only. It is that of Guejok, It is not of the tongue only. (Shorter, 1975, pp. 70–1)

Hearne (p. 59) thinks that this gives 'a solid basis in African tradition for the Christian concept of memorial, especially if this is seen as the memorial of the "First Ancestor", Jesus Christ'.

Conclusion

Contextual issues centre around two dominant symbols, community and sacrifice. From these poles, points of discussion have arisen related to the transference of a symbol from one culture to another. This transportation raises the question of the authenticity of the symbol in the new context. The question is also raised of the influence of the understanding of the culture in which the symbol is transplanted on ritual, sacrifice and the cluster of issues discussed above. These issues will recur in the chapters that follow.

Anthropology and Inculturation

Various anthropological models have been used in this chapter to examine something of the nature of the issue of inculturation. The grid–group theory of Mary Douglas has shown some of the problems of the transference of a symbol system from one culture to another and thus illuminates the growth of a protest movement that the received wisdom does not fit. Turner's definition of symbol, particularly his observation that there are two poles of meaning of a symbol, has been used to approach some of the complex issues relating to the use of materials to be employed for the eucharist as well as to tackle ideological issues in the African context. This chapter forms only a preliminary exploration of these problems and of the anthropological approaches. Further chapters will concentrate on particular case studies. The previous chapter looked at the theology of symbol from an ecumenical perspective. Thus Protestant, Catholic and Orthodox theologians were studied. The case studies to follow will be equally ecumenical, examining Ethiopian Orthodox, African Independent, Roman Catholic and Anglican eucharistic practice. The first two of these Churches have been described as indigenous, in contrast to the Catholics and Anglicans who, perceiving themselves not to be indigenous, have proposed a programme of inculturation. Each of the different Churches will be examined in the light of the theological and anthropological models introduced in chapters 2 and 3.

CHAPTER 4

The Ethiopian Orthodox Church

One method of elucidating the meaning of the term 'indigenous' is to examine the problem of alienation, which is the perceived foreignness of worship, but another approach is to identify churches that can be described as authentic to Africa. The next two chapters will therefore examine those churches that have been declared as indigenous, beginning with the Ethiopian Orthodox Church. The meaning of 'the inculturation of worship' is a problem of culture and thus a problem within both theology and anthropology. This chapter will examine the culture of the Ethiopian Orthodox Church and its eucharistic liturgy. Subsequently a more theological model, that of the 'holy' as developed by Rudolf Otto will be examined in relation to the Orthodox Eucharist.

The Integration of Symbol Systems

'Ethiopia is the only black African country with an indigenous church' (Arnold, 1971, p. 142). This comment is a common one about the Ethiopian Orthodox Church, but what are the criteria of such an evaluation? Is the Orthodox Church indigenous because it has its own leadership? But the 'Abuna' was an Egyptian until the 1950s. Is it indigenous because it has been present in the country for two thousand years? But there are cases where length of time in the country has not led to a decrease in the foreignness of the Church. Or is it indigenous because there is not the dual religious system of Christianity and traditional religion existing side by side, as is common in much of the rest of black Africa? Sperber (1975, p. 75) commented that symbols, no matter what their origin, tended to become integrated within a single system. Is this church indigenous because there has been an integration of the different symbol systems?

The Jewish influences on the Ethiopian Orthodox Church have been commented on many times (Pawlikowski, 1971–2, p. 72). This Jewish influence is distinctively strong in the Ethiopian Church and may be traced back to the time of the advent of Christianity in the country. It would appear that the religions in the country before the preaching of Frumentius were the worship of the Serpent and a variety of Judaism. It is not clear if the Judaic elements in the Church are a result of the influence of this original Judaism on a Gentile Christianity, or the result of the preaching of Jewish Christians in the country, or a product of the hermeneutical approach of the Church to the Old Testament. Whichever is true, Ethiopian Christianity is 'an excellent example of a Semitic-based Christianity ... the interpenetration of Judaism and Christianity' (p. 179). The integration of the Church with other symbolic systems in the country can be examined in three areas: Judaism, the state and magic.

The Judaic Spirit of the Church

The Orthodox Church has a strong tradition of keeping the Sabbath. Thus the eucharist is celebrated both on Saturday and Sunday and the faithful are supposed to keep both. The keeping of the Sabbath was commonly enjoined in the fourth century, but in Ethiopia this tradition has survived where in other places it has died out. It has been a matter of dispute in history and was settled in the time of Zara Ya'aqob who enforced its observance. The argument of the Church is that both the Old and New Testaments honour the Sabbath and that there are no explicit commands in the New to abolish it. Thus it is still binding (Haile, 1981).

The *Mashafa Berhan* lists what the faithful are allowed to do on the Sabbath. Hard work is not permitted but the restrictions are not as severe as the *Mishna* or the *Talmud*, for the Ethiopian principle is that the day is a feast day and thus any work needed to keep the festal character is permitted (Hammerschmidt, 1965). The terminology used for the Sabbath is confusing and 'the Sabbath and Sunday or even a general feast day are not always clearly differentiated' (Hemple & Hammerschmidt, 1965).

One of the most striking influences on the eucharist of the role of the Sabbath is found in the Anaphora of Athanasius 'an original work of Ethiopic poetry' (Hammerschmidt, 1965, p. 9). A great part of the prayer is devoted to the praise of the Sabbath. The preface includes:

> Come, let us exalt; come, let us praise; come let us honour; come let us celebrate the chief of the holy days which is the holy Sabbath of the Christians...
>
> Oh, this day is the first but not the last. Oh, this day is the last which exists forever. Oh this day was declared to Abraham and caused him to desire, prophesy and rejoice...
>
> Oh, this day is what the Father hallowed...
>
> Let us rejoice and be glad in it and sanctify it...
>
> Oh, other days of the week... come ye, let us praise the holy Sabbath of the Christians which is the chief day of the week. (Daoud, 1959, pp. 181–3)

Before the people receive communion the praise of the Sabbath is resumed:

> Oh, this day, the holy Sabbath of Christians, thou art glorious like the Father, ruling like the Son, and living like the Holy Spirit.
> Oh, this day, the holy Sabbath of the Christians, offer prayer and supplicate towards the Lord our God on behalf of us... (p. 194)

After communion there is more praise:

> Come, let us exalt; come let us praise; come let us honour; come let us celebrate the chief of the holy days which is the holy Sabbath of the Christians. As we rejoiced yesterday at its entering so also let us bid it farewell rejoicing as it departs . . .
>
> Again let us say, Pray for us and intercede towards the Lord our God . . .
>
> Oh, holy, come unto us every week that we may rejoice in thee, world without end. (p. 196)

Such praise of the Sabbath is also found in the *Talmud* and the work of Solomon Ben Moses Halevi Alkabez but these are almost certain to have had no influence in Ethiopia (Hammerschmidt, 1961). More important is the role of the Sabbath among the Falashas, who in the *Te'ezaza sanbat* 'endow the Sabbath with a mystico-metaphysical character by regarding it as a female person embodying the heavenly world' (Hammerschmidt, 1965, p. 10). A Falasha is reported to have said, 'Marie est la médiatrice des chrétiens, notre médiateur est le Samedi' (Buxton, 1970, p. 117).

Thus the keeping of the Sabbath, its praise and the personification of the Sabbath to the point of asking it to pray in a similar way as one would ask a saint to intercede, all these together signal the integration of Jewish elements. Elements of praise to Saturday and Sunday are bound together, the anaphora of Athanasius being celebrated on ferial Sundays. The two systems of Jewish Sabbath and Christian Sunday have grown together in a unique way in Ethiopia.

The layout of the churches in Ethiopia are also said to be of Jewish inspiration. Churches are, in general, either square, hexagonal or round. Their layout is of the same pattern whatever the exterior shape: that is of three concentric areas divided by walls (Ullendorff, 1968). The central square is the *maqdas* also called the *qeddusa qeddusan*, that is the holy of holies, and only the clergy are allowed to enter this place. It is separated from the rest of the church by a wall. Surrounding this, and also often walled off, is the *qeddest* or the *'enda ta'amer*, the place of miracles. The people use this part of the church, when they receive communion. The outer part of the church is the *qene mahlet*, the place where the hymns are sung, and is open to all. The organization of space is said to be modelled on the temple in the Old Testament. 'In part the Judaizing tendency . . . may be due to an uncritical reverence for the Old Testament' (Jones & Monroe, 1935, p. 39), and this may explain the layout of the churches, but it is also interesting to note that the Falashas had exactly the same architectural design, the only difference with them being that there is no cross on the top of the building (Flad, 1869).

The *Kebra Nagast*, the chronicle of the history of Ethiopia, reports that the son of Solomon by the Queen of Sheba (an Ethiopian queen), stole the Ark of the

Covenant from the temple and brought it back to Ethiopia, to Axum, where it has remained ever since (Budge, 1922b). In each church there is a replica of the ark, the *tabot*. This may be a complete replica or it may be a replica of the tablets of Moses, whichever, it is regarded as the most holy part of the church. To consecrate a new place of worship, a new *tabot* is taken to the Abuna who blesses it. This is the consecration. The church is functional once the blessed *tabot* is placed in the building. On the feast of *Timkat* (Epiphany) the *tabot* is processed to a nearby stream or pond with great pomp. The *tabot* is wrapped in colourful cloths and carried on the head of the priest, who is accompanied by clergy carrying bells, crosses, and incense. Other clergy with sistra and prayer sticks perform a special dance before the *tabot*, which has reminded many people of 2 Sam 6:14–15, where David danced before the Lord (Isaac, 1972).

The food laws of the Old Testament are strictly observed by the Church, both the prescriptions of Lev 11 and Gen 32:33 concerning the forbidden sinew. Again it is difficult to distinguish between this practice as a continuation of original Jewish practice and the result of a particular hermeneutic. The latter certainly bolsters the continuation of the laws for 'Ethiopia unlike most Christian nations has rejected the traditional doctrine of Pauline Christianity which claims that Biblical law lost its binding force at the coming of Jesus' (p. 227).

The Church also practises circumcision. Thus male children are both circumcised and baptized. It is not clear whether this is a Jewish influence, for the practice is common in the Near East and in the rest of Africa. Perhaps the date is significant, 'of all the peoples that circumcise their males, only Jews and Ethiopians limit the ceremony to the eighth day after birth, as decreed in Genesis 17' (p. 226). All of these show a strong Semitic influence that makes the Church distinct.

The Church and the State

Until the revolution there was a strong integration of Church and state. Orthodoxy was established by the monarchy and the Emperor had great influence in Church affairs. The integration of Church and state is found in the acceptance and propagation by both parties of the Solomonic mythology. The emperor traced the dynasty back to the Queen of Sheba and thus to Solomon. The *Kebra Nagast*, which records the coming of the ark to Ethiopia and chronicles the history of the kings, is a 'repository of Ethiopian national and religious feelings' (Ullendorff, 1968, p. 75). Thus the loss of the ark by the Jews symbolized that God had abandoned them and that the Ethiopians were now the people of God, the new Israel, and that God chose the kings. The influence of the *Kebra Nagast* on the people is seen in the incident in 1868 when an important copy of the book was taken to the British Museum. Emperor Yohannes IV had to write to Lord Granville to request its return because the people would not obey him without the presence of that book (Isaac, 1972). Thus the book itself was regarded as sacred and gave legitimacy to those in power. The Church, by putting the *tabot* in the centre of its ceremonial, was supporting the ideology of the state and the whole mythology of Menelek and the Ark of the Covenant.

The Church and Magic

'One of the most notable features in Abyssinian Christianity is the survival of magical practices' (Ullendorff, 1968, p. 79). The magic is based on the idea of words of power. The greatest magicians were given these words, which by repetition are able to accomplish the desired effect. Moses and Solomon were great magicians, but greatest of all was Christ who gave some of his powers to his mother. 'The magical names and words-of-power known to Christ were thought absolutely invincible, and Satan and his devils were rendered powerless when they were uttered' (Budge, 1928a, p. 583). The most common form is found in the amulet. This is often a strip of parchment 2 inches to 6 inches in width and 6 inches to 6 feet long, which is rolled up and put in a leather pouch and hung from the neck or attached to a garment. Amulets are supposed to protect the wearer from demons and are produced by the clergy. They may have names of God, names of archangels, magical names of Christ, legends or words of power on them. Budge (1930, p. 188) reports that one amulet had on one side of the parchment a story of Michael and the Virgin and on the other side spells, magic drawings and charms, 'fusing Christianity with paganism and its religious magic'.

Magic has also had an influence in the eucharistic liturgy. In the epiclesis of the anaphoras of Jacob of Serough and Cyril mention is made of *Melos*, e.g. Jacob of Serough says:

> Let the gate of light be opened . . .
>
> Let the Lamb of God descend and sit on this holy table . . .
>
> Let <Melos> the fearful sword of fire be sent and sit over this bread and cup: to fulfil this offering. (Daoud, p. 285)

One explanation of the origin of the sword (Burmester, 1959/60, p. 60) is that it is a sword that is coming out of the mouth of Jesus. Thus the petition is for the consecration of the elements by the logos. But this explanation does not account for the word *Melos*. It would seem that this is a magic word for Solomon, a variation on that name spelt backwards. *Melos* is connected with a sword of fire in other Ethiopian magic texts, and is regarded as meaning in the secret language Christ (Hammerschmidt, 1961).

A United Symbolic System?

The Church is thus integrated with the different symbol systems in Ethiopia. The Jewish roots find expression in the Sabbath, church buildings, food laws and circumcision. The state was linked to the Church through the ideology of the Solomonic dynasty and the *tabot*. Magic found its niche in the Church. However, there has been little integration between Islam and the Church in Ethiopia. The following petition in the anaphora of Athanasius may be directed to the Muslims:

> Draw out thy sword and stop the way against all of them that hate thy holy name, and let the earth which they tread be a slough and swallow them up that they may go down alive into hell. (Daoud, 1959, p. 191)

Ethiopia in many ways is a remarkable confirmation of Sperber's comment about the tendency of symbol systems to integrate. This can be a synthetic process as in the case of the Church and Judaism, and in the case of magic. The relationship to Islam shows that the integration can be one of accepted mutual hostility. The two symbol systems are reacting against each other rather than synthesizing. Thus there can be either a relationship of cross-fertilization or there can be an enduring tension and hostility between different religious systems. Yet perhaps Sperber's insight does help to clarify the nature of an indigenous church. A mission church is one that is not integrated into the prevailing culture. There is a lack of coming together of symbol systems. There may even be a dual religious system. An indigenous church is one that is integrated into the culture because the symbolic systems have harmonized. Ethiopia in that sense had an indigenous church when it was part of a Christian nation. The Church has even survived the end of the monarchy.

The Ethiopian Orthodox Eucharist: A Symbolic Analysis

Introduction

Victor Turner (1969) applied his method of processual symbolic analysis both to rites of passage and to rites of affliction. Later (Turner & Turner, 1978) he turned his attention to the Christian equivalents and was particularly interested in the phenomenon of pilgrimage in the Church. In this chapter a symbolic analysis will be applied to the Ethiopian Orthodox eucharist. In the Orthodox Church the eucharist is the dominant ritual. There are others, including baptism, chrismation, marriage, funerals, ordination, monastic profession, confession and the celebrations of the year, but often these are performed in the context of the eucharist.

The dominant symbol in the eucharist is the bread and the wine. These are carefully prepared and manipulated throughout the service. They are the body and blood of Christ and the service can be seen as the recapitulation of the life of Christ. Isaac comments (1968, p. 39) 'the Keddasse is thought of in the Ethiopian Church as the re-enactment of salvation, because it is the worship of the life of Christ, his teachings, death and resurrection, narrated dramatically'. Thus the bread is taken from Bethlehem and progresses through the service to Calvary until consumed by the people, as the body and blood of the risen Lord. This method of interpretation of the liturgy is common to many of the Eastern Orthodox and Oriental churches. It has deep roots and can be seen, for example, in the commentary on the liturgy of Theodore of Mopsuestia and its influence can be seen in the prayers and actions of the Ethiopian Church. The approach was once popular in the west but fell out of favour in both the Protestant and Catholic churches (Power, 1984). That the elements represent the life of Christ does not mean that at different parts of the service there is a symbolic re-enactment of a particular episode in strict historical progression. That would be to turn the symbols into signs. At each stage of the service the bread and wine have a multiplicity of meanings that may result in an exegetic meaning (as revealed in the prayers) that would seem out of sequence. Thus the covering of the bread at the beginning of the service is seen to symbolize the burial of Christ. Nevertheless there is a general progression in the service from Bethlehem to the death and resurrection of the Lord and the exegetical interpretation is directed towards a particular event in the life of Christ at different parts of the rite.

The symbols of the body and blood of Christ are powerful. Thus there is a complex of secondary symbols that cluster around them. These may be manipulations of the bread and wine as in the mingling, elevation, fraction and the commixture. They may be associated with purification, for example the censing of the clergy, the censing of the hands, confession, absolution and the lavabo. They may include the use of other elements to those of the primary symbols, in this case water, incense, vestments, crosses, bells, linen. The building used, the use of space in the building and any processions around the building all contribute to the symbolism of the service and are secondary to the elements. The power of the primary symbols is therefore shrouded in a plethora of secondary symbols, as a result of a gradation of symbolic power. This does not mean that the people do not participate in the body and blood of Christ. Rather these secondary symbols both protect the people from direct and unprepared contact with the deity, and also draw out the gravity of the primary symbols by emphasizing the danger of the ritual. Therefore it is in the nature of any primary symbol to attract and develop a collection of secondary symbols.

The liturgy of the Ethiopian Orthodox Church falls into two sections: the preparatory service and the anaphora. The preparatory service is one of sanctifying the people, elements and the ornaments. It includes the ministry of the Word, intercessions, the creed and the peace. During the latter part of this section the catechumens are called to depart, even if the catechumenate has ceased to exist. The service follows the same pattern as the preparation in the Coptic Church in Egypt, but has Ethiopian embellishments. This part of the service is invariable, the only difference from one service to another being the readings. The anaphoras vary according to the season. There are 14 different anaphoras in regular use and perhaps some six more used occasionally. The exact number is hard to tell, as there is variation in different manuscripts. Hammerschmidt (1961) divides them into three groups:

1 The original liturgies. The use of these anaphoras is supposed to go back to the founding of the Church in the fourth century. These include the Anaphora of the Apostles, which is an elaboration of the Apostolic Tradition, and the Anaphora of our Lord, which is derived from the *Testamentum Domini*.
2 Translations. These include St Basil and St Mark from the Coptic Church, and St James the Lord's Brother.
3 Local productions. These may be free developments of foreign anaphoras, for example those of Cyril and Gregory, and those that seem to be composed in Ethiopia, e.g. Athanasius, the 318 Orthodox, Epiphanius and those to Mary (Haile, 1983).

As the last category includes 13 different anaphoras, it can be seen that one area of creativity in the Ethiopian Church has been the production of eucharistic prayers. Some have not regarded these prayers very highly. Bouyer (1968, pp. 358–9) comments on them that 'all continuity of thought is destroyed by a succession of exclamations and digressions that are practically limitless ... the whole eucharist is dissolved ... in a sentimental farrago in which the only thing floating on the surface is disjointed debris'. This is a superficial statement that does not take into account the unity of the rite and the repetition of cycles of symbolism that are uncovered by symbolic analysis. Also they are an example of African theology well before the African theology movement; the product of an African church grappling with the symbol of the eucharist and expressing itself in its own terms, even if heavily relying on patristic tradition.

Various methods of the anthropological analysis of a rite are possible. One way to examine a ritual is to divide it into three phases: separation, limen and reaggregation. This parallels the three phases of Hubert & Mauss (1964), of entry into the sacred, consecration, and exit from the sacred. These phases are also found in Leach with his rite of separation, marginal state and the rite of reaggregation. All of these models have their basis in Durkheim's dichotomy of the sacred and the profane, which itself originated in Robertson Smith's distinction between the holy and the common. The religious rite is a separation from the profane, an entry into the sacred, and a return to the profane. Both Hubert & Mauss and Leach acknowledge their roots in the work of Durkheim. Turner points more to the influence of Van Gennep. A processual analysis concerns the interrelationship of the different symbols used in the service, and of the passages of the people involved. Its common roots with these other models can be seen in the phases. Turner was particularly interested in the way the ritual empowered a change of status for the participants and its results on society.

Drawing on Van Gennep, Turner states that a rite of passage has three phases:

separation, limen and reaggregation. The Ethiopian eucharist can be seen to follow the same pattern:

1. Separation. This begins for the elements in the preparations in the Bethlehem. In the church the vessels are prepared, then the clergy, and finally the people.
2. Limen. This comes in three phases. Firstly there is the voice of the holy in the lessons, which forms a preparation for, secondly, the presence of the holy in the eucharistic prayer. Then, thirdly, comes the contact with the holy in the sacred meal. This is the climax of the service.
3. Reaggregation. This includes all the post-communion material such as the drinking of the water, distribution of the blessed bread, the blessing and the dismissal.

In each part of the service there are various ritual symbols. The bread and the wine of course are consumed at the end of the liminal phase. The whole service will be analysed within this framework.

Separation

The preparation of the bread and the wine is a complex ritual in itself. In many western churches the bread is purchased by the priest or by the laity and no specific ritual is associated with its procurement. Not so in Ethiopia. Wheat is not a common crop. More important are *t'eff*, sorghum, barley and maize. Details of the preparation of the bread are given by Drower (1956). The preparation of the bread is done in a separate house in the church compound, Bethlehem (which means the house of bread). Often the deacon does it in the evening or the morning before the service. The flour is the best, often sifted through fine silk. While making the bread shoes are removed, hands are washed, a special vestment is put on, and prayers are made to the Virgin. The leaven is saved from the previous batch. Before the bread is put into the oven it is stamped to put a pattern onto it. So the bread is a 'round, flat, leavened cake, four inches across by three-quarters of an inch thick. It is stamped with a cross of nine squares, with four squares added in the angles of the cross' (Woolley, 1913). It might be added that in each of these 13 squares is a cross. These become important in the fraction and the communion. A number of loaves are prepared but only those that are without blemish are used in the liturgy. The rest become the blessed bread that is consumed at the end of the service.

The wine is also prepared in Bethlehem. Grapes do grow in Ethiopia but wine is not a popular drink. Some priests ferment their own wine but the more common method is for raisins to be steeped in water. Bruce (1804) commented that the grape was 'bruised with the husk together ... so that it [the wine] is a kind of marmalade'. Thus the wine is often an orange colour rather than red. The use of raisins led the Jesuits to question the validity of the matter and in 1706 the Vatican declared this to be invalid.

The elements are brought to the church in procession. They are carried around the church on holy days otherwise they are taken direct to the sanctuary. The priest is accompanied by two deacons in collecting the elements. One of the deacons carries a bell, which he constantly rings. One carries a censer in one hand and a cross in the other. The priest is vested in white. The elements are put in special containers that have been prepared and the procession enters the church by the north door. Thus the Lamb is born in Bethlehem.

The preparatory service is one of sanctification for the ministers and the vessels. The three functions of a minister – of contact with sacred symbols, ascetic piety, and religious learning – are divided in Ethiopia between the three religious specialists: the priest, the monk and the *dabtara*, a lay teacher of religion (Levine, 1965). Thus the priest has primarily a cultic role, the one who enters the holy of holies and brings the presence of the holy. He begins his separation by the recitation of prayers of penitence and Pss 25, 61, 102, 103, 130, 131, and he continues with the prayer:

> O Lord our God, thou alone art holy, who hast bestowed thy holy things on all of us by thy invisible power ... we pray thee to send the Holy Spirit upon this church and upon this ark and upon all the holy vessels whereon thy precious mystery will be celebrated. And now, bless them, sanctify them, and purify them from all uncleanness. (Daoud, p. 9)

The power of God must also fall on the ministers afresh and thus make them worthy even to enter the sacred space of the sanctuary. The holiness of this space is viewed in Ethiopia by the use of the Old Testament analogy of the sanctuary of the church representing the Holy of Holies.

The vesting of the priest also emphasizes his separation. Deacons are required because once the priest is vested he is not allowed to disrobe to go out of the temple nor to 'wander about on the business of the world' (Daoud, p. 20).

The faithful prepare themselves in ascetic ways. They are expected to fast if they are to receive communion. Those who intend to receive are expected to come clothed in white. The men stand separate from the women. All remove their shoes on entering the church. Bruce (1804, p. 3) commented on this: 'when you go to the church, you put off your shoes ... but you must leave a servant there ... or else they will be stolen'. Alvarez (1881, p. 30) also found that his conduct in the church was regarded as inappropriate, 'they also were surprised at our coming into the church with our shoes on, and still more at our spitting in it'.

The bringing of the bread and wine into the church is accompanied by a variety of prayers. The host is taken by the priest and covered while this prayer is said:

> Jesus Christ, the High Priest, like as Joseph and Nicodemus wrapped thee in linen cloths and spices, and thou was pleased in them, in like manner be well pleased in us. (Daoud, p. 23)

The priest then processes around the ark preceded by a light and followed by a deacon. The wine must be good and the water added is not to be more than one third. The prayer links to the miracle at Cana:

> Christ our God ... who didst go to the wedding ... in Cana ..., and didst bless for them the water and change it into wine, do thou in like sort unto this (*pointing*) wine. (Daoud, p. 24)

The Lord is then blessed in a Trinitarian prayer and benedictions are made over the elements.

Prayers of confession, absolution and intercessions may begin. An apotropaic element occurs in the Thanksgiving of St Basil and enhances the separation of the people from this world:

> all the working of Satan ... and all the uprisings of adversaries ... remove far from me + and from thy people + and from this thy holy place +

This is a distinct element in the Ethiopian liturgy. Apotropaic prayers are common in baptism, but are rare in the eucharist.

Incense is also used in great quantities in the service. Alvarez (p. 30) commented 'they do not think that mass is properly said without incense'. This is seen as conveying a blessing and as a sacrifice:

> Accept ... this pure incense as a sweet-smelling savor for the remission of my sin, and forgive the sins of all thy people. (Daoud, p. 37)

Mary is asked to let 'this incense, ... our prayer, ... ascend' (p. 37). Mary is seen as 'the golden censer which didst bear the coal of fire' (p. 41). Indeed both Mary and Christ are seen as incense, 'Mary is the incense, and the incense is He, because he who was in her womb is more fragrant than all chosen incense' (p. 48). Thus a rich diversity of Old Testament imagery is used with reference to the incense and this is connected to elements of Christology and Mariology.

Thus there are a host of secondary symbols in the separation phase. The dominant symbols of the bread and wine are themselves re-emphasized by the lights and the incense. The covering of the bread is analogous to the burial of Jesus. The use of benedictions, processions and other customs all emphasize that the person is leaving the everyday world and passing into the eternal realm. The separation completed, intercessions can begin and above all the Holy can come in the ministry of the word.

Limen

The liminal phase itself has three parts to it. The first is the voice of the holy in the lessons. The second, and a development of that, is the presence of the holy in the eucharistic prayer. The third, and the climax of the sequence, is the contact with the holy in the fraction and in the communion.

The lessons form the first contact with the Holy. In the rites of passage there are often times of instruction. The lessons take on the same function in the eucharist. They instruct the candidate in the correct morals, understanding and disposition for the approach to God. Four lessons are read: from Paul, the Catholic Epistles, Acts and the Gospel. The readings also have a positional meaning in that they form the teaching of the Christ. The preparation has been the birth of Christ in Bethlehem. The water into wine was his first miracle. Now the people are to come into contact with Christ the teacher.

The deacon is blessed with the laying on of a hand and 'May the blessing of Paul be upon thee' (Daoud, p. 42), as he goes forth to read Paul. After the reading, the intercessions of Paul are requested by the people:

> Holy Apostle Paul, good messenger, healer of the sick, who hast received the crown, ask and pray for us in order that he may save our souls. (p. 44)

Thus approach to the deity is aided by the intercessions of those who have gone before. One does not rush into the presence of God, and the power of the readings is emphasized by the use of incense and the saints who protect us.

The Gospel is read with particular ceremony. Before it is read there are intercessions to the Virgin. This is positionally meaningful, as before one is to hear the Saviour one should remember the Mother. The Virgin Mary has a very strong role in the Ethiopian Orthodox Church. There are collections of legends of the Virgin that are used in the Church (Budge, 1923). The *Weddasse Maryam* is a daily office of prayers to the Virgin (Budge, 1922a). Perhaps the most interesting aspect of the Marian devotion is that of the four eucharistic prayers addressed primarily to Mary. Only one has been translated into English but it shows the nature of the devotion to the Virgin. After the dialogue and Sursum Corda, rather than a preface addressed to the Father one gets the following:

> My heart is inditing a good matter . . .
>
> I speak the praise of the Virgin . . .
>
> O Mary, for this we love and exalt thee, because thou didst bear for us the True food of righteousness and the true Drink of life . . .
>
> O Interceder, intercede with thy Son for the sake of each . . .
>
> O Virgin, full of glory, with whom and with what likeness shall we liken thee? Thou art the loom from which Emmanuel took his flesh . . . Thou wast the hope of Adam . . . the ark of Noah . . . the tablets of Moses, the bush of Sinai . . . the harp of David . . .

> O Virgin, the wicked young men could not entice thee, but the angels of heaven visited thee...
>
> There abode in thy womb the inestimable and unsearchable fire of the godhead...
>
> O Virgin who giveth the fruit that can be eaten, and the spring of that which can be drunk. (Daoud, p. 130)

Thus the preface of the prayer is taken up with a meditation on the role of the Virgin in the economy of salvation drawing from biblical imagery and from various legends. The eucharistic prayer has changed from a prayer that is in the category of strict theism and has moved into the category of asymmetrical mediation.

In the ministry of the word the Virgin is remembered before the Gospel, the Mother before the Son:

> Rejoice ... Oh holy ... ever-virgin, parent of God, mother of Christ, offer up our prayer to thy beloved Son that he may forgive our sins.
> Rejoice, O Virgin pure, very Queen; rejoice O pride of our kind ... O thou that bearest for us Emmanuel our God ... We ask thee to remember us, O true Mediatrix before our Lord Jesus. (Daoud, p. 48)

The saints are also important. As the clergy process out of the sanctuary various graces given to the saints are remembered:

> To Michael was given mercy...
>
> To David was given understanding...
>
> To our father Peter were given the keys, and virginity to John...
>
> To Moses was given the law...
>
> Thou art the incense, O our Saviour ... Have mercy on us. (p. 49)

Prayer is said before the reading of the Gospel, the four quarters of the earth are blessed. Incense is offered, and the assistant priest intercedes and the priest reads. 'When reading the word of God ... there must be silence and awe ... for hearing the word of the holy gospel of the heavenly King' (p. 58). People are to uncover their head for this reading and no one is to go out of the church.

All this elaborate ceremonial emphasizes the awe of hearing the voice of the holy. The Jesus who taught in Galilee speaks to us now as the great King from heaven. We listen in the presence of the ancestors who have received blessings from the same King and we ask them to intercede to him for mercy. The speaking of Christ from heaven is emphasized by the procession from the Holy of Holies with incense, candles and vested ministers. The use of space is important in the symbol system.

There is a development in the closeness of the participant to the deity. In the first stage the holy is apprehended primarily through the ears. The second phase is that of the presence of the holy in the elements. The elements are unveiled and manipulated by the priest. Thus there is a progression of the use of the senses from the ears, to the eyes and touch, to the climax of the eating of the gifts and the entrance of the holy into the body of the communicant.

The diversity of eucharistic prayers in the Ethiopian Church makes the study of each impossible. The Anaphora of the Apostles is often regarded as the basic eucharistic prayer. The ceremonial for each of the prayers is broadly similar and thus it is possible to comment on this one prayer as an example of all the others.

The opening dialogue shows Egyptian and Syrian influence, and is the moving of the spirit of the people outside their earthly existence. Cyril of Jerusalem, commenting on 'lift up your hearts', said 'the priest is virtually commanding you at that moment to lay aside the cares of this life ... and to keep your heart in heaven on God' (Yarnold, 1971, p. 89). The phrase is the inducement to the rupture of paramount reality.

The Narrative of Institution is a re-enactment of the Last Supper with actions also appropriate to the crucifixion superimposed. It begins with the censing of the elements and the removal of the veil. At the words 'he took bread' the priest raises the bread. Then at 'he blessed and broke' three benedictions are made and five wounds are made in the bread. The bread is not broken in half (as would happen if a repetition of the Last Supper were being enacted) but rather the focus shifts to the cross and the wounds of Christ. At the words 'my blood which will be shed on behalf of you ...' the chalice is raised and moved with the right hand in the sign of the cross, again ceremonial to recall the crucifixion. At the same time the responses of the people in the narrative reflect their belief in the transformation of the elements. The response to 'this bread is my body ...' is 'Amen ... we believe ... that this is he'. Likewise for the cup, to 'this cup is my blood ...' there is the same response. Thus three events are happening at once: the now, the cross and the Last Supper. There are links between the presence of the holy in the primordial event of the cross, the foundation of the Supper on the night he was betrayed, and the recapitulation of these events now.

The bread and wine are offered and the sending of the Holy Spirit is requested to transform the elements into the body and blood of Christ. This highlights the transformational understanding of the epiclesis: 'Whatever the Holy Spirit touches is sanctified and transformed' (p. 91). Theodore stressed that they become the resurrection body 'free from death, corruption ... like our Lord's body after the resurrection' (p. 246). This provides the logic for the dipping of the finger of the priest in the wine and the signing of the body with the blood. The uniting of the body and blood are the uniting of the body and soul at the resurrection, for 'the blood is the soul'. An umbrella may be brought over the elements during the epiclesis, the interpretation being that it is symbolic of the tabernacle, the epiclesis being analogous to the entering of the *shekinah* at the consecration of the tabernacle.

Thus the Holy is present. By the descent of the Spirit the bread and wine are transformed into the body and blood of Christ. The deity has come and the next stage can begin, contact with the holy.

The final part of the liminal phase is the contact with the holy in the fraction and the communion. Once again a complex network of prayers and actions have developed that surround these rites. The simple action of breaking the bread, which was one of practical necessity, has developed into a complex manipulation of the bread. The eating of the elements is accompanied by penitence and the use of the sacred space of the *qiddist*. The people may have been protected from the presence of the holy by the wall that separates the sanctuary from the people, but there is no separation if the people are to eat of the bread and drink of the cup.

Prayers that express the fear of the danger of eating unworthily surround the Lord's Prayer, a preparatory prayer for reception:

> Grant us to take of this holy mystery with blessing . . . and not to condemn any of us, but make us worthy all that partake of the holy mystery. (Daoud, p. 76)

To enter the presence of the holy is dangerous. To eat the holy, requires proper care and preparation.

The breaking of the bread is begun with the following exclamation: 'Let us draw nigh the face of the Saviour of the world ye ye ye'. This is repeated, with variations, three times. The repetition of 'ye ye ye' is the cry of those who weep for the dead. The people participate in mourning the death of Christ. The fraction is thus linked to the death, rather than to the unity of the body as in modern fraction rites. The gates are opened and the people bow in honour.

The fraction of the bread is a complicated procedure. At the end of the eucharistic prayer the priest separates the 13 crosses from one another and from the base of the bread. At the invitation to communion, 'Holy things for the holy', the priest rearranges the crosses in the bread. The whole host is raised and a bell is rung continuously. The people can now get a view of the elements. The proclamation is then made 'This is the body and blood of Emmanuel our very God', and the people prostrate themselves. Before the reception the priest takes the *asbadikon* (the central part of the host) dips it in the wine and then makes the sign of the cross with it on the other 12 squares. The movements of the *asbadikon* are supposed to represent the descent of Christ from heaven and his wandering on earth. The salvific events are recapitulated in this action just before reception.

The priests receive first, after washing their hands and offering prayers of confession and self-abasement. The top of the loaf, with the 13 squares on it, is for the communication of the clergy. Each square is designated for a different minister and the *asbadikon* is dropped in the chalice after the signing. The assistant priest administers the wine, communicating the people by a spoon.

The participants receive in order of their degree, the priests first, then the deacons, and then other clerics, followed by children, men and women. Each receives in the part of the church assigned to them. Thus the clergy partake in the sanctuary, the men on the west and the women at the south. The clergy come out of the sanctuary in full pomp with an umbrella over the celebrant. The people enter the *qiddist* also called the *'enda ta'amer* the place of miracles. This is a space surrounding the sanctuary that is only used for the people to receive communion. While chewing the bread, 'he shall put his hand on his mouth. He shall chew in fear and trembling without making any sound' (Daoud, p. 86). The division of the people and their separate reception is contrary to much theory. It might be expected that in the liminal period the normal social hierarchy would be broken down, for it is this breaking down of hierarchy that allows the experience of communitas. In this eucharistic rite, however, the orders of people remain distinct, the clergy, men and women receiving separately. The service concludes with a few brief ceremonies: the phase of reaggregation.

Reaggregation

The post-communion rites are simple and brief. First they centre on the consumption of any elements that are left. The clergy eats the remains for 'the Body and Blood can never turn again into the bread and the wine' (Daoud, p. 90). Water is used to rinse the mouth and drunk, and the water of ablution, which is seen as holy water, is taken out and given for the people to drink. The assistant priest now distributes the remaining loaves that were baked before the service, but were not spotless and were therefore rejected from use, as the blessed bread. Thus all the elements are consumed.

The people are blessed before they are dismissed. This begins with a general blessing using the sign of the cross. Then each of the faithful comes to the priest to be individually blessed. Finally the deacon finishes the service with: 'Go in peace'.

> After partaking of the Holy Communion a man shall not wash his hands or feet, shall not take off his clothes or bow down or kneel, shall not spit, or let blood, or cut his nails, or cut his hair, or go on a journey, or sue in the court, or go to a bathing place, or eat too much, or drink too much, or lie with a woman. (p. 96)

All of these actions would seem to profane the contact with the holy that has taken place in communion.

The Eucharistic Rite

The model used to analyse the Orthodox liturgy has been from anthropological studies. This has been a useful tool in terms of delineating the three phases of the ritual process, that of separation, limen (or margin) and reaggregation. Turner developed this model from Van Gennep's work on rites of passage. He also applied it to rites of affliction, and then went on to use it when discussing ritual in the western world. In the latter application there were seen to be differences in the liminal phase, not least being the lack of use of sacred space. So he developed the category of liminoid. Turner saw one of the major distinctions between the liminal rites of passage and the liminoid Christian sacraments being that the latter is a transitional interstate but it is fragmentary, being outside central economic and political processes. Thus he searched for the liminal in pilgrimages.

The eucharist is not a rite of passage as there is no transition from one social status to another. Also, at two significant moments in the liturgy, the peace and the reception of the elements, there is no anti-structure, the sacred hierarchy is not broken down, rather it is encapsulated within the rite, each level of the hierarchy performing in due order. If rites of passage and the eucharist are seen in a broader theoretical context, then similarities and differences between the two are clearer. The need for such an analysis is apparent from the work of Turner, for he was forced to develop the category of liminoid in the application of his theory to the west. Rather he might have looked for a more fundamental approach to ritual than the rites of passage model.

Leach (1961, p. 66), in returning to the work of Durkheim, gives a broader framework in which passages and sacraments can be analysed. The theory rests on the distinction of the sacred and the profane, which is helpful in this context in illuminating the process of ritual. Figure 4.1 is a diagram of the model.

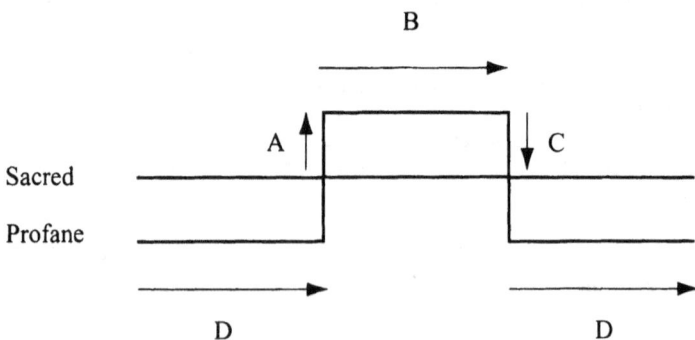

4.1 The ritual process

Life is normally lived in the profane realm. Phase D is normal secular life, the interval between festivals. Phase A is the rite of sacralization or separation. This is a transfer from the secular-profane world to the sacred world. This may even be conceived in terms of a death. Phase B is the marginal state. Ordinary social time has stopped and the person is in sacred time. Phase C is the rite of desacralization, or aggregation. The person is brought back from the sacred into the profane. This may be seen as a kind of rebirth. This model underlies rites of passage and the eucharist.

Rites of passage (or rites of initiation) are distinguished by their effect of social transition. They raise one up the social hierarchy, for example from infant to adult or, in the case of baptism, of incorporation into the sacred community. They are triggered by the phases of life (childhood, adolescence, adulthood) and are performed on the whole community (to be a part of the community is to have experienced the initiation). The marginal state is characterized by liminality, betwixt one social status and another social status. The reformulating of status occurs through anti-structure; the structure of the liminal state that may be at variance with the normal social structure. In this period the initiate experiences communitas, social bonding between the initiands that may result in an age group brotherhood for the rest of life. Tribal initiation and baptism-confirmation would be included in this category.

Rites of affliction may effect social passage, if they initiate one into a healing group, but that may not be universal. They are triggered by a particular problem and are not performed on all those who are a part of the community. It is not necessary to go through the rite to be a full member of the society. This category includes rites of healing and responses to natural disasters such as lack of rain.

Rites of intensification, according to Chapple & Coon (1942), are those that reassert paradigms of the group world-view. There is no development of anti-structure in the marginal state but rather the reinforcement of the sacred hierarchy. Indeed this may be the period in which the sacred hierarchy asserts its raison d'être. There is no social transition in the rite, but rather the rite repeats (intensifies) the core values and myths of the group. Communitas is experienced in the rite but this is often a communitas primarily with the deity and as such does not fall into the sociological category of communitas, only into a personalized analogy of such a state. Bonding of the group as a result of the ritual is a bonding of the whole community as socially intact, rather than the formation of an age group. The whole community is expected to participate in the ritual rather than a select few. The eucharist and communal prayers would be included in this category.

This classification clarifies the differences between the rites of passage and the eucharist. The difference is primarily in the lack of social transition in the eucharist and the different effects of this on communitas and anti-structure in the marginal state. Those who have wanted to argue that the eucharist is a rite of passage have had to point to the eschatological nature of the passage. 'It is the ritual stage on which we act out the eschatological drama of the journey we are undertaking'

(Goodwin, 1979b, p. 351). This, however, is a mythologization, not an application of the rites of passage model. Passage in Turner's terms is social not mythological. Rites of passage are a particular application of a more general approach as exemplified by Leach above.

Ethiopian Inculturation

While the Ethiopian eucharist shares much in common with other Oriental churches there are many distinct elements. The Church has had a particular place in Ethiopian society and culture. There are Ethiopian traditions of music, dance and vestments. There are particular styles of art and architecture. There is a distinct Ethiopian liturgy. The Church acted as a symbol in the rest of Africa with a number of Independent Churches using the word 'Ethiopian' in their title. While until recently the Abuna was always a Coptic monk, the Church now has full autocephalous status. All of this has been a long historical process. It has included local creativity even in the production of eucharistic prayers. Perhaps this is the most vital element for inculturation.

In chapter 3 various contextual issues were raised. Does this study of the Orthodox Church illumine any of these issues? In both Traditional Religion and in the Orthodox there is a strong sense of the closeness of the ancestors. Prayer to the ancestors is common in both. The Ethiopians are clear in their practice. The prayers of the ancestors (in this case the enormous list of saints) are for us and invocation of the saints is ultimately directed to God, a matter of symmetrical, or more properly, asymmetrical mediation. Even the Virgin, who receives high exaltation, is still seen as one of us. In African Traditional Religion prayers have a tendency to become directed to ancestors as an end in themselves in a number of tribes, modifying strict deism to relative deism. However there are examples of both in both types of prayer in both religious systems. Sawyerr had suggested that sacrifice was a concept that would be important in the integration of the mission churches with their culture. Although the concept of offering is very strong in the Ethiopian liturgy, there is less direct reference to the sacrifice of the eucharist than in the modern Roman Catholic services. Perhaps Sawyerr has overstated his case and that sacrifice will be significant only in some contexts. The comments about the role of the danger of reception of the elements due to the magical view of the world, as outlined by Mbiti, are seen as significant in the Ethiopian service. Numerous prayers ask that the reception might be not for the condemnation of the communicant but for his salvation. This perhaps is strengthened by the role of the concept of awe in the liturgy, something that will have to be pursued further.

The Numinous and the Eucharist

Introduction

Central to the anthropological discussion has been the category of the sacred. Durkheim's dichotomy of the sacred and the profane was seen to be the conscious presupposition of Leach and the unconscious or at least unacknowledged presupposition of Turner. The essence of a rite is seen as the exit from the profane and the entrance into the sacred, which is then followed by a re-entry into the profane. Part of the core value of any religious ritual is thus contact with the deity and in the particular case of the eucharist of contact with God through Christ. The sacred is a category that is not unique to anthropology. Schleiermacher focused the interest of theology on inward experience. Rudolf Otto refined his 'feeling of absolute dependence' in his 'knowledge of the holy'. Thus the discussion of the anthropologists can be developed through the work of theologians and in particular the theology developed from the seminal work of Otto.

Rudolf Otto

In *The Idea of the Holy* Rudolf Otto (1917, 1959, p. 59) emphasizes two aspects that exist in Christian experience: the rational and the non-rational. The two interpenetrate one another in an analogous fashion to affection and sex. According to Turner (1967, p. 30) symbols bring the different levels of experience together. 'The ritual symbol ... effects an interchange of qualities between its poles of meaning'. For Otto any such interchange would occur in the experience of awe, which is associated with a feeling of overpoweringness, energy and the presence of the wholly other. The experience of awe is not just an excitement of the emotions within everyday consciousness, but is a drawing out of everyday consciousness into a realization of the presence of the other. Such an experience is not taught, 'it must be awakened from the spirit' (Turner, 1967, p. 75). But there is a significant role for symbols in that they may reawaken the sense of the holy, once it has been experienced in the first place. This sense of otherliness may be expressed in a liturgy by the use of an archaic language such as Latin or Ge'ez, and the use of words and actions that do not have a direct rational content for the participant, for example the use of the word 'hosanna'. In most churches there has been a debate as to the role of the rational and the non-rational in worship. The emphasis in the churches of the Reformation has been on the intelligibility of worship and thus the rational. Turner criticizes reforms of the liturgy as being carefully arranged but lacking in a pointing to the holy. Such sentiments are shared by Mary Douglas (1970, 1973) concerning the reforms of the Roman Catholic Church in the Second Vatican Council. In western technological society the rational has tended to dominate the non-rational. Otto provides a corrective to this way of thinking, and in the African continent the non-rational has a much greater part to play in the worship of the Church. This is so of the Ethiopian Orthodox Church.

The Numinous in the Orthodox Liturgy

There are many ways in which the holy is evoked in Orthodox worship. Firstly, the use of incense that fills the church and hangs around shimmering in the light. Then, the chanting of the service, which has a hypnotic effect and draws one outside of oneself. Also, the careful covering of the bread and the protection of the worshipper from the presence of the deity save for the consumption at communion. All are in some ways non-rational but evoke the presence of the holy to the worshipper. In Ethiopia parts of the service are conducted in Ge'ez, the ancient liturgical language, and this too gives a sense of contact with the ancestors and the primal revelation.

The words of the service emphasize the presence of the holy and warn the worshippers. At the reading of the Gospel the rubrics direct: 'When reading the word of God ... there must be silence and awe ... for hearing the word ... of the heavenly King' (Daoud, p. 58). The holiness of God is emphasized in the sanctus and the numinous nature of the epiclesis is reinforced by the exclamation of the deacon in the anaphora of St Basil: 'Worship the Lord with fear'. Speaking it in a low voice indicates the power of the epiclesis further. It is too holy to be heard by all. Holiness is the theme of the words of invitation, 'Holy things for the holy'. The contact with the holy in the consumption of the elements is a time of awe: 'He shall chew in fear and trembling without making any sound until he finishes'.

The liturgy of the Orthodox Church is deeply evocative of the holy. It is rooted in a village society that is in deep contact with the natural world and a strong system of shared values. That is not to say that there is a lack of the rational in the service. Rather the rational and the non-rational are not opposed and there is emphasis on both.

Development of the Numinous in Eucharistic Worship

The tradition of the evocation of the holy in the liturgy has deep roots in history. Bishop (1909, pp. 92–3) comments that in the fourth century there was 'a great change in religious sentiment in regard to the eucharist – a change which found outward, and as it were material, expression, especially in the east, in ritual or ceremony ... The sacrament of love became ... invested with attributes of cultural dread'. Cyril talks of the eucharist as 'the most holy and awesome sacrifice' (Yarnold, 1971, p. 92). Chrysostom develops this:

> When you see the Lord sacrificed and lying before you, and the High Priest standing over the sacrifice and praying, and all who partake being tinctured with that precious blood, can you think that you are still among men and still

standing on earth? Are you not transported to heaven ... [and] with soul naked and mind pure look around upon heavenly things? ... Can anyone ... despise this awe-inspiring rite? (Chrysostom, 1964, pp. 70-71)

Jungmann (1965) suggests that the change is a result of the conflict with Arianism: the change of the view of Christ from servant to King. Davies (1970/71) develops the reasons to include a development of the doctrine of the real presence, the view of buildings as temples, and the adoption of the Old Testament view of the holy. Perhaps the change in social circumstances is an important catalyst in this. But before this can be developed Brabant's criticisms of Otto must be examined.

Brabant

Brabant (1932) suggests that there are two assumptions behind the work of Otto: firstly that worship is merely a sense of the numinous; and secondly that there is no mystery properly so called except the holy. With regard to the latter, Otto distinguishes between the absolute, 'that which exceeds our power to comprehend', and the mysterious, 'that which wholly eludes it'. But the differences are not so clear. Is the Trinity only absolute and not also mysterious? Brabant concludes 'we reach mystery by any road, if only we go far enough' (p. 18). If other aspects besides the holy bring one to the numinous then the introduction of the numinous into worship is not evidenced by the development of the mysterious in the sense of externally otherworldly ceremony. Thus there was not an introduction of the numinous in the worship of the Church in the fourth century to which the Ethiopian Church has been faithful, but a change of expression of the numinous due to the change in the social circumstances of the Church. The Church changed from a persecuted sect to an established Church. This entailed a shift in ideology of worship. The small group that met behind locked doors experienced the numinous in the joy which took them outside of themselves into the presence of God. The size of the Church in the post-Constantinian era and the influx of the partially committed led to the externalization of the feelings of awe and their association with the primary symbol of Christian worship: the eucharist. With a root metaphor of mystery, the numinous is expressed in veneration of the symbols of that mystery. This was the paradigm that Chrysostom and Cyril emphasized in response to being swamped by the influx of those wanting to join the Church. Previously there was more emphasis on the small group of the committed who experienced the numinous in the joy of salvation.

This opening up of the concept of the numinous by Brabant is important as it entails a contrast not between churches that emphasize the numinous in worship, for example the Ethiopian Orthodox, and those that do not, for example African Independent Churches, rather the question is of the way the numinous is experienced and thus the root metaphor of that type of worship. The contrast would then be one of the power of God in the cult and the power of God in the heart.

Worship and the Numinous

Thus there has been a tendency to identify the holy with the development of ceremonial and the sense of mystery in the service. This sort of analysis fits in very well with the liturgy of the Ethiopian Church. It is an heir of the teaching of Chrysostom, even if it has developed in an independent way. Yet to follow this line is to ignore some of the inconsistencies of Otto that Brabant has disclosed. The opening up of the category of the numinous to more than the holy enables it to be used in those churches with a different ethos of worship. If the numinous is experienced in the Orthodox Church in its ceremonial, then it is experienced in the Independent Churches in a different way. The contrast lies not in the numinous being in one church and not in the other, but in the way it is experienced. The Orthodox Church puts the concentration of its worship in the objective. The Independent Churches concentrate on the subjective. In the committed fellowship of such a church the power of God is experienced directly in the heart. This is the nature of such sects. This observation also points to the relationship between attitudes to society and the churches. The state church tends to emphasize the cult and the numinous in the cult. The sect tends towards emphasis on fellowship and the power of God in the person. In each the numinous is expressed in a different way.

The holy in Otto's usage (Brabant is not denying the importance of the holy but rather the exclusive leading of the holy to the numinous) is particularly relevant to the Orthodox Church. The service is one of complex symbolism evoking awe in the faithful, leading one through a pattern of segregation to the limen of the voice of the holy, the presence of the holy. The system of symbols in the service warns the participant of the danger of such an activity, and insists on purity for approach. To be naked before the deity is a dangerous thing.

Thus the category of the holy or the sacred is an important link in the dialogue between analysis in anthropology and theology. The analysis of Otto takes the discussion one stage further than most anthropologists go, for he wants to talk not just of an experience of 'the other' or of being drawn out of the profane realm, but of this experience being overwhelming and of taking the person out of the self into intimate encounter with 'the other'. Perhaps this is to provide a platform for a particular set of doctrines of the nature of God and the methodological agnosticism of most anthropologists would cause them to be cautious over such an analysis. However, such an important discussion has enabled the development of the work of Otto such that it can be applied not only to the Orthodox liturgy, but also in principle to any form of worship. Thus the next chapter will continue to study the eucharist in those churches that are declared by some to be indigenous, the case of the African Independent Churches.

CHAPTER 5

African Independent Churches

The African Independent Churches are the second group that Mbiti (1969) defines as indigenous. They mostly originated as breakaways from the Mission Churches for a variety of reasons, partially to do with indigenous leadership, or with style of worship, or because of a vision or sense of call by a charismatic leader. They have mostly come from the Protestant denominations but there are examples from the Roman Catholic Church, e.g. the Maria Legio Church in Kenya (Dirven, 1970). There are thousands of these Churches in Africa today. Barrett (1968) analyses 6 000 of them in the continent and they form a large percentage of the 224 denominations he then lists in Kenya. Barrett notes that at one time on average there was one new denomination a month formed in Kenya, many of these being Independent Churches.

These Churches raise important questions for the Mission Churches. Why have so many African Christians left the mainline Churches to form their own denominations? Why have so many left the Anglican Church in particular? In what way do they provide 'a place to feel at home'? To what extent are they an example of the way that the Mission Churches should go? As worship has proved to be one of the factors for new religious movements, in what way is the worship of the Independent Churches more indigenous? What is the role of the eucharist in their life?

The Churches as breakaways are an example of the development of the tradition of the Mission Churches. In the formation of a new church often elements of the old are included in the new. Thus in Methodism the eucharistic liturgy was a simplification of 1662 but not a radical departure. The African Independent Churches are a conscious departure from the parent body in a more African direction. They are both in dialogue with that tradition in reaction to it. They are also in dialogue with their social setting, which is infused with Traditional Religion. In fact they are freer to react to immediate surroundings, as they are rarely affiliated with any overseas body and so do not have the constraints of a parent body or of an international communion. They vary in size from a group that may be only a handful of people to the Kimbanguists who number millions.

Wilson (1973) notes that the new religious movements in Africa tend to fall into two categories: the thaumaturgical and the revolutionist. His classification is determined by the response of the group to the world. The thaumaturgical response looks for salvation from present ills. There is a stress on healing and assuagement of grief. Supernatural help is personal and immediate. There is often a 'magical' element in the operation of healing. There is an expectancy of miracles and oracles. God works through the direct intervention of the Spirit in the life of the believer.

The revolutionist looks for the destruction of the social order. He does not see this as his work but the work of God. He is not there to hasten it by social action. Salvation, rather than being present, is immanent. The day of salvation is dawning; the revolution of God is about to come. The revolutionist group is less common than the thaumaturgical, and a group may change from one to the other. The vast majority in Africa today are thaumaturgical.

The stress on the imminent salvation of God has led many of these groups to emphasize the Holy Spirit, healing, visions and strong fellowship. In Europe this might be expected to be accompanied by a suspicion of symbol and an emphasis on the verbal (the word). In Africa there is often the emphasis on the word but also an openness to the use of symbol. Water is an element of great importance to many of the Churches, used not only in baptism (in some Churches a repeatable experience), but also as holy water, and to drink for healing. The worship may include the use of incense and candles. Dancing may form a part of the service. There is often a church uniform to be worn by all church members. The leaders may have particular clothing, which indicates their rank. The vast majority of these Churches have rejected infant baptism, which is significant in that they have mostly originated in paedobaptist missions. The eucharist is of differing importance to the various groups. Some do not have it at all. Most are infrequent in celebration. This is for a variety of reasons, not least being the influence of the mission. Many evangelical missions were not practising a frequent eucharist until the liturgical movement affected their parent bodies in the liturgical revisions of the last century.

In the following pages three case studies will be examined: the Church of the Lord (Aladura), the Cherubim and the Seraphim, and the Kimbanguists. The first two churches are both thaumaturgical and from Nigeria. They both departed from the Anglican Church and have churches in other countries in West Africa and even congregations in Britain. Kimbanguism is found in the Congo and was very much a revolutionist movement for a part of its history. It is now one of the largest of the Independent Churches and has affiliated to the World Council of Churches. As the eucharist is celebrated infrequently in all of these churches the position of the sacrament will have to be examined in relation to the whole ritual system of the Church. Do other activities of the Church function in such a way as to compensate for the infrequency of the eucharist? What is the doctrine of Holy Communion in that particular group? Are other sacraments regarded as more important? What is their attitude to symbol and how does this compare to the original body? Are there any similarities between these groups and the other churches on the African continent? Is there evidence of a dialogue with Traditional Religion even if unconscious? These sorts of questions are raised by the Independent Churches.

The Church of the Lord (Aladura)

History

The Church of the Lord has its roots in the Aladura movement of the early part of the last century. There had been movements of independence before this, most notably in the life and work of Garrick Braid, who in 1909 began a ministry of prophecy and healing. However, the main impetus for the Aladura movement was the 1918 flu epidemic. This crisis led, through a vision, to the formation of the prayer-people (the meaning of Aladura). They were often members of the Mission Churches but began to have visions and to have experiences of healing. The Faith Tabernacle, an American Pentecostal Church, was influential in the early period and when the Aladura left the Anglican Church in 1921 there was an affiliation with this denomination. The message was not only of salvation but also of healing. 'I had found that Christ was not only a saviour, but also a healer', was the testimony of one of the founder leaders (Turner, 1967a, p. 12). The 1920s saw the continuation of the movement and the rise of different prophets. In 1925 Moses Orimolade Tunolashe and Christiana Abiodun Akinsowon began a ministry of prayer and the use of holy water, which led in 1928 to the formation of the Church of the Cherubim and Seraphim. The Church of the Lord was the result of the visions received by Oshitelu, a first-generation Christian who was employed as a pupil-teacher in the Anglican Church and was training as a catechist.

Oshitelu took the Christian name of Josiah at his baptism in 1914. In 1925 he began to receive visions and began to work as a travelling evangelist. He recorded all these visions and in nine years received over 10 000. In 1926 he was suspended from the Anglican Church and devoted his time to prayer and preaching. In 1927 he received his holy name, Arrabablahhubab. Holy words continue to play a part in the church. He married and had seven wives. The Church began in the 1930s and spread to Ghana, Liberia, Sierra Leone and even to England. It has had many offshoots; Turner documents 26 different secessions (pp. 108–9).

Worship in the Church of the Lord

The Church of the Lord has produced a number of booklets that are sources for its approach to worship, some in English and others in the vernacular. The English sources include *The Bible Speaks on the Church of the Lord* (Adejobi, 1950), *The Observances and Practices of the Church of the Lord (Aladura) in the Light of the Old Testament and New Testament* (Adejobi, n.d.), the *Book of Rituals* (n.d.), *99 Questions and Answers on the Church of the Lord Doctrine* (Krow, 1961), and the Church *Hymn Book* (1958). These and other Church publications illuminate their understanding of worship and the eucharist. In some ways the Church continues in the Anglican tradition in that parts of the *Book of Rituals* are directly from the

Book of Common Prayer and many of the hymns are traditional to the west. But it is in its divergences from the parent body and the reorganization of the material that the new path is revealed. Not all the theological changes were necessarily conscious and the teaching of the Church has modified within its history. It is also impossible to determine to what extent all the services found in the *Book of Rituals* are regularly used, just as there are great variations in the use of the prayer book of any denomination. One of the most noticeable divergences from Anglicanism of the low church CMS tradition is the use of symbols in worship. There is much greater use of material symbols in the Church, often gleaned from the Old Testament or the book of Revelation. An analysis of the material also shows there is active dialogue with local culture. Various aspects of the worship will be examined to illustrate this and to provide the background to see the eucharist within the ritual system.

Prayer and Fasting

Prayer is given a high priority in the Church. There is daily morning and evening prayer and the Sunday service is a more extended form of that which occurs in the week. Fasting is an important part of prayer. It is done 'for the purpose of punishing and sanctifying the body in preparation for the imbibing of the Holy Spirit, as penance for the conferment of God's favour' (Adejobi, 1950, p. 7). The Mission Churches are criticized for their laxity in the practice. Members are expected to fast on Wednesdays and Fridays and in Lent. Lent is a time for special prayer and the use of the litany is encouraged. This is an adaptation of the Anglican litany but much simplified. The words of the priest (the name of the leader given in the book but not an official church title) are shortened to a brief sentence. The litany is divided into three sections by the triple repetition of:

> Priest: We use our mouths like a broom before Thee.
> Cong.: Good Lord have mercy on us.

Turner comments (167a, p. 168) that this is accompanied by the prostration of the congregation and that it is a traditional practice of humiliation and penance before a Yoruba King. The petitions also reflect the concerns of the culture in the petitions with regard to witchcraft:

> Priest: From the attacks of wizards and witches.
> Cong.: Good Lord deliver us.
> Priest: Over those who employ spirits against us.
> Cong.: Good Lord give us victory.
> Priest: Over all bad and wicked juju-men.
> Cong.: Good Lord give us victory.

This also reflects the strong reaction of the Church against Traditional Religion as comes out in the baptism service:

Question: Dost thou promise to renounce the devil . . . the use of Juju?

The Church rejects all traditional healing and calls its members to come to it for healing. There is also a strong apocalyptic section:

Priest: In the days of wars and the rumours of war.
Cong.: Good Lord deliver us.
Priest: In the days that the moon shall be troubled and it shall become blood.
Cong.: Good Lord deliver us.

Thus the litany is a radical adaptation of the Anglican rite reflecting the culture of the Church and a dialogue with Traditional Religion.

Symbolic Space

There are a variety of holy places in the Church. Firstly, there is the village church or temple. Most are simple structures with the sanctuary railed off. It is a holy of holies. It contains a light wooden table with an altar cloth, a seven-branched candelabrum, some paper flowers and a wooden cross. The lectern is outside the sanctuary, and there is a table for the blessing of water. God is believed to be specially present in the temple and people may sleep there. Secondly, there is a special area attached to the church called the mercy ground. This is a holy place for prayers. People may go there before the service. Thirdly, there are home altars. These often contain a cross, candle and a Bible. Turner comments (p. 103) that there is a precedent for this in Yoruba household shrines. Fourthly, the city where the visions first took place is regarded as holy. Ogere is not a place of pilgrimage, but a large cathedral is built there. Fifthly, there is the holy hill of Mount Tabora where there is a large pilgrimage every year. Preparation for this may include a retreat at the seashore for quiet, purification and fasting.

Symbolic Objects

The members of the Church are expected to wear white apparel as an 'emblem of purity and chastity Rev 7:9'. Candles are used and justified from Ex 25:31. Palm leaves are used as 'emblems of victory . . . Rev 7:9'. An iron rod is used as a staff of office: it is 'a visible omen of the victory through Christ'. A turban may be worn by some leaders according to Zec 3:5. All manner of objects may be used in healing, including handkerchiefs, oil, salt, water, clay and incense. Many of these objects are justified by the Old Testament and by the book of Revelation.

Symbolic Actions

Church services are not as static as the mission parent. Besides kneeling there are prostrations, kissing the Bible, clapping, shouting, use of the sign of the cross, anointing, laying on of hands, the sprinkling with Holy Water, and usually at some point in the service there is dancing. Apostle Adejobi interprets some of these uses: 'Palm leaves are given and water sprinkled on people as a visible sign of sanctification as Moses sanctified the children of Israel with water and ointment. The blood of Jesus represented by water, we now apply has a super sanctifying and cleansing force' (Adejobe 1950, p. 8). Shoes are removed on entering the temple and there may be water provided to wash the feet.

Time and Symbolism

The use of time follows the pattern of the Mission Churches with the observance of Sunday and the major Christian festivals. Adejobi also recommends 6 a.m., 9 a.m., 12 noon, 3 p.m. and 6 p.m. as the hours of prayer, based on the New Testament, but it is not clear to what extent these hours are kept. There are no official forms of prayer for these times.

A particular use of time in this Church is the Mount Tabora Season. This is a festival that begins on 10 August with a period of fasting and reaches its climax on 22 August. This is the main event of the calendar. The mountain is chosen by revelation, each branch of the Church has its Mount Tabora and it is sometimes called the Feast of Tabernacles. In Nigeria a hill is used at Olorunkole near Ibadan and this is shared with other Aladura Churches. Turner (1967a, p. 21) suggests that the Aladura have developed the Yoruba tradition of sacred hills to their own ends. People come to the mountain for fellowship and to receive visions. All the revelations are recorded and those by the primate are published. The climax is the final day, which is for the fulfilment of vows, the giving of the iron rod of ministry (the equivalent of ordination), the blessing of water and the making of cross-bearers. People are not allowed to wear shoes on the mountain and women who are ritually unclean are banned. There is the consecration of holy food and the event finishes with the consumption of the food by the whole Church. In this activity hymns are sung such as 'Love feast in heaven tonight', and one including the line 'foretaste of the festal joy, the Lamb's great bridal feast of bliss and joy'. This type of feast is also known on Easter Monday but no connection is made with the eucharist.

Symbolic Persons

There is a well-developed hierarchy in the Church. Among the men the pattern is as follows:

                Primate
Apostle Bishop
Rev Apostle   Rev Deacon
Senior Prophet   Senior Evangelist

Prophet   Evangelist
Acting Prophet   Captain
              Teacher

The two columns represent two different types of ministry, those with spiritual gifts and those with pastoral gifts (preaching and administration). This seems to be an example of dual sovereignty (Needham, 1980). There are also six grades of women's ministry:

Rev Mother
Rev Deacon
Prophetess
Lady Evangelist
Lady Captain
Sister

All these ranks have their own particular vestments and their ranks and duties are carefully prescribed. Whereas in England there has been a reaction against rank and title, the African Church finds that this accords with the traditional value of giving honour to the elders.

Holy Words

This is 'one of the most bizarre features of the Church of the Lord' (Turner 1967a, p. 272). Strange words are spoken, sung and incorporated into the liturgy. There is no special relationship of these holy words to glossolalia; the church does allow the gift of tongues. The holy words are meaningless in themselves, in the sense that normal conversation cannot be conducted in them, but they do convey various suggestions to the church members. They are regarded as revelations from the Lord, a special gift from God. Often the services in the *Book of Rituals* are prefaced with a statement that they are by the command of Jehovah and a holy name is used, e.g. at the naming of a child 'by the Command of Jehovah Abbilal', and at weddings 'By the command of Jehovah Gorrabbuttallah'. At the consecration in the Holy Communion the priest offers 19 holy words including 'Jehovah, Yaawaanniei, Yaawaarraa . . . Labieussas'.

Similarly Ositelu (n.d.) directed a distinctive use of the Psalms. Individual Psalms are recommended in particular circumstances: Ps 5 should be read over olive oil 'for gaining favour of all men', and the oil is then rubbed over the body, Ps 9 is to be read over a pot of water, and then the person is to bath in the water if he is impotent. On Ps 7 it is said 'If enemies rise against thee, recite this Psalm, standing facing East in midnight with the Holy Name Ell Ellijjon. You will be naked. And the enemy will be defeated at will.' This is 'pure occult magic', comments Turner (1967a, p. 74).

Holy Water

The use of water for the washing of feet on entering the church has already been noticed. However, there are more extensive uses of water for cleansing and healing. 'We make no use of medical aid besides the use of Holy Water' (Adejobi, 1950, p. 8). The Church had its origins in the experience of the power of God in healing, that Christ was not only Saviour but also Healer. This has led to a rejection of western medicine, which for much of its history was in the hands of the missions. The separation of the Independent Churches was a rejection of the dominance of the west in the running of the emerging African Church, and the attraction of the medicine of the missions was responded to by a thaumaturgical gospel: hence the use of holy water for healing. 'The Lord has provided and established this water for the Healing of all diseases, body and spirit. The water may be likened to the Ark amongst the children of Israel in those days provided for them for their redemption' (p. 5). This water is blessed towards the end of the service and may be taken away to be drunk or applied to the body.

Water is also used for purification. After the general confession, water is sprinkled on the people using a palm branch, which 'stands for an outward sign of that continuous cleansing pool which flows still in the blood of Jesus Christ. Lev 8; Ez 36:35'. Water is used in the confession at communion and also is sprinkled on a child at his or her naming. This of course should not be confused with baptism, as the Church rejects infant baptism.

The Eucharist in the Church of the Lord

The first constitution of 1938 mentioned the Holy Communion but there was no actual celebration until 1952 and then in Sierra Leone. Nigeria followed in 1953 and Liberia in 1955. The service is held only three or four times a year and the rubrics direct that it be done at night between 9 p.m. and 11 p.m.; often it is held behind closed doors. Ordinary wine is used and ordinary bread, which is broken into small pieces. Only those who are apostles have the mandate to celebrate but they can delegate their authority down to the rank of prophet.

The catechism in the *Book of Rituals* follows that of the *Book of Common Prayer*. However, there are some major differences when it comes to the sacraments. There is no definition of a sacrament. The questions associated with baptism explain the rejection of infant baptism (infants cannot confess). There is nothing about Holy Communion at all. Instead there is a section on the Water of Life. 'What is required to drink the Water of Life? Self examination'. It would seem that holy water has taken on the function of the eucharist. This is compounded by the use of the image of the blood of Christ associated with holy water, as has been quoted above.

However there is a flexibility in doctrine, for the catechism from Ghana has a section on the eucharist. A sacrament is 'a sacred act instituted by Jesus Christ in which fixed and visible tokens connected with its word of promise God offers and gives us great spiritual blessing' (Krow, 1961). There are two sacraments, and baptism has such power because of the word of God, which is 'in and with the water'. The Lord's Supper is also called the Sacrament of the Altar and we are said to eat the body and blood of Christ 'under the bread and the wine'. The catechism rejects both the Catholic doctrine and the Reformed view, which it interprets in a Zwinglian way. However, the Real Presence is affirmed and the benefit is the forgiveness of sins. The last two questions are concerned with the worthiness of the communicant and the warning of 1 Cor 11:28–29 is expounded.

The order of service in the *Book of Rituals* is as follows:

1 Sentence
2 Rubric directing the unworthy not to participate
3 Hymn – 'I hunger and I thirst'
4 Ps 51 followed by a prayer of absolution
5 Hymn – 'Jesus, my Saviour look on me'
6 The Ten Commandments
7 Pss 65, 32, 130, with a prayer of absolution
8 Hymn – 'There is a fountain filled with blood'
   During the hymn holy water is sprinkled on everybody
9 Pronouncement of the absolution of sins
10 Prayer of consecration. This includes the use of 19 holy names and, 'Consecrate . . . all these vessels . . . and also the bread and the wine . . . that we may not be killed by them. Let the bread become changed to the flesh of Christ and this wine the blood of Jesus Christ . . . may we for ever live in Thee, Amen'.
11 The Narrative of Institution is read
12 Hymn – 'Come the feast is ready'
13 Distribution using the words of the *Book of Common Prayer*
14 Hymn
15 Closing prayer
16 Benediction

As the service is held at night there are no children present: The atmosphere is subdued, there is no clapping. The people have to be clean to receive. The water for sprinkling is consecrated by the passing of the iron rod over the water and the hymn is often sung that includes the lines:

> What can wash away my stain?
> Nothing but the blood of Jesus.

The iron rod is used in the consecration of the elements. Each of the elements is touched with the rod during the consecration prayer. The closing prayer often gives thanks for 'the power of life, healing, salvation, and eternal life given to us', and there is often an element of self-oblation.

The origin of the rite is the *Book of Common Prayer* but there have been some radical changes. A number of motifs in this service show the changes that have occurred.

Firstly, there is a strong emphasis on purity. The first half of the service stresses the need for cleansing from sin. The Ten Commandments remind of sinfulness. The psalms are penitential, there are three absolutions and this is sealed by the use of holy water. This in itself is seen as a symbol of the cleansing blood of Christ. The impure are not allowed to partake. The danger is that the rite might become something only for those who view themselves as worthy.

Secondly, there is a strong emphasis on consecration. Much of the material in Cranmer, which emphasizes praise (e.g. the sursum corda), and that which emphasizes the service as a holy meal (e.g. the prayer of humble access), has been omitted. The consecration prayer in Cranmer is a prayer for fruitful reception. The Church of the Lord has changed this back into a prayer of consecration of the elements, 'Let this bread be changed into the flesh of Christ'. Indeed the prayer begins with a prayer for the consecration of the vessels, which has more in common with the Ethiopian Orthodox Church than with Cranmer. This emphasis on consecration is associated with an embryonic doctrine of awe concerning the consecration. The rubrics direct that 'everybody shall kneel by the altar reverently and with awe and receive'. This parallels the development of Cyril of Jerusalem's doctrine of awe (Bishop, 1909) as outlined in chapter 4 above. It is also the undoing of the Anglican doctrine of receptionism, which tries to avoid an objective view of consecration. This was the product of the Reformation revolt against symbol and the desire to control symbol with careful explanation in the text. The ambiguity of the Prayer Book, as to if the bread is the body of Christ and the wine is the blood of Christ, has been removed by a clear prayer of consecration. This perhaps reflects a culture that is more able to appreciate symbol and contrasts with the recent revisions in the Church of England where the notion of consecration has been one of the moot points, not least over the inclusion of a consecratory epiclesis and any reference to the blessing of any inanimate object.

Thirdly, the words of Paul in 1 Cor 11:27–30 have a much stronger influence in this rite than in Cranmer. The prayer of consecration specifically asks, 'Thy children who shall partake thereof may suffer no stomach trouble thereby nor become ill through same, that we may not be killed by them'. This supports Mbiti's assertion, quoted in chapter 3 above, of these verses being interpreted in a 'magical' way.

Conclusions

The Church of the Lord has developed its own ritual system in reaction to its Anglican roots, in dialogue with its environment, and in debate with the other

Aladura Churches. The system may seem to be a cross between the Catholic and the Pentecostal. This is only superficially true. It would be better to say that there has been the development of a more 'restricted code' using symbols suggested by the Bible and also coming from traditional culture. The latter are taken not from Traditional Religion as such, but from the rites associated with kingship.

Peculiar to this Church is the use of holy names, which may have some links with the 'occultish' use of the Psalms and a desire for power over evil forces. The fear of evil is certainly a strong feature of the litany, but this feature has caused criticism not least from the other Aladura Churches. Before further conclusions are drawn, another Aladura Church, The Cherubim and the Seraphim, will be examined, to provide a contrast with the Church of the Lord and to clarify some directions of the Aladura movement as a whole, for the Independent Churches are in dialogue not only with their parent and with their culture but also with one another.

The Cherubim and Seraphim

The examination of the Cherubim and Seraphim will complement the Church of the Lord (Aladura), and show some of the differences in the Aladura movement. They both come from Nigeria, both out of the ferment of the 1920s. The Cherubim and Seraphim was founded by Moses Orimolade in 1925 and, like the Church of the Lord, has branches in other countries including Britain. In some ways it is closer to the parent mission, CMS, but it also has its own ethos. The services follow more of the Anglican pattern (Peel, 1968) but within the ritual there is space for free prayer. The Church produces its own liturgy, 'The Order', constitution, and various pamphlets to explain the reason for the Church and the doctrine of the Church.

Worship in the Cherubim and Seraphim

Abana (1956) devotes a large amount of space to items related to worship. This was one of the central features of the Aladura breaking away and it is in its relevant worship that the Church is perceived to be indigenous. The Mission Churches had not led the Africans to true worship and the examination of the Bible, as directed by the revelation of God, has revealed those areas that are the way that the Christian should worship. Once again the Old Testament and the book of Revelation provide the most fertile sources.

There has been a development of the use of many objects in worship as in the Church of the Lord. Candles are used and justified by Rev 3:1–3. Rods are included because of Rev 2:26–27. Incense is used (Mal 1:11; Rev 5:8, 8:4) to drive away the demons. Bells are rung as a sign of victory. White garments are the dress of the faithful in worship, Rev 7:9 'this is the uniform of Christian worship here on earth'. Worship on earth is to be an imitation of the worship of heaven.

There is a greater emphasis on purity than we have so far seen. Menstruating women are to stop coming to church in line with Lev 15 and men who have had an emission are to wash themselves. No dead bodies are to be allowed in the church, following Num 19:11–13. These may well be traditional taboos that have parallels in the Old Testament and have been adopted by the Church. The basic command is to keep the 'temple' (church building) holy. 'All churches will be one if the temple and altar are kept holy as commanded by God.' Holiness does not involve monogamy, for the Church allows polygamy.

Morning and evening prayer are held in the church three times a week. One of the most important services is the Saturday vigil, which is held from midnight to 2 or 3 in the morning. This service begins ritualistically but after one hour there is often an outbreak of the use of charismatic gifts. Tongues and visions are highly valued.

The Church follows the main features of the traditional Christian year and encourages fasting in Lent but it has also developed its own feasts. These include Founders Day, Consecration Day, Virgins Day, and then a set of feasts associated with angels: Cherubic Anniversary, Seraphic Anniversary, Michael, and Gabriel. This interest in angels is the distinguishing feature of the Church and finds parallels in Africa in the Ethiopian Orthodox Church.

There are often no chairs in the church building, or 'temple' as it is called. The floor may be covered with carpets and the room is bright and clean. Religious mottoes are often painted on the walls and over the chancel arch. The altar may have a sevenfold candlestick and a triptych of Christ and two angels. There are usually banners of Holy Michael and of Orimolade. There may be a baptismal pool and the temple always contains a lectern.

Dreams

Abana says that the Church needs to be directed by dreams and miracles. The way this leads to the reform of worship can be seen in the pamphlet (Abana, 1972) that explains how the Church was led to receive the Ark of the Covenant. On 12 June 1972 the praying members of the Cherubim and Seraphim in Amatta-Ikedura were told in a vision that they were to pray and to prepare to build the Ark of the Covenant. They went on praying and fasting for seven days and were told to march round the town with the Ark once it was built. On 25 August the Ark was completed and the procession was made. The Ark went first, and then people carrying bamboo with palm leaves tied on top, followed by a thurifer. As the congregation processed they prayed Psalm 23 and shouted halleluiah. The Ark is now kept in the altar of the temple at Amatta. A white candle is put on it every Friday. Access to the Ark is not allowed to every member of the Church. More processions of the Ark were planned. The Ark is seen as 'the enfleshment, suffering, crucifixion and resurrection of our Lord and Saviour Jesus Christ. This is the testimony of Jesus Christ calling all mankind to fellowship with him' (p. 2). All this is an interesting development in the light of the Ethiopian legend of the Ark being taken to Axum by Menelek I and the procession of the Tabot on the Feast of Temkat.

Initiation

The style of worship in the Church can also be illustrated by examining the services of initiation. The Cherubim and Seraphim retain many features of Anglicanism but reject infant baptism. At eight days old the babe is to be brought to the temple for the service of 'circumcision'. Materials to be used are a white gown for the babe, candles (3 or 7), which are set on the table, and incense, which is used throughout the service. There are various Psalms and lessons including Luke 2:21–40. During the song 'Jesus proceeds to Jordan' a Lady Leader in a prayer gown dances with the child in her arms. The babe is given to the leader and the Cherubim and Seraphim are invoked. John 4:1–14 is read and the leader uses the middle finger of the right hand to drip water into the mouth of the babe. This is done three times. Honey is also dripped three times into the mouth of the child (compare Is 7:14–15). Then the child is blessed with the Aaronic blessing. Although the service is labelled 'circumcision' there is no actual circumcision performed.

Baptism is done by immersion and the minimum age is 13. A river is the preferred place. Confirmation is done after the age of 16 by an apostle and is seen as the receiving of the Holy Ghost. Here is an adaptation of the Anglican pattern. The services of baptism and confirmation follow the style of the Anglican service. The service of circumcision is an indigenous construction. The use of holy water parallels its use in healing in the Church and is logical in a land of high infant mortality, but there may also be links to traditional customs. What is noticeable is that there is no emphasis on the giving of the name in the ceremony in contrast with the Church of the Lord.

Healing

Emphasis is placed on the need for faith in Jesus the healer. Thus the traditional methods of talismans and charms are rejected. The water is consecrated not in the church but in the vestry or some other reserved place. The service involves the reading of Psalms and the singing of hymns. After the consecration, prayers are offered for the departed brothers and sisters. This is a significant departure from the teaching of CMS but one that comes naturally to the African as much of Traditional Religion is to do with the departed and interceding both for and through them.

The Communion of Saints

The Church's identity is associated with the angels and there is felt to be a link to the departed. How is this explained? In a comment on the Apostles' Creed, Abana (1956, p. 16) says 'we are now communicating with the saints and they are forgiving our sins'. He explains this further 'when you are communicating with the saints, it means you receive messages from them in the way of visions or dreams' (p. 27). Dreams are very common in Africa and are given great significance. Passages in the Bible, e.g. Joel 2:28, are seen by the Church to reinforce the belief in dreams and visions. The importance of ancestors was discussed in a previous chapter. Here is an example of the way a Christian Church has given the Creed an African interpretation.

The Holy Spirit

The Holy Spirit receives particular emphasis. The teaching of the Church is (Abana, 1956, p. 27):

> The first covenant started first from Egypt . . . the second started from Jerusalem on the day of Pentecost. In the third covenant we are made to understand that Moses was the first and Moses also shall be the last Dt 18:12, Acts 3:22 . . . Jesus is greater than Moses . . . the third covenant started from Ikare in Nigeria. This covenant was sent down on a hill, which was divided into three, which goes again to signify the Blessed Trinity.

There is a tendency here for the Holy Spirit to become more important than Jesus, for there is no mention of the cross as the beginning of the new covenant. The Church conceives of the Christian message as incarnate and thus has developed the notion of the third covenant. The significant fact here is not the arrival and preaching of the missionaries, as would be the view of the Mission Churches but the revelations received by Moses Orimolade, the last Moses. The role of the founder as icon of Christ becomes more acute in the Kimbanguist Church and in those Independent Churches where there is a Black Messiah.

The Eucharist in the Cherubim and Seraphim

There are a number of pamphlets that specifically explain the view taken of Holy Communion. In *The Key to Salvation* Abana (1956, p. 18) rejects infant communion: 'Whosoever gives it to an infant is only poisoning him; rather it is better to give it to a full grown person both in age and reason'. This is rather surprising in that infant communion was not an issue in 1956. It may be that he is thinking of the first communion of the Catholics and saying that the age is too low for admission. It may also be that he is thinking of infant baptism (the motif of the cleansing blood of Jesus often being linked to water) and rejecting this on the grounds of discernment.

Whatever the reason, there is a strong reliance on Paul in 1 Cor 11 'whosoever takes it unworthily shall be guilty of the body and blood of Jesus'.

The *Lenten Season and The Feast of Passover (Revised and Enlarged)* (Abana, n.d.) suggests that Maundy Thursday is the particular day in Lent when there should be Holy Communion and then in the evening. This is done in remembrance of the events of the Last Supper, which suggests a 'rememorative' or 'historicization' approach. The major teaching of the Church on the Holy Communion is found in Abana's pamphlet (n.d.) *Holy Communion Ordinance (Revised)*. It is seen as 'the oath of God' and as a feast. Its origins are the Old Testament, the manna in the wilderness, which Jesus came to restore. 'Our fathers cried unto God in the Wilderness for the bread out of aching need, in the same manner the Jews cried unto the Lord Jesus to give them the bread of life. And we of the present generation have followed their footsteps.' Thus the biblical interpretation follows the motifs from Numbers and John 6. The communion is eating the bread of heaven, the manna, the living bread. Therefore, there needs to be great precaution in participating. Usually the service is at night and the communicants should fast afterwards until daybreak. Infants, the sick and the wicked are barred. 'When the holy communion enters into the person's body and meets evil, it brings death or sickness, to the person.' The example given is that of Judas. 'But when it meets goodness it restores goodness.' The example given is the other apostles. Thus the communion is good for any believer,'but it is better for those who have grown in wisdom and understanding of God'. The emphasis on eating Christ has turned the eucharist into a service for the pure and wise rather than the feast for all.

The order of service follows the Anglican 1662 pattern:

1 The third exhortation
2 Ye that do earnestly repent . . .
3 Confession
4 Absolution
5 Comfortable Words
6 Sursum Corda
7 Preface and Sanctus
8 Reading – John 6:33–58
9 Prayer of consecration (without manual acts)
10 Administration (1662 words)
11 Collection and the blessing of the almsgivers
12 Lord's Prayer
13 First post communion collect
14 Gloria
15 Benediction

The service being in the evening would probably be after evening prayer, which explains the loss of the synaxis. The third exhortation is full of warning of the dangers of unworthy participation, which is one of the themes of the communion ordinance. It is unfortunate that the second exhortation is not used instead. The prayer of humble access has been replaced with the reading from John. Presumably a reading immediately before consecration was thought necessary and rather than choose 1 Corinthians 11, as is common in the free churches, John 6 is used, a paradigm passage in their eucharistic theology. It is rather strange to have the collection immediately after reception of the elements but it enables a practical response to the love of God in the sacrament.

If the Holy Communion is an infrequent service, for the mature then there is a service to which there are fewer restrictions and which may act as a substitute, the Love Feast: 'The church shall institute Love Feast and the Holy Sacrament among its members. Love Feast shall be taken by all and Sunday Members ... The Holy Sacrament shall be administered to workers and such members have received the baptism by immersion'.

The service is thus open to all people who are members of the Church, but they do not have to be baptized.

The service is as follows:

1 Bread and water are prepared
2 Singing of three or seven songs
3 Lesson – 1 Cor 1
4 A song
5 'Consecration of the Feast'
   (i) Ps 24
   (ii) Reading – John 4:6–15
   (iii) Prayer by three members for love and unity to descend
6 'Distribution of the Feast'
   Words of administration of the bread: 'I am the food of salvation he who partakes of me will no longer be hungry.'
7 Words of administration of the water: 'I am the Water of Life he who partakes of me will never be thirsty, Amen.'
8 Songs, testimonies, prayers and hymns
9 The grace

The rubrics say that the service is to be held a minimum of twice a year.

It is significant that John 6:48 is referred to in the words of administration of the bread. The bread of life, manna theme has already been used in the explanation of the Holy Communion and now it is being used again in the Love Feast. There is a danger of the blurring of the two. Water was used by the Aquarians in the eucharist (see chapter 3, above) and is often seen in the Independent Churches as having sacramental power. Now it is used in this service, which could become a quasi-eucharistic rite, a substitute for the holy communion.

Conclusions

The Cherubim and Seraphim Church tends to celebrate the eucharist infrequently. This is partially due to the view that only the worthy can participate and that there is great danger in receiving the sacrament. However, the attitude of the missions that they departed from should not be neglected. There was a tendency to stress infrequent communion, perhaps quarterly, and many were barred from communion because of polygamy. Thus the Aladura Churches may have accepted the situation of communion being only at special times of the year. Turner comments (1965, p. 169) 'The Lord's Supper or Eucharist is usually neglected among the independents. Some have discarded it altogether; others celebrate it infrequently and without understanding or as a special rite for an inner circle of sanctified members'.

Ideologically the symbol of the eucharist is seen as the Living Bread, manna, the body and blood of Christ. There is a shift from the receptionism of CMS to, in the case of the Church of the Lord, an acceptance of the real presence. The teaching of Paul in 1 Cor 11 has led to the fear of unworthy reception and the drinking of judgement which discourages frequent communion. The churches emphasize the power of the Spirit and the new life, but no connection is made between the eucharist and healing, or between the elements and the resurrection body of Christ, which brings us the new life. These churches are strong on the Holy Spirit but their Christology is weak, compare the three covenants' doctrine of the Cherubim and Seraphim, and this can easily result in the founder becoming a Black Messiah, as happened amongst the Ngunzists.

Turner also says (p. 167) 'There is a danger that the holy water, etc, can become a new magical power acting apart from God, and that the sacramental use of wine and bread in the Lord's Supper ... will be replaced by a different sacramental use of water'. The drinking of holy water, the Love Feasts and the church picnic can all end up functioning as a substitute for the eucharist.

One noticeable feature of the Aladura Churches is their adoption of numerous symbols in terms of objects and actions. The worship of the Mission Churches did not reach the heart of the people because it reflected the reformation suspicion of symbol. The Aladura Churches have developed their own restricted code with a level of symbolism that is appropriate to the village tribal life of modern Africa. Unlike the Pentecostal movement, to which they bear some resemblance, they are open to symbol and much of the justification for the existence of the Church centres on the use of the right symbols in worship. Hence they can seem to western eyes a curious mix of the Pentecostal and the Catholic. In fact they are a genuine attempt by African Christians to make a 'place to feel at home'.

The Kimbanguist Church

The Church of Jesus Christ on Earth through the Prophet Simon Kimbangu or, to use the abbreviated form of the official name, the Kimbanguist Church, is one of the largest Independent Churches in Africa found mostly in The Congo and numbering several million members. The Church has become a member of the World Council of Churches but does not have any other denominational links outside of Africa. The Church today is a thaumaturgical denomination but in its history has been a revolutionist sect. The eucharist has become a part of the life of the Church but for a long period it was not celebrated at all. Indeed it was the seemingly unorthodox position of the Church on the sacraments that raised questions with some members of the WCC, as to the suitability of the Church for membership of that organization (Crane, 1970). The Church is a product of the short ministry of Simon Kimbangu and the devotion of his much-persecuted followers. The pattern of study will be the same as for the other Independent Churches, first a brief history of the Church, then a study of the ritual system, and finally an outline of the eucharist in the life of the Church.

History

Simon Kimbangu was born c.1889 (Martin, 1975). Shortly after his birth a Baptist (BMS) missionary blessed him. His aunt brought him up after the death of his parents. In 1915 he and his wife were baptized in the river Tombe and the marriage was solemnized in church. One night in the flu epidemic of 1918 Kimbangu heard a call from God to lead the Church. He fled to Kinshasa but found that he could not escape the call. Due to lack of success in the city he had to return to his own town of N'Kamba. On 6 April 1921 (which is seen today as the date of the founding of the Church) Simon reluctantly began a ministry of healing. At first there was suspicion but soon crowds were flocking to N'Kamba to be healed. Simon not only healed but also began a ministry of preaching salvation through Christ, rejecting the use of fetishes and polygamy.

The impact of the preaching and miracles on the Africans and the numbers coming to N'Kamba with subsequent neglect of the plantations led to the authorities taking an interest. They were afraid that the prophetic movement developing around Kimbangu might cause an uprising. They called a meeting of all missionaries, who were happy to denounce the new movement. On 6 June 1921 an attempt was made to arrest Kimbangu but this met with resistance. The spread of the movement led to a state of emergency being proclaimed on 12 August. Because of a voice from God, Simon returned to N'Kamba and allowed himself to be arrested on 12 August. He was accused of sedition and hostility to whites and was sentenced to death. The Catholic missionaries had accepted the ruling of the court but there were some questions in the minds of the civil authorities and King Albert commuted the sentence to life imprisonment. Kimbangu was transported and spent the remainder of his life in prison until he died in 1951. Thus the active ministry of the prophet was a mere five months.

From 1921 to 1957 the Church was persecuted. In fact the Church did not exist as a separate organization in this period, and there were unclear lines between the Kimbanguists and other prophetic groups. It is estimated that 37,000 heads of families were banished, but this process of banishment only helped to spread the movement. There was severe persecution in 1925 but the period 1934–36 was a time of revival associated with the ministry of the Salvation Army. The Church was an unofficial part of the Protestant Churches until 1956 when Kimbanguists were ejected from the Mission Churches and they were forced by circumstances to form their own organization. The onset of independence enabled the Kimbanguists to obtain freedom from religious persecution.

In the era of persecution there was an overlap with another prophetic group, the Ngunzists. Their view was that God 'sent us Simon Kimbangu a Saviour who belongs to the black race. He is the Chief and Saviour of all the blacks and has in fact the same authority as the Saviours of the other races, such as Moses, Jesus Christ, Mohammed and Buddah' (Martin, 1975, p. 141). The hope was that God would liberate the people from the colonialists by a Kimbangu who would come with Jesus on the clouds. The thaumaturgical Kimbangu was turned into a revolutionist by the actions of the government. There were rumours of the return of Kimbangu and the healer was transformed into a Messiah.

In 1957 the Church was granted toleration and in 1959 it was recognized and able to make a statement of its position. While the Church was being persecuted there was no official leadership, now the prophet's son Joseph Diangienda became its head. Thus the Church was forced to regularize all the patterns of worship and to train pastors, whereas previous to 1957 it had been a movement that had taken refuge in the missions and had participated in their life and worship.

The Ritual System

The church building is

> extremely austere . . . [and] those officiating do not wear special dress . . . The service is largely Protestant in type . . . [but] is essentially communal. Everyone takes part in it and it is when the community really lives . . . The festive atmosphere is enhanced by the palm leaves that the people like to wave above their heads. (*Ecumenical Review*, 1967, pp. 31–2)

People take off their shoes as they enter the church or for any prayer. Also purses, watches and other objects are removed in order to be poor before the Lord (Martin, 1974). There is daily morning and evening prayer and members are expected to pray if possible at noon. The morning prayer includes prayers for those who have died in the night, e.g. 'as Mama Mwilu comes to Thee we pray that Thou accept her' (Ndofunsu, 1978, p. 580). A special day is Wednesday when no work should be done and the members should gather for a prayer meeting. The services are long by western standards but they are full of life. Dancing is not permitted, which is in contrast to many of the Independent Churches, but the Church points to the controversy that the introduction of dance has caused in the Mission Churches.

Besides the Holy Communion, baptism, marriage and ordination are regarded as sacraments. The first baptisms were performed in 1957. The service is held twice a year and baptisms are performed according to Mark 1:8. The rite is done without water. The candidate kneels before the pastor who takes him by the hand, invokes the name of the Trinity and raises the person to his feet, which is regarded as baptism. This is in strong contrast to the use of water for healing in the rest of the ritual life, but it should not be forgotten that the Salvation Army had a strong impact on many Kimbanguists in the era of persecution. Baptism is regarded as the time when the candidate receives the Holy Spirit. It is through being united with Christ through the Holy Spirit that a person receives the forgiveness of sins. Nevertheless the primary motif of baptism is the reception of the Spirit (Diagienda, 1980).

Holy water is used in many contexts for blessing and healing. People use the water daily on themselves, and to bless houses or cars. The water is obtained from the well at N'Kamba, which is regarded as a holy well. N'Kamba has become a place of pilgrimage and part of that includes bathing in the well and collecting the holy water.

N'Kamba is regarded as the New Jerusalem for the Church, an anticipation of the glory and peace to come. A pilgrimage there is expected of all the members of the Church. Along the way pilgrims sing and pray. It is the place where there was a new outpouring of the Holy Spirit in 1921, and it is the place of the burial of the prophet. It is a place for ritual washing; the bathing is done by kneeling in the pool, praying, and immersing three times in the name of the Father and the Son and the Holy Spirit. Not only is water collected in bottles from the well but also the earth of N'Kamba is taken home. Finally the pilgrim visits the mausoleum of Simon Kimbangu, the prophet who is regarded as risen with Christ and interceding for his followers.

Members of the Church are expected to take part in a five-day retreat each year. These retreats are held in a remote spot and there are specially chosen teams who lead them. On the first evening everyone is expected to make an open confession of his or her sins in front of the whole group. Many fast for the duration of the retreat: all are supposed to fast for at least one day. There is intensive Bible study, prayer and meditation. In the retreat many are strengthened in their faith, make new commitments and receive new visions. On the day of return a special service is held and the participant is not allowed to resume normal relationships until this rite is completed. All this is highly liminal, with the first day being a rite of separation via the hymns and Bible study, leading to the liminal phase when the individual is able to receive new direction through visions and new commitment to a particular course of action. Finally there is the re-integration at the service of return.

Invocation of Simon Kimbangu

The traditional ending to the prayer of the Kimbanguist is: 'In the name of the Father and of the Son and of the Holy Spirit, who has spoken to us through (or descended on) Simon Kimbangu'. This has caused a certain amount of controversy and it would seem certain that the role of Kimbangu has been one of a messiah or god in the minds of some of the members (Wainwright, 1971). Diagienda (1980, p. 231), however, sees the role of Simon as comparable to the saints in the Catholic Church. The elders are before the throne of God (Rev 4) and Simon Kimbangu is one of those:

> Although the Kimbanguist as a Christian has no need of intermediaries, to convey his woes and supplications to Christ by prayer, he can solicit the special aid let us say of Saint Paul, Saint Peter and above all of Simon Kimbangu so that they may support his case with Christ ... Simon Kimbangu ... is an advocate on our behalf with Christ.

Here the unity that the African feels with the elders has overcome the Protestant influences in the past and led to the adoption of a more 'Catholic' position on the role of the saints.

The calendar of the Church follows the major festivals and there are special days linked to the life of Kimbangu. April 6 is the anniversary of the beginning of the ministry of the prophet and is also seen as Easter. October 12 is celebrated as the anniversary of the death of Kimbangu (Manicom, 1979). The prophet is seen as the living image of Christ, hence the combination of Easter and the ministry of Kimbangu. This is taken further in that Diangienda is both a representation of Christ and of Kimbangu, his father.

The Eucharist in the Kimbanguist Church

Diagienda (1980, p. 236) say the primary significance of the eucharist is:

> That the Lord Jesus Christ once more humbles himself by coming to dwell in the being of the communicant ... at the same time forgives the sinner his/her faults. It is one of the very rare moments at which the human being almost attains sanctification, for at the precise moment at which a person receives communion, he or she is united with Christ. By this union the contrite sinner ... benefits from the sanctity of Christ who is present.

This may seem rather receptionist but the book of services says, 'Le superviseur fait la prière afin que les gâteau et le miel soient transformés par le Seigneur en corps et sang du Christ' (Diagienda, 1974, p. 2). In the prayer before administration, 'le Seigneur Jésus Christ est invité à venir participer au saint sacrament avec l'assemblée de son Eglise, comme il fit avec ses Apôtres' (Diagienda, p. 2). Thus there is not a doctrinal emphasis on the transformation of the elements but the *lex orandi* certainly includes it and there is no receptionism in the Kimbanguists. Manicom (1979, p. 40) says that their view is that after the prayer of benediction, the honey and cake become in reality the Body and Blood of Christ. To receive communion is very much more than to remember Christ; it is really and truly to eat and drink the Body and Blood of the Lord. The emphasis is on the sacrament as a rite of sanctification Christ comes to dwell in the believer, who is united to Christ and almost attains sanctification. This is the reason for the intense spiritual preparation that Kimbanguists are expected to perform before they receive the sacrament. This includes vigils, retreats, confession of sin, so that 'at the moment of communion the Lord may be welcomed into a "house" which has been put in order as far as possible' (Diagienda, 1980, p. 236). Weekly communion would not enable this intense preparation. One has to be as holy as possible before receiving, a table for saints rather than sinners. Once again the passage of Paul in 1 Cor 11 is explicitly mentioned.

Orectic Issues

The Kimbanguists came out of the Baptists and were much influenced by the Salvation Army. The Protestant missions tended to use white bread and grenadine syrup for the elements. There was much discussion as to the correct elements to use. 'Bread is not indigenous to Central-Africa, and no vines grow nearby. Moreover all alcoholic drinks ... are condemned by the Church' (Martin, 1971, pp. 4–5). It was not until 6 April 1971 that the Church first celebrated the Communion, the 50th jubilee of the movement, and there had been five years of discussion on the correct way that it should be done.

The foods chosen were a cake made of maize, potatoes and bananas, and a drink made from honey and water. Luntadila explained it this way: 'the foods used to make the elements are found in Zaire and the neighbouring countries. In order to be obedient to the spirit of the Gospel our church has chosen African foods, just as Christ in His day used bread and wine, the daily foods of Palestine' (Martin, 1971, p. 180). This argument contrasts with Cyprian who said that it was necessary not only to be faithful to the spirit of the gospel but also to the event. We do what Jesus did. The concept of daily food has overcome the desire to use the same food.

For wine the Church uses honey and water. Honey is seen as having biblical roots in the manna tasting of honey (Ex 16:31) and Ps 81:16 is seen to provide a parallel between honey and blood: 'But you would be fed with the finest wheat; with honey from the rock I would satisfy you'. This is an example of analogical logic (Needham, 1980, pp. 41–62). From this verse a polythetic form of classification is set up:

wheat : honey
bread : wine
cakes : honey-water
body : blood

The homologous chain complex is often one of sporadic resemblances. In this case a form of logic is built up:

honey : rock
rock : water
water : wine
wine : blood

The connection between rock and water is common in the Old Testament. Water and wine are combined in the miracle of Jesus. A link between water and blood is a common one in the Independent Churches, as we have seen in the Aladura movement. Thus it is entirely logical to substitute honey-water for wine. The exegesis of the verses follows the system of analogical classification. The next justification is in the fact that John the Baptist ate honey and that it is full of nourishment. The link to the Baptist is used to justify the idea that honey is 'the food which encouraged meditation, prayer and purity' (Martin, 1975, p. 180). This is then confirmed by the fact that the monks of the Ethiopian Orthodox Church use honey. Luntadila continues to argue for the validity of honey on the grounds of Luke 24:42 that in some texts has Jesus eating honey rather than fish at this resurrection appearance. The transformation of the pollen by the bee is seen as an illustration of the necessity of inward transformation by the Holy Spirit. Finally it is argued that the bee is an ancient Egyptian symbol and as such is a profoundly African symbol.

It is significant that the arguments are African centred. The use of the Ethiopian Orthodox Church as an authority provides an African Christian rationale. That this Church does not use honey in the eucharist is irrelevant to the Kimbanguist. The important thing is that there is an African justification. This is shown by the next argument, for the bee in Egypt is not a Christian symbol but a pagan one. A Church that rejects the Traditional Religion of Zaire today ends up justifying the substitution of honey for wine by an Egyptian pagan symbol. Thus the logic used suggests the primacy of the motif 'daily bread' and that this here is interpreted as meaning African staple. Thus the analogical classification can be extended:

wheat : rock
bread : wine
cake : honey-water
foreign food : African food
European : African
colonialist : indigenous
mission : independent
missionary : Kimbangu

The second set of dyads from the political sphere strengthens the choice of local foods, as the whole raison d'être of the church is tied up with the persecution of Kimbangu by the colonialists and the missionaries.

The use of a cake made of maize, bananas and potatoes is justified on the grounds that 'maize and potatoes have saved millions in the world' (Martin, 1975, p. 181). The mixing of the ingredients shows that the Church is a mixture of all the races and the spread of the potato from America is a sign of the need to spread the gospel over the entire world. In these arguments no direct reference is made to the life of Jesus and the events of the Last Supper, but they are an allegorical interpretation of the matter used in making the cakes. Such a method of interpretation has been used in the need to put yeast in the bread or to put water in the wine.

It is, however, important that the Kimbanguists have developed their own justification for the elements used. This is African theology in the making. The primary motif of daily (African) food is one that the Church may have unconsciously accepted from the Baptist roots but the particular materials used are unique to Kimbanguists. The Church is a poor one without the links of the Mission Churches to the west and thus with less chance of donations from a parent or sister body. It is also a Church that has received persecution from the state with the acceptance of this by the missions. It is hardly surprising therefore that the solution to the problem of what to use did not follow the pattern of those organizations from which it had broken away.

The first service in 1971 was at N'Kamba and the consecration was done at the tomb of the prophet. The elements were borne in solemn procession to the people by people clad in white garments. The cakes were put on simple wooden platters and the wine was put in individual cups. As there were 350,000 pilgrims and 100,000 were eligible for communion the celebration took 1½ days. The normal order of service is:

1 Sermon
2 Prayer for transformation of the elements in an enclosed place
3 Procession of the elements to the faithful
4 Prayer from pastor in the serving team
5 Reading from 1 Cor 11:13–29
6 Two prayers by pastors
7 Prayer of benediction by the president with hands held in orans position
8 Reception, the people first and the serving team last
9 Final common prayer by the president

There are no set prayers in the service but there are directions at 2 to pray for the transformation of the elements, and at 7 to pray that Jesus would come and share the sacrament with his Church as he did at the Last Supper.

At the inauguration of this service a special ceremony was added before communion. This was the sealing of the communicant with holy water. The sign of the cross was made on the head of the faithful with holy N'Kamba water, according to Rev 7:1-4. The seal was given to all who came, irrespective of denomination, even if communion was given only to Kimbanguists in right standing. The seal is an unrepeatable sign and thus will not be used again in further services unless it becomes a rite used in the administration of first communion.

Conclusions

The Kimbanguist Church is an example of the development of a particular restricted code more appropriate for Africa. This Church has developed its own solution to the appropriate form for the eucharist; one which may find support in African theologians such as Uzukwu, but that has not found support in the practice of the Mission Church leaders. The strongest argument for the use of local materials is the daily food–daily bread motif. The Church is unusual in that considering the influence of the Salvation Army on its history, there has been a conscious move away from the rejection of the sacraments. This may also be a response to the criticisms in the WCC about the poor sacramental theology. There is also an adoption of a less Protestant view of the eucharist with the clear direction to pray for the transformation of the elements. Once again, the Protestant hesitation about the use of symbol has been replaced with a more open approach, which is found in all areas of worship. Holy water takes a paramount place in the ritual system with all the dangers mentioned above. It was even used in the inauguration of the eucharist, thus in some way validating the new ceremony? Certainly holy water has a day-to-day use that the eucharist does not have. Indeed the reception of the eucharist is surrounded with the rites of retreat and preparation, emphasizing the need for purity before participation. No connection is made between eucharist and healing, and only a weak link is made between the eucharist and the forgiveness of sins. It is not seen as making people holy, rather it is for holy people.

African Independent Churches: Adaptations to Africa

This chapter has been able to study only three of the many Independent Churches. The older ones came into being for a number of reasons, not least the lack of African leadership in the colonial context. However the movement has not ceased with the transfer of power to local people in the Mission Churches in the postcolonial period. The movement has continued to gain strength in independent Africa. One factor here is a perceived weakness in the worship of the Mission Churches. The document outlining the raison d'être of the Church of the Lord (Aladura) is primarily a discussion of the distinctives of the worship of that Church. The point of departure is not the *lex credendi* but the *lex orandi*. The Mission Churches have failed not in terms of their doctrine but in their worship, their symbol system. Many of the Independent Churches are broadly similar in theology to the parent body. Thus there is a contrast to the west where the centre of interest in the production of a new movement is the theology of the group. The focus for the Independent Churches is the praxis of the worship experience. The issue is one of African worship rather than African theology.

In chapter 3 of this book the work of Mary Douglas was introduced. Her theory as to the relationship of symbol and culture gives a theoretical background for the analysis of the symbol systems of the Independent Churches. Douglas commented that, as grid and group change, the type of symbol system changes. The dynamic dimension is in two directions. Firstly, a culture changes through time. The symbol system has to adapt to these historic changes. An example of this process is the rites produced as a result of the modern liturgical movement, not least the *Alternative Service Book* and *Common Worship* in the Church of England. The change in the structure of the society has led to the reformulation of the symbol system. The second dynamic dimension is the movement of a symbol system from one culture to another. The modern missionary movement is a prime example of this. All the churches involved exported their rites intact. The reason for the minimal adaptation to the host culture has been looked at above and need not be re-examined. The important point is to see how the symbols have coped with the culture shock. Tillich commented that symbols live and die. The transfer of a symbol across a cultural barrier and its incorporation into the host culture is a challenge to the symbol and a test of its ability to open up new levels of being.

The ties of Mission Churches with the parent body are still very strong. An example of a Mission Church adapting to a new culture will be dealt with in the next chapter. In breaking the ties, the Independent Churches have been able to develop their own symbol system, or looked at from the point of the symbol, the symbol has been able to find its form in the new social structure. Societies in Africa tend to have stronger grid and group than those of the north Atlantic. The Reformation also built into the rites an ambivalence towards symbol. The worship of the Independent Churches is more open to symbol. There is not only the development of a nexus of symbols that speak to the people, for example the growth of the use of holy water and of uniforms for all the different strata of the Church, but also a greater realism in the approach to symbols. Thus in the eucharist the Church of the Lord (Aladura) prays openly for the transformation of the elements. This is a stark contrast to the *Book of Common Prayer* service (the parent rite), which calls the prayer one of consecration but is in content a prayer for fruitful reception. Perhaps the difference between the two positions is a part of the degree of condensation of symbols that Douglas mentions. Thus with a weaker grid and group, as in north Atlantic cultures, symbols are, in the terms of Douglas, diffuse. This seems to mean that symbols are open towards greater personal interpretation, and in the case of the rites as received in the Protestant Churches, there is a built in reservation to the use of the symbolic, hence Tillich's reaction to the statement, 'a mere symbol'. The transfer of the symbol to a context with a stronger grid and group has led to the strengthening of the symbol system. The most dramatic example of this is the resurrection of the eucharist in the Kimbanguist Church. It has also led to the symbols being more condensed, which can be seen in the realism of the Aladura Churches to the bread and the wine. All these examples seem to corroborate the Douglas grid–group model.

Turner (1969) developed his concept of liminality in a temporal direction, suggesting that there are liminal periods. This would seem to be a variation on the idea that there are stable periods of history interspersed with periods of change. This is not to say that there is not constant change but that the rate of change varies and that particular periods of rapid change can be seen to be paradigmatic in some cultures. This period of change in which there is a restructuring of society and the production of new symbols is the liminal period. Langley (1982) has applied this concept to the charismatic movement in Britain and perhaps it is only one step further to relate it to the Independent Churches. These churches could be seen as anti-structures in the development of a truly African Christianity. The growth of contextually appropriate symbols could be seen as the natural result of such a state, the matrix of symbol production being found in the liminal period. There is the danger here of a degree of circularity. Liminal periods are when symbols are produced: thus, if a period is seen to produce symbols then it must be liminal. In that the long-term position of the Independent Churches in the history of Africa is not clear, then the liminal period theory is of limited value. However on a micro scale the Independent Churches have built into their systems scope for change as a result of visions and dreams. This can be seen in the importance of the retreat in the Kimbanguist Church, and the church pilgrimage to the holy mountain, the place of visions and prophecy, in the Aladura movement.

The importance of the vision is closely related to the surfacing of the charismatic leader. Kimbangu is a prime example of this. The prophet leads to the rise of a new Church. There is an African twist to this in that it is the son of the prophet who is expected to take over the leadership of the movement. At this point it is worth mentioning that there seems to be an affinity between the Old Testament and the emerging Africanized Church (Pobee, 1983). Perhaps this is because there is the common tribal motif. Thus two possible alternative theoretical interpretations to the rise of a new symbol system have been discussed, and these are complementary rather than mutually exclusive models. One is more structural; the model of the liminal period, and the other examines the actors in the social drama, the charismatic leader. Both seem to be operating in the case of the Independent Churches.

Turner emphasized the importance of the orectic material in a symbol. The same emphasis comes from the stress in liturgical theology that *lex orandi est lex credendi*. Collins (1979, p. 307) has commented 'the issues underlying licit bread choice and use are fundamentally christological and ecclesiological'. Thus a church with a living black icon, Simon Kimbangu, was able to develop its own approach to the eucharistic elements. The choice of elements was a mixture of the analogical exegesis of scripture, and the assertion of the importance of being African, for 'what is judged appropriate bread form and use is ... determined according to an operative but non conscious system of meanings which reflect cultural experience' (p. 306). In Christianity the term 'the body of Christ' is applied to both the physical body of Christ, the Church, and the elements in the eucharist. Thus there is the possibility that 'the order achieved in ... the ecclesial body will be replicated not only in choices about the eucharistic assembly but also in choices about the bread of the sacrament' (p. 315). This is based on the theory of Douglas that our bodies are the primary symbol in our apprehension of social reality. In the case of the Kimbanguists there may have seemed to be a degree of circularity in their justification of their choice of material: we are an African Church, thus we use African materials. But this is to be expected, if there is a relationship between the body as eucharistic elements and the body as social reality. The orectic issue is thus not peripheral.

The Independent Churches have the scope to adapt their approach to worship according to their own perceptions of worship, theology and culture. This is often done in a less formalized way than the councils and assemblies of the Mission Churches. Independent Churches do not produce formal statements of faith or books systematically explaining their beliefs. Nor have there been consultations discussing the need to adapt to Africa. Any adaptation has been spontaneous. Yet most Christians on the African continent belong to a Mission Church, not least the Roman Catholic Church. This Church has strong overseas links, both through the great dependence on expatriate personnel and in the structural ties to the Vatican. Thus this Church is an important point of departure for the study of the relationship of worship and culture in the Mission Churches of contemporary Africa.

CHAPTER 6

The Roman Catholic Church

Introduction

The previous chapters have examined the eucharist, using various anthropological models. The Ethiopian Orthodox liturgy was approached through processual symbolic analysis and the system of its eucharistic ritual studied. The African Independent Churches illustrate the development of symbols in a liminal period and can be looked at by the application of Mary Douglas's theory of grid and group to the worship of different churches. The contemporary discussion in the Roman Catholic Church about inculturation takes the subject of ritual and culture one stage further. The focus of discussion shifts to the process of adaptation to culture.

Changing to a new culture can be approached from different positions. Diffusion has been one of the models. A functional approach was developed by Malinowski (1945). The issue was linked to ritual in the work of Clifford Geertz (1973). These studies have had the primary focus on the process of westernization, the impact on the culture of the strong forces unleashed as a result of contact with the west. This is a major factor in Africa, not least as a legacy of the colonial period, and it is a process that continues today. There have been currents of reaction to this force, for example the rise of black nationalism and Africanization policies, which have achieved some success not least in the rise of the independent nations of Africa, even if they perpetuate some of the structures of the colonial period. The African theology movement and the attempts at the indigenization of worship are movements against neo-colonialism in the church. But they are also the institutional readjustment of a colonial structure, the Mission Church. The study of the indigenization of the eucharist thus differs from other studies of culture change in that it is not the study of the impact of the west on an African tribe or nation. Rather it is the study of the impact of Africa on a western institution. It is the study of the reverse process.

Malinowski saw the interaction of cultures as that of conflict, cooperation and compromise. This parallels a periodization of the history of the Catholic approach to liturgy and culture in Africa as one of antagonism, adaptation and incarnation. It may seem that to use aspects of the approach of Malinowski is passé. However, his analytical scheme emphasizes the importance of structures, a useful position in the case of the Catholic Church. The Independent Churches are often the spontaneous response of an individual or small group. The problem before the Catholic Church is one of adjusting as an institution. Indeed, of all the Mission Churches the Catholic Church is perhaps the most ideologically committed to a system of control with the final authority outside of Africa. This makes structural adaptation – and the Mass is a structure that is regulated by a Sacred Congregation in Rome – all the more difficult. An approach that highlights the structural is therefore all the more apposite. The interface of the two cultures, in this case between traditional religion and the Catholic Church, is leading to adaptation in the Church. The tension of cultural contact has produced different approaches. Historically the first reaction has been that of the Church rejecting African religion in the phase of evangelization. Vatican 2 responded to the call to be more sensitive to local culture by the adaptation of the liturgy. The greatest impact in this area has been the translation into the vernacular. The Council also points to the possibility of more radical adaptation of the liturgy, a so-called incarnational approach, the aim of which is to produce a rite that is African not only in language and song but also in thought form and ceremonial.

From the point of view of the actors in the Church this entails a change in approach to cultures. R. Niebuhr (1952) has outlined different attitudes of Christians to culture in *Christ and Culture*. The pre-Vatican 2 position can be seen as Christ against culture. African culture is rejected; the missionary is there to preach the gospel and to bring civilization. The present phase is one of Christ and culture in some form of tension. That there has to be adaptation is acknowledged, but there is great uncertainty as to how to do it and how far this should be, and is, allowed to go. The liturgical incarnationalists are working on a Christ in culture model, African culture and traditional religion being seen as one sphere of the operation of Christ, and the Church needing to see and incorporate into her worship this cultural realization of Christ (e.g. Hillman, 1993).

This is a debate that the Church has had before. Chupungco (1982) has said this occurred with the collapse of pagan antiquity and thus the establishment of the Church in the post-Constantinian era. Rowthbotham (1942) shows the debate about culture in the Chinese Rites controversies. Vatican 2 put radical adaptation on the agenda worldwide and has led to various proposed eucharists, e.g. for Aborigines and the Indian Mass (see Thurian & Wainwright, 1983). The process is that of the transformation of a symbol as it crosses cultural boundaries: the birth and death of new symbol systems.

This chapter will look at the inculturation of worship from the point of view of cross-cultural change. In examining the Roman Catholic Church one focus is of the changes to the 'invading body', rather than of change of the parent culture. At the same time the acceptance of the receiving culture needs examining, for change is not only a conversion seen as a discontinuity – there are also continuities and hidden agendas in the process. The resulting synthesis is a 'compromise' between two symbol systems, the result of the desire to have a religion that is authentic.

The approach of the Roman Catholic Church to evangelism in Africa in the past may seem the most culturally imperialistic of all the Mission Churches. The general practice was of hostility to African Traditional Religion and the introduction of the Roman rite. Thus Africans were taught western music and the Mass was conducted in Latin. The attitude of *tabula rasa* has been touched on before, and the desire to introduce both Christianity and civilization. This may not seem the best missionary approach, but the Roman Catholic Church has been one of the most successful of churches in gaining African converts. Despite arriving after the Anglicans, losing a war, not having vernacular liturgy, and not being favoured by the colonial government, the Catholic Church in Uganda is of about equal size to the Anglican. There are many reasons for this, not least the numbers of personnel, their length of stay, and the resources put in. But more important is the interaction of the symbol systems. Africans accepted the Latin Mass because it struck chords in the African soul. It produced a Church that reacted both against it, in response to Vatican 2, and at the same time feels the pulls of the attractions of the old Catholicism that is more than a reactionary traditionalism. The Church came and brought the gospel, and thus the liturgy to Africa, and so the mission will be examined first.

The Roman Catholic Church and African Culture

The Mission

The position of the mission may seem clear: its role was to preach the gospel and convert the African to Christianity. In fact the position was more complex. There was a consciousness by the missionaries that they were not only bringing Christianity but also civilization. The burden of the white man was to go to darkest Africa and take people out of heathen darkness. The methods used were preaching and education, particularly through the schools. It was realized that there would be few results from a mass campaign to the existing population, and thus schools were built to take the children out of their culture and train them in Christianity and western education. The assumption was that the European culture of the day was Christendom, the Christian culture. The divine sanction for this came from the representative of Christ on earth, the Pope, who guided the Church and ensured that the teaching and worship were free from error. The expansion of colonial imperialism encouraged the view even further.

The relationship of missionaries to colonial authorities was complex. In the scramble for Uganda, for example, each Church tried to get the country taken over by a colonial power that was perceived to have a policy that would be favourable to their particular mission. Thus the Anglicans supported the British and the Catholics the French. The Mass was seen as the product of centuries of Christianity and the product of a Christian culture. Thus any concept of adaptation was anathema. Liturgy was a part of the package of Christianity, almost a part of the gospel. In fact Chupungco (1982) shows this to be untrue. The Latin rite is an amalgam of various symbol systems. There are links to the religious roots of the Church in Jewish prayer, developments of this in the Greek Church, the unique synthesis of the rite with Roman religion, links to the cult of the Roman state, and the ceremonial of the medieval and Tridentine Church. It is not necessary to unravel all the strands of the rite and only two areas will be looked at to illustrate this: the links with the Roman state, and the links with Roman religion.

The conversion of Constantine led to a great change in the Church. It was no longer a proscribed group but became the cult of the empire. The Church now received the blessing of the state and was an open organization, with many flocking into the Church because of the official patronage. The Church was evolving from being a sect to being an established Church. The effects on the worship were vast. In Jerusalem the influx of pilgrims led to the development of the Holy Week rituals (see Wilkinson, 1981). In Rome Chupungco (1979, p. 132) says 'former antagonism towards the pagan cult gradually softened and finally turned to something just short of benevolence'.

It was the imperial cult that had the most impact, 'the ceremony from the court of the emperors ... passed over not only to the court of the pope ... and hence to the episcopal liturgy, but even into the ordinary solemn Mass' (Jungmann, 1959, p. 132). Once again the two major symbolic systems, religion and state, merged together. For 'if two symbolic systems are confronted, they begin to form, even by their opposition, a single whole' (Sperber, 1974, 1975, p. 88). The Church had followed the way of various pagan sects in adopting the basilica, originally an imperial palace, as the style of architecture for its buildings. The dress of Roman officials became the dress of the clergy; hence the stole was worn which derived directly from a scarf worn by Roman officials as a sign of rank. But, more importantly, the ceremonial use of incense and processions in the Church's worship were an assimilation from the imperial cult. Previously incense had not been used. Christians had had to give an offering of incense and say 'Caesar is Lord' as a part of the test in the persecutions. Now, with the Christian monarch, incense became acceptable to the Church.

There were also borrowings from the general culture of the day. *Ite missa est* 'Go, this is the dismissal' was a formula used at the end of any gathering, either imperial or for any other social event. It was put at the end of the service and gave the eucharist the Roman name, the Mass. The style of prayer adapted by the Church was also an encapsulation of the Roman genius. 'Shortness and conciseness, clarity and austerity are significant characteristics of the Roman orations. In addition is what may be styled "a juridical way of thinking"' (Jungmann, p. 127). These became the marks of approach to and style of the Latin liturgy.

The canon of the Mass was also influenced by the establishment of the Church: 'A preference for language based on pre-Christian cultic expressions and the Latin of the imperial court in the Roman canon, [resulted] in a tendency for the prayers to be cast in a supplicatory manner' (Kelfer, 1976, p. 46). The canon minimizes the direct use of scripture apart from the institution narrative. The oblation language of the canon was shaped by pagan cultic practices. Offering had to be for something. 'In the *Momento* of the living, the very words, *reddunt uota sua, pro se suisque omnibus, salute et incolomitatis*, can all be shown to derive from pre-

Christian cult' (p. 45). The petitionary nature of the prayer parallels the way emperors were addressed. '*Prex*, or prayer of petition, gained currency in the fifth and sixth century as a Roman technical term for the eucharistic prayer. At the same time, *prex* was the term used to describe petitions to the emperor' (p. 45). The pattern of prayer to the divine majesty thus followed the pattern to address the imperial majesty. This is one of the reasons for the emphasis on petition and offering. 'The Roman canon insists so strongly on this point and returns to it so often that it falls into the error of excess' (Vagaggini, 1976, p. 88). It is 'a patchwork of a number of prayers put in some sort of an order' (p. 93). The pattern of oblation from pagan Rome and petition from the imperial court had relegated the *berakah* of the preface in Hippolytus, and thus the Jewish roots of eucharistic praying, to the background of the eucharistic prayer.

Thus the Latin Mass was an indigenous rite to Europe, an integration of symbols from Judaism and the imperial cult of Rome. The missionaries were exporting the total package of Christianity and culture, and their liturgy had deeply embedded in it the link of Church and state, even when this had pagan roots. Thus the colonial situation required little or no adjustment of liturgy because the integration of colonial state and Mission Church reflected sufficiently the home integration of the two systems. But there is another side to the question: the acceptance of the religion by the Africans.

The Africans

The conversion of the African was as a result of various factors. In the preaching there was a god who was close and accessible. This contrasts with the remote high god of much Traditional Religion. The colonial powers had pacified resistance and thus the traditional authority had lost power. The chief or king was responsible to the colonial master. This was apparent to the African in the necessity to pay taxes, which introduced people to the money economy and obligations beyond the tribe. In this new world the route to success was education provided by the missionaries who were linked to the colonialists in colour, education and often nationality. If life in this new world required Christianity along with the education, then that was seen as a necessary cost (cf. Russell, 1966). Okot p'Bitek (1980b) believes that the weakening of the power of the chiefs and clan leaders may have led to the decline of particular clan rituals. But maybe the same functions have been taken over by bishops, the great feast being instead the gathering of the tribe at the annual ordination service.

There was also a perceived affinity between the worship of the Church and Traditional Religion. Idowu (1965, p. 29) comments 'the liturgical unsuitability [of the Roman Catholic Church] is compensated for by the impressive paraphernalia of a dramatic, ritualistic worship ... [Catholic ritual] strongly appeals ... as a European system of incantation and magic'. There are two points from this. Firstly, that there is a perceived link between Catholic worship and magic. The importance placed by Protestants on the comprehensibility of worship and thus on the vernacular may not have the same significance in a context that was used to the chanting of medicine men or secret rituals and languages. Comprehension does not have the same priority. Secondly, in a world where beliefs are danced rather than written, the significant advantage of Catholic worship was the movement and colour.

In some ways the African Church looked like a copy of the home Church, but that is a superficial analysis, for the Church had selected aspects of the mission package. Turner (1971, p. 46) said 'It is no longer possible to assume that Africa received Christianity passively. All influences from Europe have been filtered through a grid of more traditional ideas and assumptions'. Thus some characteristics of being conservative, legalistic and pragmatic are a genuine African expression of Christianity. The Church is conservative in worship because this is to honour the founders of the Church (the Christian ancestors); legalistic in a culture that emphasizes taboo; pragmatic, for the focus of interest in Traditional Religion is not in discussing theology but in responding to immediate personal problems.

However, even the majority of converts rejected some parts of the mission package. Thus the problem of marriage continues in the Church. Few come forward to receive the sacrament of marriage and therefore, as they are only traditionally married or polygamous, they are barred from Mass as they are seen by the Church to be 'living in sin'. Christians continue to pray to their ancestors and maintain the family shrine. In the event of sickness it is common for the faithful to go to the diviner and to wear charms. These are some of the indications that the preaching of the missionaries has resulted in the formation of a dual religious system (cf. Schreiter, 1985, pp. 144–58). On the one level there is religion, in this case Christianity, and on the other level there is Traditional Religion. The two symbol systems sit in tension and are not integrated. The pressures of such a situation led the Church at Vatican 2 to greater cultural sensitivity and thus to address the contextual issues. The implementation of this policy has followed a number of twists and turns.

The Second Vatican Council

Introduction

Pressure built up in the Church, not least with the realization of unsolved contextual problems, which were not going away, and the Africanization of the leadership in the Church. The Roman Catholic Church has been slower than most of the Mission Churches in the transfer of leadership to Africans. One of the causes of this is the desire to have one standard for the education of priests around the world. This entails the expenditure of more resources than the other churches on the production of priests. But this is only one factor in the shortage of priests in Africa, which Hickey (1980) said resulted in the Church having to rely on the catechist. The problems related to worship were expressed in the Second Vatican Council, not least in the document *Sacrosanctum Concilium*, the Constitution on the Sacred Liturgy. In this document are found attitudes both of the desire to adapt to culture and to incarnate in a culture. This section will examine these attitudes. The Church in transition is no longer the Mission Church in the mission state. By the time the Council began it was clear that the European domination of Africa was over and the post-colonial period was about to begin. There are two approaches – adaptation and incarnation – which exist together in the documents of the Council. Both can be seen to express a different attitude to culture.

The Council Documents

The attitude of the Council to culture is found in a number of documents. One of the most important with regard to the liturgy is *Sacrosanctum Concilium*, the Constitution on the Sacred Liturgy (Flannery, 1975). This was one of the first documents to come from the Council, promulgated on 4 December 1963. But there are other important documents with respect to culture, not least *Ad Gentes*, *Lumen Gentium* and *Gaudium et Spes*. *Sacrosanctum Concilium* is the primary document concerning itself with the liturgy of the Church including the relationship between worship and culture, but the attitude of the other documents to culture will affect its interpretation.

One of the major achievements of the Council through *Sacrosanctum Concilium* was the vernacularization of the liturgy. In fact the documents of the Council do not propose the total replacement of Latin but rather the possibility of the vernacular alongside the Latin:

> The use of the Latin language, with due respect to particular law, is to be preserved in the Latin rites. But since the use of the vernacular ... may frequently be of greater advantage to the people, a wider use may be made of it ... (*Sacrosantum Concilium*, §36; Flannery, p. 13)

A concession was also allowed for the clergy:

> In accordance with the age-old tradition of the Latin rite, the Latin language is to be retained by clerics in the divine office. But in individual cases the ordinary has the power to grant the use of a vernacular translation to those clerics for whom the use of Latin constitutes a grave obstacle to their praying the office properly. (§101; p. 28)

The rites are called Latin rites. The Council still considers the bond between language and the rite to be such that the distinguishing feature of the rite is the language. However, the concessions gained at the Council were such that the Bishops were able to petition for the vernacular in such strength that by 1971 the authority to decide to have Mass in the vernacular was delegated to episcopal conferences (Flannery, p. 39). Thus in Africa today one of the few branches of the Catholic Church that continues to use Latin is the Mario Lega Church, an African Independent Church that broke away before the Council (see Dirven, 1970).

The Council was also interested in revising the rites. A number of principles were outlined in order to do this:

> The liturgy is made up of unchangeable elements divinely instituted, and elements subject to change. These latter not only may be changed but ought to be changed with the passage of time, if they have suffered from the intrusion of anything out of harmony with the inner nature of the liturgy . . . rites should be drawn up so as to express more clearly the holy things which they signify. (§ 21; Flannery, p. 9)

The model of unchangeable core and changeable packaging has been a popular one since the nineteenth century. However, it is a severely limited model for, what is this unchangeable core and how is it determined? Are not all aspects of liturgy and of doctrinal formulation an expression of a particular cultural form? Although this seems to provide a suitable model for the adaptation of worship, it proves to be false. The only way it can work is by the decision of religious authority, in this case the Papacy, and the danger is that these decisions become arbitrary when there is no clear methodology of adaptation. Yet some principles are easier to apply:

> Mother Church earnestly desires that all the faithful should be led to that full, conscious, and active participation in liturgical celebrations which is demanded by the very nature of the liturgy. (§ 14; p. 7)

Vernacular liturgy has been one of the outworkings of this principle.

There was also the principle of a simplification of the ritual such that it should be more comprehensible:

> The rites should be distinguished by a noble simplicity. They should be short, clear, and free from useless repetitions. They should be within the people's powers of comprehension, and normally should not require much explanation. (§34; p. 12)

In saying this the Church has reasserted Roman values. Some cultures do not value noble simplicity. Ethiopia has a number of eucharistic prayers that are written in a poetic form that is far from simple and encourages repetition. This is one of the cultural distinctives of that rite. The issue facing the Council was how to adapt the liturgy not only to places that have Roman influence in their cultural heritage, but also to places that have no Roman influence at all. Noble simplicity is an inculturation of the Roman rite; it is not in and of itself culture free.

In the Council scope was made for adaptation:

> Provided that the substantial unity of the Roman rite is preserved, provision shall be made, when revising the liturgical books, for legitimate variations and adaptations to different groups and peoples, especially in mission countries. (§38; p. 14)

This is cautious in that adaptation is within the unity of the Roman rite. How is there to be suitable adaptation, if the essentials of the Roman rite are adhered to? For the Roman rite incorporates Roman cultural values as to the nature of worship, not least 'noble simplicity, short and clear' (Vagaggini, 1976, pp. 89–90).

Sacrosanctum Concilium also allows for a more radical development of the liturgy (§40; Flannery, p. 14): 'in some places and circumstances ... an even more radical adaptation of the liturgy is needed, and this entails greater difficulties'. Debate about what this means will fill much of the rest of this chapter.

Lumen Gentium, promoted on 21 November 1964, sees the Church as a pilgrim on earth. The relationship of the Church to culture is not seen in a negative way. The Church 'fosters and takes to herself, in so far as they are good, the abilities, the resources and customs of peoples. In so taking them to herself she purifies, strengthens, and elevates them' (§13; Flannery, p. 364). Thus this expresses the spirit of adaptation in the previous document.

Ad Gentes Divinitus tells something of how this process is seen to happen. Through the missionary activity of the Church, which includes the preaching of the gospel and the celebration of the sacraments, the Church 'purges of evil associations those elements of truth and grace which are found among peoples ... it restores them to Christ their source who overthrows the rule of the devil' (§9; Flannery, p. 823). The relationship of the Church to culture is therefore one of purification. The seeds of faith are already sown in the culture and the proclamation of the gospel is a baptism that brings judgement to some elements and purification to others. The Church is seen as the vessel that brings this purification. It is essential to be in the Church for this is necessary for salvation, and the tradition of the Church stands above particular cultures. Thus there is the dichotomy that, 'the faith should be imparted by means of a well adapted catechesis and celebrated in a liturgy that is in harmony with the character of the people ... but they must graft elements of [the Church's] tradition on to their own culture' (§19; pp. 835–6).

Gaudium et Spes has a most important section on culture and even attempts a definition. '"Culture" in the general sense refers to all those things which go to the refining and development of man's diverse mental and physical endowments' (§53; Flannery, p. 958). These are seen in terms of structures such as science and art. This relates to an elitist definition of culture, e.g. high culture vs. popular culture. There is little discussion of culture as providing identity, and man is seen as the author of culture rather than being in culture. This definition of culture continues in the Catholic Church (e.g. Gallagher, 1997).

Anthropological Reactions

Mary Douglas (1970, 1973) was a trenchant critic of the reforms of the Council. She sees them as expressing anti-ritualistic trends among the clergy, in contrast to the ritualism of the faithful. The English hierarchy are particularly attacked for their approach to Friday abstinence. The American bishops are commended for their greater socio-cultural sensitivity. The difference would seem to be that the latter have gone to the root of the ritual and recognized the sociological context of such a symbolic expression, rather than be iconoclastic. Douglas sees the presupposition behind the approach of the clergy as 'a rational, verbally explicit, personal commitment to God is self-evidently more evolved and better than its alleged contrary, formal, ritualistic conformity' (p. 4). In the desire of the Council to foster the participation of the faithful, has the Church opposed ritual commitment to personal commitment and thus opposed the rational to the symbolic? Douglas's book develops the theory of grid and group to show the relationship between culture and ritual, and thus to explain that such an opposition is only one approach and one that it is culturally determined. Recent research on the way the brain operates could also be added to Douglas's analysis, as this would imply that ritual commitment uses one side of the brain and rational commitment uses the other. Based on her grid–group theory, Douglas comments:

> many of the current attempts to reform the Christian liturgy suppose that, as the old symbols have lost their meaning, the problem is to find new symbols or to revivify the meaning of the old ones. This could be a total waste of effort if, as I argue, people at different historic periods are more or less sensitive to signs as such. (p. 9)

From an African perspective the analysis of Mary Douglas would seem to be particularly significant. If the Council has opposed the rational to the symbolic, then it would be particularly insensitive to the variety of African culture. The success of the Christian ritual in the continent has been seen as due to the link with the symbolic system of the colonialists and unconscious links to traditional values. The fact that the liturgy was in Latin was not a difficulty in that some traditional ritual may have been carried out in a sacred language, or have been done in a secret way, or have been incantations of an incomprehensible nature. The difficulty of the meaning of symbols in the African context is not a loss of meaning because of a post-Christian culture, but the foreignness of symbols and thus their lack of integration into the culture. The centralized authorization of the rite from Rome means that it embodies aspects of Roman culture and that it expresses ritual for a grid–group of a European context.

Victor Turner (1976a) was also critical of the Council. He sees a link between the rituals of Ndembu Traditional Religion and the Mass. Both have fundamental structural resemblances, for both rituals are ordered by the dramatic representation of a sacrifice. In both instances the victim is a deity, and in both the adepts and the candidates are ritually identified with the victim. Traditional Religion 'and the pre-Conciliar Mass have much in common. Both were charged with potent, multivocal symbols' (1976, p. 519). Recent liturgical changes have abandoned depth for breadth. 'Rituals ... have been jettisoned in favour of ... verbal formulations which are thought to be "relevant" to the experience of "contemporary man"' (p. 524). This may be so, but Crichton (1980, p. 29) criticizes the Roman rite until the reform as being 'over symbolised'. Also Balthasar Fischer has defended the modern reforms of the liturgy because the new symbols incorporated into the liturgy are in fact mostly modern applications of ancient symbols. Two of the eucharistic prayers have drawn on models older than the Roman Canon. Thus eucharistic prayer 2 looks back to Hippolytus and prayer 4 draws from the Coptic Basil. The peace is found in the New Testament and the modern revisions have opened it up as a dramatic symbol rather than the fossilized verbal exchange of the Tridentine rite. The offertory prayers have reduced the elements of oblation and replaced them with two *berakah* prayers that go back to the very roots of the eucharist in Jewish table prayers.

But Turner's (1972a, p. 392) criticisms are not only about the abandonment of powerful symbols in the liturgical revision, but also the anthropological theory that such a change embodies:

> The Constitution on the Sacred Liturgy was clearly influenced by structural-functionalism, which holds that ritual structure reflects social structure – hence should change *in response* to social structural changes ... It was also influenced by behaviourism with its assumption that the faithful can be 'conditioned' by 'reinforcement' to accept what Establishment theoreticians of liturgy regard as being sociologically appropriate ... Both structural-functionalism and behaviourism are obsolete formulations since they depend on the metaphor or model of society as a closed integrated system ... rather than regarding it as a *process*.

Turner wants to establish that ritual is a dynamic process within society rather than a reflection of the social structure. The latter approach he sees as a product of positivism and rationalism. Yet Turner did not apply his theories to the Council itself. Was the Council one of those examples of a rite of passage for the whole of the Catholic Church: a creative anti-structure in a liminal period? That being so, the quest for 'relevance' is not a mere application of structural-functional theory, but the promotion of a powerful symbol that has arisen in a liminal context.

Local Liturgical Experiments

The words of the Council encouraged all manner of experimentation. Alward Shorter (1970) proposed four eucharistic prayers. Uzukwu did a similar thing for Nigeria (1980a). A lively debate on these prayer and other proposed inculturations of liturgy occurred in the pages of *AFER* and in other places. They often included adaptation of prayers from a number of tribes set in the structure of the Roman eucharistic prayer. There was an increase of reference to creation in the preface and experiments with greater congregational dialogue in the prayer. Uzukwu (1979, p. 340) was critical of some of the approaches: 'Prayers of African religion cannot be transplanted wholesale into the Christian eucharistic prayer without establishing the role these prayers play in their original contexts and their appropriateness for their new role'. The greatest criticism of the prayers is that they did not emphasize the salvation history revealed in Jesus. This is a result of the method employed. In that – apart from the Narrative of Institution – they are based on traditional prayers, then there is bound to be nothing of salvation history, for this is a part of what the missionaries brought, that which is lacking in Traditional Religion. The mythical approach of African religion is encapsulated in the prayers but not the historical insistence of Christianity.

There were some group attempts at the production of an indigenous liturgy. One such example is the Tanzanian rite produced by a group of Tanzanian students at the AMACEA Pastoral Institute in Eldoret in 1977 (Shorter, 1977). The eucharistic prayer continues in the style of the other prayers examined; thus it is highly responsorial. There is extended thanksgiving for creation:

> O God our Creator . . . you created us differently from all other created things – those that are alive and those that are without life . . . You have blessed us with a beautiful land with valleys and mountains, rivers and lakes, thickets and haunts of wild animals.

The purpose of this blessing is not, however, for selfish enjoyment but, 'in order that we can use all these things to build a good society'. This is an expression of Tanzanian socialism, and further expressions of socialism are found in the prayer. Thus sin is expressed in these terms (p. 8):

> many times when we seek to do this [attain perfection] we follow the path of profiting ourselves, not bringing to each one in our community.

One of the results of the coming of Christ is (p. 9):

> He has shown us that if we volunteer and serve others in our society even to the point of being ready to give up our lives . . . we are building blessedness and your loving intentions in our midst.

The expression to volunteer in particular would have strong political connotations. Tanzania has had a strong socialist tradition through the long presidency of Nyrere. This is socialism with an African face emphasizing the importance of brotherhood. There is also a strong Christian component in it, Nyrere being a devout Catholic. The prayer is an example of the integration of the religious system and the political in contemporary Africa.

After the Council there was a proliferation of unauthorized prayers that were used illegally. The response of the Vatican was the 1973 document *Eucharistiae Participationem*. This notes the desire for greater variation in eucharistic rites than the four prayers provided entail:

> many have manifest a desire for further adaptation ... by the composition of new formulae, not excluding new eucharistic prayers ... They say that the choice ... does not yet fully meet the needs of the diversity of congregations, regions and people. Thus this sacred congregation has frequently been asked to approve new texts ... (§ 4; Flannery, p. 234)

The Vatican's response to this was:

> the time ... [is] not ripe for granting to episcopal conferences a general permission for the composition of approval of eucharistic prayers ... (§ 5; p. 234)

> there are at the present four eucharistic prayers ... It is not permissible to use any other eucharistic prayer which has not been composed by permission of the Holy See or approved by it. (§6; p. 235)

Episcopal conferences are expected to request the Vatican for permission to begin the process of composition. The attitude of the Roman tradition to the stability of a text is stressed: 'It is a part of the Roman tradition to lay great store by the immutability of texts and yet not to exclude changes where appropriate' (§10; p. 237). Thus the unity of the Church is seen as obedience to the Papacy expressed in use of the Roman rite. It is somewhat difficult for the Vatican to maintain immutability of texts, as it had recently introduced eucharistic prayers that were not traditional (prayer 3 was a new composition) and had introduced novelties in these prayers not found in the traditional Roman Canon (for example the split epiclesis, and the oblation of the body and blood of Christ in prayer 4). Reassertion of authority has not halted the desire for more prayers in Africa; Uzukwu has produced a proposed prayer after *Eucharistiae Participationem*, but there has been slowness in granting permission for experimentation.

Post-Conciliar Policies

Introduction

The Roman Catholic Church did not cease to produce policy documents with Vatican 2. Perhaps more than any other Church it has poured out documents that touch on inculturation. These include documents from the Pope (John Paul II has been called the father of inculturation), synodical documents, and instructions from pontifical councils and congregations. It is almost impossible to review all these documents here and so only a selection will be taken. However, it does show a vigorous consideration of issues of gospel and culture and the place of liturgy in that discussion.

Evangelii Nuntiandi

Evangelii Nuntiandi, promulgated in 1975, took up a positive note with respect to culture. It picked up *Gaudium et Spes* but said that 'only the kingdom ... is absolute, and it makes everything else relative' (Paul VI, 1975, p. 14). This raises the important question of the relationship between the tradition of the Church and culture. Is tradition a part of the kingdom or is it a part of the relative? If tradition is a part of the latter, then there is the possibility of radical adaptation. Indeed, the target for evangelism is not individuals but cultures. 'Every effort must be made to ensure a full evangelization of culture, or more correctly cultures' (p. 30). In so doing what matters 'is to evangelize ... (not in a purely decorative way as it were by applying a thin veneer, but in a vital way, in depth and right to their very roots)' (p. 29). If the very roots of a culture are to be evangelized, and the celebration of the eucharist is seen as a part of the evangelization process, then the Church must address aspects of culture in the liturgy. 'The building up of the kingdom cannot avoid borrowing the elements of human culture' (p. 29), so presumably this would include borrowing in the eucharistic celebration. In this document there is a move towards seeing the gospel as needing to be realized in particular cultures. In so doing a cultural form comes into being incorporating not just the cultural tradition of the Church but also elements from the evangelized culture.

The African Synod

In 1994 a Synod of all the African bishops was called by the Pope. In working towards this the bishops had a clear agenda to bring to the Synod (Uzukwu, 1982, pp. 27–8):

> Our theological thinking must remain faithful to the authentic tradition of the Church and, at the same time, be attentive to the life of our communities and respectful of our traditions and languages, that is of our philosophy of life ... The Bishops of Africa and Madagascar consider as being completely out-of-date, the so called theology of adaptation. In its stead, they adopt the theology of incarnation. The young Churches of Africa cannot refuse to face up to this basic demand.

Thus the bishops expressed their desire to go along the more radical road. The message of the Synod put inculturation in the context of evangelization of culture.

Liturgical inculturation is put alongside the other incultural demands, section 18 says:

> The field of inculturation is vast; the Synod which has so strongly insisted on its spiritual dimension by the place it accords to witnessing demands that none of its dimensions, theological, liturgical, catechetical, pastoral, juridical, political, anthropological, and communicational be lost sight of. It is the entire Christian life that needs to be inculturated. A special attention should be paid to liturgical and sacramental inculturation, because it directly concerns all the people who are already participating in it. Among the other basic conditions that will enable it to touch the lives of the people, there is the translation of the Bible into every African language. We also need to promote the personal and communal reading of the Bible within the African context and in the spirit of Tradition.

As an outside observer I can't help feeling that while on one level putting inculturation in a wider context is important, the effect is to gradually lose sight of specific attempts at liturgical inculturation.

The Pope himself has taken up inculturation (Udiodem, Makozi & Thompson, 1996) and talks about it in his addresses. However while this is linked to evanglization of cultures there is conservatism with regard to the liturgy. In *Ecclesia in Africa*, just after the Synod, he said:

> On several occasions the synod fathers stressed the particular importance for evangelisation of inculturation, the process by which 'catechesis "takes flesh" in the various cultures.'[86] Inculturation includes two dimensions: On the one hand, 'the intimate transformation of authentic cultural values through their integration in Christianity' and, on the other, 'the insertion of Christianity in the various human cultures.'[87] The synod considers inculturation an urgent priority in the life of the particular churches for a firm rooting of the Gospel in Africa. [88] It is 'a requirement for evangelisation,'[89] 'a path toward full evangelisation'[90] and 'one of the greatest challenges for the church on the continent on the eve of the third millennium."[91]

Liturgical conservatism can be seen in: 'In practice, and without any prejudice to the traditions proper to either the Latin or Eastern church, "inculturation of the liturgy, provided it does not change the essential elements, should be carried out so that the faithful can better understand and live liturgical celebrations."'

The reference to eastern churches is to the Eastern Catholic Coptic and Eastern Catholic Ethiopian Churches (both very small compared to their Oriental progenitors). These have been given as examples of inculturation in the Synod. The implication of this might be that inculturation is a process that takes centuries. This statement does not develop Vatican 2 in any way, leaving an impasse between 'essential elements' and 'understanding of the participants'. However, an instruction promulgated at the same time as the Synod was to set a further tone for the issue of liturgical inculturation.

Instruction: Inculturation and the Roman Liturgy

At the same time as the African Synod an important document was promulgated by the Congregation for Divine Worship and Discipline of the Sacraments: *Instruction: Inculturation and the Roman Liturgy* (IRLI). The purpose of the 1994 Instruction is stated in section 3:

> The norms for the adaptation of the liturgy to the temperament and conditions of different peoples, which were given in Articles 37–40 of the constitution *Sacrosanctum Concilium*, are here defined; certain principles expressed in general terms in those articles are explained more precisely, the directives are set out in a more appropriate way and the order to be followed is clearly set out, so that in future this will be considered the only correct procedure.

This is a significant further interpretation of *Sacrosanctum Concilium*, which sets up further authority structures to deal with inculturation.

The document seems to go in two directions. On the one hand the earlier material makes promising statements about inculturation. Section 5 says:

> Inculturation ... has its place in worship as in other areas of the life of the church. It constitutes one of the aspects of the inculturation of the Gospel, which calls for true integration in the life of faith of each people of the permanent values of a culture

However, in setting this in the context of the whole of culture it seems at times to be saying that there can be no inculturation until centuries of Christian culture. Does this rest on an elitist understanding of the word culture? There is also some naïveté about the situation in Europe in section 8:

> in countries with a Christian tradition and ... a culture marked by indifference or disinterest in religion ... it is not so much a matter of inculturation ... but rather a matter of insisting on liturgical formation and finding the most suitable means to reach spirits and hearts.

This does not seem to take sufficiently seriously the cultural shifts that have taken place in Europe and the postmodernism that exists. It recreates the idea that inculturation is for Asia and Africa, when it is clear to many others that it is also an issue for Europe, and so seems to be filled with an implicit paternalism.

The document recognizes that the Roman Rite is itself a product of inculturation in section 17:

> The church of the West has sometimes drawn elements of its liturgy from the patrimony of the liturgical families of the East. The church of Rome adopted in its liturgy the living language of the people, first Greek and then Latin, and, like other Latin churches, accepted into its worship important events of social life and gave them a Christian significance. During the course of the centuries,

the Roman rite has known how to integrate texts, chants, gestures and rites from various sources and to adapt itself in local cultures.

This in fact recognizes that in the whole Catholic Church there has been liturgical variety, not least between east and west, but even in the west itself. In light of that statement some of the conclusions of the document are disappointing, particularly section 36:

> The process of inculturation should maintain the substantial unity of the Roman rite ... The work of inculturation does not foresee the creation of new families of rites; inculturation responds to the needs of a particular culture and leads to adaptations which still remain part of the Roman rite.

Section 37 makes clear who has the authority to make changes:

> Adaptations of the Roman rite, even in the field of inculturation, depend completely on the authority of the church. This authority belongs to the Apostolic See, which exercises it through the Congregation for Divine Worship and the Discipline of the Sacraments; it also belongs, within the limits fixed by law, to episcopal conferences and to the diocesan bishop. 'No other person, not even if he is a priest, may on his own initiative add, remove or change anything in the liturgy.' Inculturation is not left to the personal initiative of celebrants or to the collective initiative of an assembly.

This reasserts some of the statements of *Eucharistiae Participationem*, but the whole document is about tightening up the process of proposals for inculturation. Indeed the document airs a fear of syncretism, e.g. section 47:

> The liturgy is the expression of faith and Christian life, and so it is necessary to ensure that liturgical inculturation is not marked, even in appearance, by religious syncretism.

It is a shame that the document has taken this conservative tone, for there is a discussion in anthropology that is not at all negative about syncretism (see Schineller, 1992a, 1992b).

Mitchell (1994, pp. 371–2) comments, 'it is difficult to erase the impression that IRLI seeks to *re-centralize* decisions ... continued Roman discomfort with the power granted episcopal conferences ... is evident'. Thus the instruction has bureaucratized the process of radical adaptation.

Official Documents: conclusion

There have been good moves in the official documents, not least the setting of inculturation of worship in the context of the evangelization of the world. In so doing, however, there seems to be an avoidance of the hard questions of liturgical change, which both avoid having to look at radical adaptation (or at least until a lengthy process has been completed), but also ignores the reasons for the call for adaptation in the first place. This means that for the size of the Church and its resources there is a paucity of authorized inculturated rites.

Roman Catholic Inculturation

Introduction

Various proposals have already been mentioned above. These were more documents for discussion, but there are some examples of rites that have some regular usage, Lumbala (1998) mentions three, the Malawi Mass of the Poor Clares at Lilongwe, the Ndzon-Melen Mass and the Zaire rite. This section will look at the last two.

The Ndzon-Melen Mass

In the parish of St Paul de Ndzon-Melen Yaounde, Cameroon there is a long standing experimental Mass. This began with the encouragement of local music in 1958. Uzukwu (1982) explained that ten years later Fr Ngumu was appointed to the parish and the Ndzon-Melen Mass was approved one year later. It is one of the earliest experiments in incarnating liturgy.

Abega (1978) says that the Mass has been reorganized around the root metaphor of the Beti assembly (*etógán, ekóán*). This assembly is a rite of affliction, called by any member of the tribe, when they have a particular problem. There are two parts to the gathering. Firstly, the people assemble and the problem is discussed. The convener informs those who have come as to the issues involved, and the deliberations begin. There is much interaction between all parties and, when all have had their say, they respond by acclamations to the Ndzo who sums up the discussion. The second part is a communal meal. The significance of this is twofold: gratitude to those who have come to help the afflicted, and a meal of communion.

The traditional Roman Mass did not tell the people why there was an assembly and has a particular dichotomy between the people and the priest. These elements were perceived to be particularly alien and thus the Mass was reorganized along the lines of the *etógán*. The two halves of the assembly are similar to the two halves of the Mass. Thus the ministry of the word is reorganized to the pattern of the discussion, and the ministry of the eucharist along the lines of the communal meal. There is no new text but rather the reordering of the service and the development of appropriate symbolic action to accompany it. The order is as follows:

The acclamation of the book
   1 Vesting, singing, dancing
   2 Censing of the book

3 Procession
4 Enthronement of the book
5 Introduction by the commentator
6 Old Testament Lesson, followed by a song
7 New Testament Lesson, followed by a song
8 Gospel, and song of meditation
9 Homily, in dialogue form
10 Sung Credo and offerings are collected.
11 Reflection and song of supplication
12 Collect of the day, to conclude the first part

Communion Meal
1 Offerings are taken to the altar in a dance
2 Preface
3 Sanctus, with dancing
4 Consecration, with shouts of ovation (*ayangá*) and applause (*kób*)
5 Gloria, now a song of welcome
6 Continuation of the canon
7 Lord's Prayer
8 Call on the Lamb of God and the Peace
9 Communion
10 Song, purification of the vessels, final collect of the people
11 Blessing of the people and dismissal

The acclamation of the book reflects the discussion of the assembly. The commentator explains the reason for the assembly. The book is one of the participants speaking to those who have gathered. Shorter (1973a) says that great scope is given to responses by the people, not only in song but also in the homily. Elements that do not fit into this pattern have been removed, for example the Gloria. Dance has been included throughout the service as a form of expression of joy. The communion meal is in the order of the traditional Mass except for the Gloria, which now functions as a welcome song to the Lord after the consecration of the elements. This has the desired effect of giving this part of the service a greater degree of participation, but does this fit into the assembly scheme? Presumably by this time all the participants would have been welcomed.

Furlong (1983, p. 30) has criticized the service, saying 'there seems to have been no sound liturgical reason for the transposition of the introductory prayers, except the desire to make the Mass conform to the Beti assembly'. This seems to miss the point. The sound liturgical reason is the inculturation of the liturgy, as encouraged by the Church. But another comment of his reflects the problem raised by the indigenization issue in all the Mission Churches: 'the needs of a particular community are considered primary, rather than the needs of the universal Church and the transmitted body of tradition . . . to be truly "Catholic", there must be a recognizably "common" element in all rites' (p. 31). Indigenization can cause tension in an intercultural church. However it would be naive to equate the European expression of Christianity with the true tradition or the pure Catholic element. It has already been demonstrated above that the Latin Mass both in word and ceremonial was an adaptation to the needs of the Church in the post-Constantine era. Fidelity to tradition is not to the forms of the particular era but to the principle of adaptation and the concretization of the gospel in a particular culture at a particular time.

Chima (1984, p. 283) comments that this is an attempt

> at genuine creativity ... it is not just a matter of throwing a few African cultural elements into a liturgy that still remains Roman and Western, but rather to give the whole liturgy an 'African face and flesh', even if this means reshuffling some of the structural elements of the Mass.

The Roman Missal for the Dioceses of Zaire 1988

The Church in Zaire grasped the opportunity presented by the Council and began in 1969 to research into a new rite. Furlong (1983) suggested that Mobutism may have made them particularly sensitive to the issue. By 1972 they had completed their research and the experimental rite received approval. It was not until 1988 that final approval was received (see Egbulem, 1996).

The principles of the rite are 'fidelity to the values of the gospel; fidelity to the essential nature of the Catholic liturgy; and fidelity to the religious and cultural heritage of Zaire' (Hearne, 1975, pp. 216–17). Thus the service has freely adapted parts of the Roman tradition. 'What underlies the whole rite is ... a search for "authenticity": an authenticity that is truly Christian and truly African' (p. 217). Thus the assembly began in the experiments with the atmosphere of gathering as if to visit a chief. Egbulem (1996, pp. 41–2) explains that there were problems with this, not least authoritarianism, and the metaphor was changed to a family gathering. The *annonciateur* states that the celebration is about to start and the song begins. Attention has been paid to all aspects of the service. Music has been composed locally. The vestments used are those of the Roman rite (the experiments wanted to use local models). Dance is an integral part of the service. The text includes many acclamations, concrete images, repetitions and gestures. Thurian and Wainwright (1983) have published a full version of the experimental text of the Mass in English. The authorized version was published in French (Congregatio pro Cultu Divino, 1988).

The service begins with a rite of separation, the invocation of the saints. Before coming into the presence of the Holy, the ancestors who are closer to the deity are called upon to be present. After the invocation of Mary, Patriarchs and Prophets, Apostles and Evangelists, the litany continues:

> Holy people of heaven,
> **be with us.**

> You who see God,
> **be with us.**
>
> Come, let us glorify together the Lord
> **with all who celebrate this mass at this time.**
>
> You, our ancestors with a sincere heart,
> **be with us.**
>
> You who aided by God have served him faithfully,
> **be with us.**
>
> Come, let us glorify together the Lord
> **with all who celebrate this mass at this time.**

This reflects an attempt to grapple with the traditional approach to the ancestors and the Christian doctrine of the communion of the saints (see Egbulem, pp. 58–61).

In the Gloria the faithful dance in their places and the ministers dance around the altar – a sign of joy at the coming voice of the holy. For the collect all raise their hands, as sign of the oneness of the hearts of all as they pray together. The acclamation at the Gospel seems to have been simplified from the experimental text.

The penitential rite is put after the Creed and before the intercessions, as a 'ceremony of ritual reintegration' after confrontation with the word of God (Uzukwu, 1982, p. 62). This is a strange interpretation. Reintegration might be expected at the end of a rite. Here it would seem to be viewed as a response of penitence to the reading and homily, which is assumed by Uzukwu to be confrontational. It would be a better interpretation to see the positional meaning as purification for the coming presence of the holy and the sacred meal (cf. Egbulem, p. 54).

Concrete imagery is used in the litany of confession:

> Lord our God, like the insect that sticks onto our skin and sucks our blood,
> evil has come upon us. Our living power is weakened . . .

and in the absolution:

> May your Spirit take possession of our hearts, and may our sins be drowned in
> the deep and silent waters of your mercy.

During the prayers a variety of postures and actions are taken, e.g. the people express their sorrow by taking up, an attitude of repentance: head slightly bowed, arms crossed on the breast. The people may be sprinkled with holy water. Then the sign of peace is exchanged.

The eucharistic prayer follows the norms of the Roman rite (in that it follows the same structural outline) but uses African imagery and is responsorial in style. The longer prayer of the experimental period was not fully allowed, only the preface and doxology were permitted as variations from the Roman norm. Uzukwu (p. 64) says that the praise of God in the preface uses 'images which characterise traditional African experience of God':

> You, the all seer,
> You, the Master of men
> You, Master of life,
> You, Master of all things . . .
> through you Son, Jesus Christ, our mediator.
> **Yes, he is our unique mediator!**

Christ is praised as agent in creation for the world that is seen:

> Through him, you created heaven and earth . . .
>
> Through him, you created . . . the rivers . . . the lakes, and all the fish that live there.
> Through him you created the stars, the birds of the air, the forests, the plains, the savannas, the mountains, and all the animals that live there . . .
> **Through him you have created all things!**

Then thanks is given for the saving acts of the Son, leading to the Sanctus. In the experimental rite the prayer continued with the Narrative where a drum or gong is gently beaten, emphasizing the presence of the holy in the same way as the traditional bells. Even the Narrative of Institution includes acclamations:

> This is my body which will be given up for you.
> **This is your Body; we believe.**
> This is the cup of my blood . . .
> **This is your blood; we believe.**

The service continues with the Roman rite of communion and ends with the traditional Roman rite of reintegration but expressed in joyful dancing.

Hearn (1975, p. 219) concluded that 'the "Zaire Mass" can scarcely be called sensational or radical in its innovations, it represents a big step forward in that it points the way to a possible "African Rite" in the not too distant future'. Uzukwu's (1982, p. 65) view is that it is 'a genuine effort to translate the local Church's faith-experience into ritual. They have succeeded in making a translation which keeps the Zairian world, with all its dynamism, in a healthy dialogue tension with the living Jewish-Christian tradition'. But the Pope in a visit to Zaire when the liturgy was experimental had refused to celebrate this liturgy. He commented to the Zairian bishops on their visit to Rome that 'a liturgy corresponding to the soul of African culture cannot be realised except as the result of a progressive maturation of the faith' (Kane, 1984, p. 246). Presumably if the Pope took another visit he would now celebrate the rite.

Although there were certain points that the Episcopal Conference of Congo was not able to get through Rome, they persevered and have an approved rite. The title was kept as the Roman Missal ... not the Zaire Mass as is often called. Perhaps this is intended to show something about the unity of the Roman rite.

The Roman Catholic Church's Struggle with Inculturation

Vatican 2 set on its agenda the inculturation of the liturgy. The Roman Catholic Church has continued to struggle with this. For the number of policy documents and theses on inculturation of worship that exist there are a disappointing number of concrete results. This has led to a certain amount of frustration. After the Pope refused to use the experimental rite in Zaire, Kane commented (p. 247): 'Does it really need 400 or 500 years, as the Pope seems to suggest, in order to find authentic expression?' That the Oriental Catholic Churches of Africa were discussed at the Synod would suggest that there is a part of the theology of incarnation that suggests that the answer to Kane's question is in the affirmative.

Uzukwu (in Gibellini, 1994, p. 96) gives helpful insights into the contrast between Zaire and Nigeria on inculturation. Firstly, even during the Vatican Council the Zairian bishops had registered dissatisfaction with the Mass. Colonialism had been harsh in the Congo and the missionaries had actively supported it. The whole attitude was negative to African culture but there was a rejection of this by the emerging Church leadership. In Nigeria, by contrast, the Church leaders accepted the missionary–colonialist link. Secondly, in Zaire a distancing from colonial attitudes then developed in anthropologists and later missionaries. This can be seen in the new openness to African culture in the work of people such as Temples. In Nigeria the Irish missionaries were having none of this despite encouraging noises from the Vatican. Thirdly, the liturgical movement had one of its centres in Belgium and this influenced the missionaries from there. Ireland, however, was not a part of this movement and so there was no impact in Nigeria. This helpful explanation shows that historical factors are still a part of the liturgical development of a local Church.

However, having said this, considering the amount of discussion of inculturation on one level little has happened. While there have been moves in music and in translation of Bible and liturgy, there has been little production of inculturated rite that has got through the process of approval. Bujo might not worry about this for he says (1992, p. 72): 'The theology of inculturation, so often preached triumphantly in African churches, is a pompous irrelevance, truly an ideological superstructure at the service of the bourgeoisie'. I think that Bujo has missed something, which is why the issue continues to endure. But more worrying is the conclusion of Schreiter (1999, p. 116): 'The Roman Catholic Church, at the level of official discourse, encouraged inculturation ... but the complaint kept coming from many quarters that very little inculturation was being permitted, and so the rhetoric of inculturation was beginning to sound more and more hollow'. This is a worrying position for any Church.

CHAPTER 7

Anglicanism

Introduction

Anglicanism was born in the British Isles at the Reformation. The great liturgical figure of Anglicanism is Archbishop Cranmer with his Prayer Books of 1549 and 1552. While the issues of the Reformation were ones of doctrine, and so the Prayer Books were the result of doctrinal debate, there are elements of the movement that could be seen as due to cultural development and in the sphere of inculturation. These might include a number of factors. Firstly, there was technological change, in the rise of the printing press. This enabled the printing of Bibles and Prayer Books and thus their wider availability. Secondly, there was a cultural change of values to a greater desire for uniformity in worship, enabled by this technology. This can be seen on both sides of the Reformation divide. Thirdly, there was the changing political situation, in which the nation was to become a more self-consciously independent unit, not least liturgically on the Reformation side.

The Anglican formularies assert a number of principles. Firstly, Provincial independence in liturgy is proclaimed in Article XXXIV: 'Every particular or national Church hath authority to ordain, change, and abolish, ceremonies or rites of the Church ordained only by man's authority, so that all things be done to edifying'. The corollary of this is found in the earlier part of the Article, i.e. it is not necessary for Traditions and Ceremonies to be in all places one. It was at the national level that diversity was envisaged, for in the introductory material to the Prayer Book 'Concerning the Service of the Church' it is clear that the variation within England and Wales in the uses of Salisbury, Hereford, Bangor, York and Lincoln was to end so that 'the whole Realm shall have but one use'. So, uniformity was to be at the national level as against a regional or international uniformity. Secondly, Article XX asserts that the Church has the power to decree rites and ceremonies provided that what is proposed is not contrary to God's Word. Here the more moderate hermeneutic of the Reformation is enshrined in the Article, i.e. that things are lawful as long as they are not contrary to scripture (rather than they are lawful only if commanded by scripture). Thirdly, that the public prayer of the church should be in a tongue understood by the people, as stated in Article XXIV. This led to the translation of the Prayer Book into English, French and Latin. Thus Anglicanism developed with a number of Provinces: England and Wales, Ireland, Scotland, and then in the United States. Buxton (1976) shows how it developed between 1662 and 1764 into a Church incorporating liturgical variety with both a British 1662 axis and also a Scottish–American axis.

At the eve of Anglican mission the Church had some principles that were influential on missionary policy. Bible and liturgy in the vernacular was perhaps the starting-point, with Bible and Prayer Book being translated into a whole host of languages (see Lowther Clarke & Harris, 1932). Much of this was straight translation but issues at home were increasingly to influence policy. The nineteenth century saw the rise of the parties of Evangelicalism and Anglo-Catholicism. Both were involved in mission. The evangelicals tended to be wedded to the 1662 *Book of Common Prayer*. This was to be a lasting influence in some of the places they worked (see Buchanan, 1968). Anglo-Catholics were more liturgically adventurous changing in the mission field what they were unable to change at home (see Wigan, 1962). American Anglicans were to export their liturgical tradition.

In Africa Christianity and civilization became the ethos of the missions and much that was said about missionaries of the period could be said about Anglican missions. The British were a full part in the scramble for Africa. Missionary activity and colonialism had a complex interaction, e.g. Hansen (1985) has shown the informal establishment of the Anglican Church in Uganda. While the British might like to think that their colonialism was more benign than, say, that in the Congo, there are still plenty of stories of violence, racism, and land appropriation that have continued to be influential to the present day. While missionaries may have been involved in supporting the politics of colonialism, they were also involved in other movements e.g. anti-slavery, and in the development of education and health.

Africa has had its own religious movements. We have already seen the Aladura movement in West Africa and the rise of African Independent Churches. In East Africa in the same decade another movement was beginning, the East African Revival. This was to have a profound influence on the Churches (cf. Robins, 1983), as shown in Church (1981) who gives a personal history of the movement in his diaries. This movement influenced the spirituality of the Churches but was also to have an effect on the prayers and preaching and is gradually working into the liturgical text.

Anglicans have worked on a number of levels, as first indigenization and then inculturation became an issue. Firstly, there was the training of indigenous leadership leading to autonomous Provinces. This was not unconnected to the end of colonialism, but had its roots in earlier mission policy and in the revival movements. Secondly, but more importantly, there has been an emerging policy at the structural level, in the sense of a world wide movement of liturgical reform and inculturation supported by the decision-making bodies. We will see more of this later in this chapter. Thirdly, there have been a number of examples both of earlier attempts to lead to some indigenous liturgies and of others that have made a conscious effort at inculturation that are now official rites. While Provincial autonomy has lead to the production of Provincial liturgies, some of these show a fidelity to the rite as inherited or have followed the trends of the originating Church (see Buchanan, 1975, 1985a, 1985b). This latter approach has been described by some as 'liturgical neo-colonialism'. This chapter will look at the developing policy of the Anglican Communion and particular liturgies that have tried more consciously to grapple with inculturation.

Developing Policy

Lambeth Conferences

One level of inter-Provincial unity in Anglicanism is the Lambeth Conference. This is called by the Archbishop of Canterbury every 10 years. The idea of the Conference came from the Anglican Church of Canada through a Provincial Synod motion of 1865. The first Conference was in 1867 when 76 bishops met at Lambeth Palace. The Archbishop of Canterbury took the chair but only as primus inter pares and the Conference has no binding authority on Provinces. However, it is morally influential in policy making and can have profound effects.

Buchanan (1989) has given a brief summary of the Lambeth Conferences and liturgy. He particularly points to the 1958 Conference with its pan-Anglican vision. The 1988 Conference also had some substantial things to say which he comments on in his booklet. This section will look at these two Conferences for they give two contrasting models of the Communion and illustrate two key moments of change.

Lambeth 1958 included 310 bishops from 46 countries. It notes that liturgical reform is in the air (Lambeth Conference, 1958, 1.25):

> A cherished part of our heritage ... is the Book of Common Prayer, which is a bond of unity between us ... We are in the midst of a time when these forms are being revised ... We value the enrichment that comes from a variety of usage and the constant effort to keep worship close to life, though we are concerned that no liturgical innovation should make difficult that innovation ... we have tried to suggest principles which may guide gradual and careful revision ... towards a fuller unity.

This very succinctly covers a number of issues. Firstly, there is the belief in the Prayer Book as an instrument of unity. This had to some degree been romanticized by the bishops. While it is true that the 1662 *Book of Common Prayer* was used in many Provinces, it was also true that some had already undertaken serious revision by 1958. At the 1958 Conference there were 15 independent Provinces, of these six already had authorized liturgies departing from the 1662 tradition. The label 'Book of Common Prayer' may have been used, but the contents of some represented a wider Anglican tradition, and already by then one service was an attempt at inculturation. Secondly, there is vision of a pastoral element in liturgical change: worship that is close to life. This dimension is often overlooked. Small changes may be made locally to the worship event in order to fit in with local pastoral needs. This can easily build up into some major changes. This is a more organic approach to inculturation. Thirdly, the bishops are worried about Anglican identity. This is a factor that will reappear in subsequent discussion both on a world wide basis and in individual Provinces (see Stevenson & Spinks, 1991).

The Prayer Book submission in the Report of the committees looks forward to revision, realizing that many Provinces are about to make changes. It reaffirms the principal of Article XXXIV. It discusses many issues on liturgy and in one way is a snapshot of the development of the immediate post war Anglican Communion before the impact of the liturgical movement. The one key point that is relevant here is the use of pastoral necessity, mentioned both in baptism and occasional offices. Thus 1958 does not directly address issues of worship and culture save to recognize that occasionally pastoral necessity requires some adaptation.

Lambeth 1988 is completely different in feel. There are now 518 bishops from 27 independent Provinces. Liturgy is again a key concern and liturgy and culture has become a major issue. The Conference notes that the other factors for change have been the Second Vatican Council and the Liturgical Movement. Liturgy is bound to mission and links to culture. There are key statements in a section called 'Local Expressions of the Liturgy' (Lambeth Conference, 1988, p. 67).

> The liturgy of the Church must ever draw upon the past and conserve the best of the tradition ... Yet the liturgy must at the same time give authentic expression to the common life in Christ
> ... in whatever generation and in whatever country and culture. The Church has to worship incarnationally, separated from the world by the offence of the cross, but not by any alien character of culture. We affirm expressions of true local creativity ... we commend and encourage authentic local inculturation of the liturgy, and fear that ... we have been all too hesitant ...

This is a radical statement by the bishops. Buchanan (1989, p. 11), who was a part of the discussion, talks about a suspicion of a 'liturgical colonialism'. This statement encourages authentic cultural expression and recognizes liturgical alienation. It affirms inculturation and local creativity and acknowledges timidity in the past. This is a big shift in perspective from 1958 and may be because of the influence of bishops from the newer Anglican Provinces. It is also due to a growing conception of globalization and the multicultural developments in European Provinces.

The Conference tried to set up an Advisory Body on Prayer Books in the Anglican Communion. In one way this was another expression of anxiety about Anglican identity, which we have already seen in the 1958 conference. Buchanan (1989, p. 25) commented that this was absurd, showing that the body would not work. In fact it never happened and instead the liturgists of the Communion proposed another mechanism, which we will look at later in this chapter.

The Conference agreed two resolutions relating to inculturation (Lambeth Conference, 1988, pp. 219, 232):

22 Christ and Culture
This Conference
(a) Recognizes that culture is the context in which people find their identity
(b) Affirms that God's love extends to people of every culture and that the Gospel judges every culture according to the Gospel's own criteria of truth, challenging some aspects of culture while endorsing others for the benefit of the Church and the society.
(c) Urges the Church everywhere to work at expressing the unchanging Gospel of Christ in words, actions, names, customs, liturgies, which communicate relevantly in each contemporary society.

47 Liturgical Freedom
This Conference resolves that each Province should be free, subject to essential universal Anglican norms of worship, and to a valuing of traditional liturgical materials, to seek the expression of worship which is appropriate to its Christian people in their cultural context.

These two resolutions encourage a multicultural expression of Anglicanism. They try to set checks and balances, the unchanging gospel and universal Anglican norms, both of which are problematical. The place of authority for final decisions to be made is the Province.

There is a huge change from 1958 to 1988. While at both there are concerns about Anglican identity there are key differences: one has the feel of the end of the European hegemony, the other embraces global multiculturalism; one is introducing an Anglican agenda and the liturgical movement, the other embracing second-phase liturgical reform; one is barely cognisant of culture, the other puts people in the context of culture; 1958 could see the end of colonialism in sight although many of the 'overseas' bishops were expatriate, by 1988 this was all gone, indigenous leadership prevailed and the Communion was becoming increasingly black.

While it could be questioned as to the degree to which all Provinces have embraced the resolutions of this Conference there was certainly a radical air to the reports and resolutions. Some Provinces were to take up the freedom expressed in the Conference; they were also encouraged to do this by the Inter-Anglican Liturgical Consultations.

Inter-Anglican Liturgical Consultations

The Anglican Consultative Council (ACC) is a second strand of unity in Anglicanism. It is a body of delegates from each Province, which included all parts of the Church, bishops, clergy and laity. It meets every two or three years and also produces reports for discussion. Within the ACC there are a number of networks which foster developmental thinking within the Communion. The Inter-Anglican Liturgical Consultation (IALC) is one of these; it is the liturgy network. Gibson (1999) has written a history of the consultations outlining their foci. One Consultation particularly looked at inculturation, that of York 1989.

The York Consultation followed Lambeth 1988 and developed it. There were signs that inculturation was already on the agenda in that the previous meeting at Brixen, which produced a collection of papers for study, included a wide-ranging one on 'Indigenization of the Liturgy' by Eisha Mbonigaba of Uganda (1988). York produced a statement 'Down to Earth Worship' and a series of short essays. The ACC (1990, p. 107) commented that the statement was 'of central importance', and that the essays were 'timely, helpful, and illustrative of the issues raised'. While not forming an academic treatise they do flesh out the content of the statement.

The essays cover a number of issues: the meaning of inculturation, Anglican unity and worship, and inculturation and formation. The examples given cover some issues for Africa: music, ancestors and initiation. They also include issues of inculturation in inner-city England. This puts inculturation on everybody's agenda. There is not the hidden paternalism that has been unmasked in some of the Vatican documents.

Hidden paternalism is important, as there has been a discussion about inculturation being neo-colonialism (Tovey, 1988a; Mbonigaba, 1994). That might be true if the pattern were of expatriate experts telling Africans what they need (cf. *Liturgy for Africa*). York shows a fuller hermeneutic going on. Inculturation is for all of the Anglican Communion, not just Africa and Asia. In a sense those who had worked overseas at their best were following a hermeneutic that was interested not only in understanding of that which was 'foreign', but were also working on the questions of understanding themselves and their own culture. In this sense they are following the line of Ricoeur (1971, 1981, p. 158): 'the interpretation of a text culminates in the self-interpretation of a subject who thenceforth understands himself better, understands himself differently, or simply begins to understand himself'. York shows what Schreiter (2000) calls 'reflexivity'. This was already influencing the west in the immigration from former colonies. It was to affect the Church in England with, the end of an all white episcopate, in the employment of missionaries by groups such as CMS to work with these people in England, and the understanding that English culture was not uniform and always compatible with Anglican norms of worship. *Faith in the City* (Church of England, 1985) showed cultural alienation in England, which was partially responded to in *Patterns for Worship* (Church of England, 1989, 1995).

The York statement begins with the resolutions of Lambeth 1988: 'we do not yet believe they have been sufficiently grasped in our churches. But we believe them to express the mind of God for Christian worship today' (Holeton, 1990, p. 8). The statement links inculturation to incarnation and mission, as did the Roman Catholic Church. The model is dynamic with incarnational mission both adapting to cultures and confronting cultures. The criterion used for evaluation of inculturation is 'cultural appropriateness' (somewhat reminiscent of Tillich). It is acknowledged that the style of English Anglicanism has often been treated as necessary (*sic* Lambeth, 1958), but this now 'lies heavy' both in urban England and rural Africa. The result is that the lack of inculturation has fostered 'cultural alienation of some . . . and of others to live in two different cultures' (Holeton, 1990, p. 9). This seems to suggest that dual religious allegiance is acknowledged both in Africa and in the west. The scope of inculturation is not just the text but also 'the whole ethos of corporate worship', buildings, furniture, art, music and ceremonial.

The statement continues with positive statements about local culture and the need to listen to and incorporate what is good. It encourages experimentation and local creativity. This is a radical statement for a Church that has interpreted liturgical worship in such a formal way up to this point of the Prayer Book being not a guide but a norm. In England this change in mentality can be seen in the development from the *Book of Common Prayer* (1662) with only minor variations in a set text, to the *Alternative Service Book* (1980) with many variations within a set text, to *Common Worship* (2000), which has a fixed structure with great freedom and variety in each unit of the structure.

The statement tries to tackle the norms of Anglicanism. These it sees in minimalist terms, the Lambeth Quadrilateral and vernacular liturgy. This is in part because of the effect of the liturgical movement, which has made all the Churches reconsider their worship. As Provinces have rewritten their prayer books the product has been convergence in the liturgy not only within a denomination but also across denominations based on the principles of the liturgical movement. This makes the identification of distinctives more difficult. It might be that ethos rather than text, or even canonical contexts are some of the defining features today between denominations. However, it is also acknowledged that ethos can be influenced by spiritual movements, e.g. in the west the charismatic movement and in East Africa the revival.

Liturgists are often a self-confessed conservative group. The York statement and the articles with it show a development of radicalism in Anglican liturgists. They have set up a wide agenda. How far their hope for further liturgical education to foster creativity and sharing of information through inter-Anglican channels has actually happened can be questioned. There are, however, concrete examples of the inter-Anglican discussion having influence. To this we will now turn.

The Kanamai Statement

David Gitari (1994) shows how the Inter-Anglican Consultations enabled Africans to meet together and informally discuss issues. He relates the growing influence of the African contribution to the Consultations. At Toronto in 1991 it was planned that there should be a pan-African consultation. This occurred in Kanamai, Kenya in 1993, held under the auspices of the Council of Anglican Provinces in Africa, with 43 participants.

The statement is wide-ranging and covers far more than the sacraments. Five subgroups worked on these sections:

1   Principles and Guidelines
2   Eucharist
3   Birth and Initiation rites
4   Betrothal and Marriage rites
5   Death and Burial rites

In each there are wide-ranging discussions of various alternatives. Despite the variety of African cultures, delegates were able to come up with a discussion document that would be challenging across the continent. The document raises questions about the need to use local art, dress and style. Much of the document seems to push for a more spontaneous joyful celebration. The issue of the eucharistic species was raised and a very welcome stress given to listening to local culture. Listening to local culture, though raised in the writing of eucharistic prayers, is even more important in the occasional offices where there are a variety of practices that are very different from a European context.

The exact influence of the statement is hard to assess. The extent to which it has been discussed in each Province is yet to be documented. What is clear is that some of the participants were already involved in liturgical revision and that such consultations play an important part in key people meeting and being able to discuss their contextual issues. In the long run, such networks of fellowship might well prove to be more important than the production of formal statements.

Kanamai suggested that there be such a meeting every three years. A follow-up meeting was held in Kempton Park, South Africa, in November 1996. This, however, did not produce any documentation. Further conferences have not yet been held.

Eucharistic Species

The materials to be used for the bread and the wine have already been discussed in chapter 3. It is worth mentioning at this point that this is an issue that has been returned to a number of times in the literature of the Anglican Communion. Mbonigaba (1988) argues strongly in favour of indigenization in this area. The York statement (1989) raised questions and said that more work was needed. Kanamai (1993) suggested that local food and drink could be used and that the Provinces consider the matter. Quevedo-Bosh (1994) discussed the issue in preparatory essays for IALC 5. The Dublin document on the eucharist (1995) seemed to go two ways: saying that ultimately the issue was up to each Province to decide, but because of the world wide Anglican and ecumenical implications Provinces should consult, using the strands of Anglican unity. Meyers (1998) also returns to the issue.

IALC 6 at Berkeley took up some of the discussion on this topic. Gibson (2001) reports that there had been both a paper presented beforehand and then a discussion at the meeting. Gibson's report continues to list a wide variety of practice:

> The Provincial Synod of Burundi has decided that wine will not be used at the altar ... second, it is an economic matter because they do not have enough money.
> A member from Rwanda said that there is no problem in using wine at the moment, but it is very expensive and parishes often go for months without communion because they have no wine.
> In Uganda there is no problem with wine. Some local drinks are not clean, but wine is clean ... In Uganda communion by intinction was adopted by the House of Bishops because of the problems of AIDS.
> A member from Sudan said that in the church's beginning years wine was used, but later during a period of revival wine was criticized by the Christians themselves. The Synod of the church decided to find out what should be the right element. A member said that if Christ was born in Sudan would he ask his members to use wine where there is no wine? The church uses a drink made of dried fruit and a little sugar. He said that his country is in time of war and sometimes cassava is used instead of bread because there is no bread available.
> A member from Kenya said that the church in her Province uses wine imported by the government from Cyprus. When the missionaries came to Kenya they condemned the local brew ... She said the Consultation should release the Provinces from the bondage of having to do things like using imported wine from Cyprus or using wafer bread.
> A member told the meeting that Pakistan went dry but Christians are allowed to have wine. In cities the parishes get wine from the Roman Catholic Church or make their own wine from raisins and sugar. In rural areas there is more of problem because Christians do not wish to offend their Muslim neighbours ...

There has been much local discussion and a variety of issues are raised. Many of the positions expressed are pragmatic: involving cost, offending other Christians, offending other faith adherents. The Consultation resolved to do further work.

Part of the interest here is in the difficulty in making a decision. At the local level a pragmatic decision will have to be made by the bishop to enable a eucharist to happen. Provincial synods may also have to make such decisions. However, agreement at a wider level seems to be very difficult. The narrative of institution goes back to Jesus who took bread and wine. A part of Anglican tradition has been the use of bread and wine, and in the west to reject the temperance arguments and use grape juice. Biblical and traditional arguments have given some people caution even in the light of pastoral necessity. It is clear that cultural differences influence the weight given to the argument of pastoral necessity.

Anglican Policy

Anglicans have gradually become more aware of being in a global Church. This has resulted in culture coming to the centre of the discussion of liturgy and Anglican liturgists affirming some radical positions. At the same time there are real practical problems that are scattered in the papers of the conferences and consultations, e.g. education in liturgy, the creation of liturgical teachers, the economics of the Province, language complexities (some Provinces work with more than 10 languages), and printing problems (see Gibson, 2001). When all that is put together there is no surprise that progress seems slow. However, if Lambeth 1988 was the Magna Carta for Anglican liturgical inculturation, then there has been some progress around the Communion.

Inculturated Rites

Introduction

A whole range of texts in the Anglican Communion could be pointed to as signs of inculturation: the rise of inclusive language texts where English is spoken, *Patterns for Worship*, the use of Maori influence on worship in New Zealand, the possibilities for 'Alternative Worship' under the Service of the Word in *Common Worship*. Before I go on to look at two examples of work from Africa, I want to go back and suggest that there were people pushing for a new approach well before 1988.

Early Examples

Jack Winslow engaged in an early example of inculturation in *Christa Seva Sanga*. He argued that there was a need for a distinctive Indian style of devotion. He even got a liturgy approved by the Church, the so-called Bombay Liturgy (Wigan, 1962, pp. 94–113). This was heavily influenced by the Syrian tradition in Kerala and in some ways the argument for this approach has continued today, not least that the Syrian tradition is an eastern tradition that fits in with the eastern nature of worship in India. This is still the argument of the more traditionally minded in the Syro-Malabar Church and of some in the West Syrian Churches. Colin Buchanan (1968) sees the liturgy as 'contrived' and it is true that it did not get used widely. However, further reflection could suggest that this was a bold experiment of the sort that was to later be encouraged. The Church of India, Burma and Ceylon were to write into their constitution the need for 'congenial' forms of worship. Both the Church of South India and the Church of North India now have authorized experiments in inculturated liturgy. However, such official experiments are still controversial, as are the experiments in the Roman Catholic Church (see Mathew, 1991).

Another abortive experiment was the *Liturgy for Africa*. This was produced in 1963 as a result of a request of the then primates of the Anglican Churches in Africa. The problem with this liturgy is that it was produced by a group of expatriates who wanted a pan-African service. Gitari (1994) rightly says that there is little African in it. It can be seen from the accompanying book *Relevant Liturgy* that Brown, who was then Archbishop of Uganda, was still very taken up with his Indian experience. However, one can also see in that book Brown struggling with what would be indigenous African worship. He says (1965, p. 34): 'The only indigenous form of worship I know in Africa is the fellowship meeting of the Revival groups.' This liturgy has only had a regular use in Bishop Tucker Theological College in Uganda, but is of marginal significance except that it is another indication of early struggles with indigenous worship. Brown's comment on African worship is to be seen as insightful in the light of the later history of two key services that have received Provincial approval.

A Kenyan Service of Holy Communion (1989)

The Anglican Church of Kenya (ACK) has been involved in a process of liturgical revision. This began in 1987 with an experimental eucharist, which received some published critique (Tovey, 1988b). This text was revised and authorized in 1989 as *A Kenyan Service of Holy Communion*. It was followed by *Modern Services* 1991, which includes Morning Prayer, Evening Prayer, Baptism, Admission to Holy Communion, and Confirmation and Commissioning. The story then seemed to slow down, but Gibson (2001) included a report from Joyce Karuri of the way the project was developing:

> The intention was to produce services that are authentically Kenyan, biblical, while on a par with those of other provinces, and that meet the needs of both old and young. There was a lot of discontent with the old BCP in its various translations, which were compiled when literacy was very low. On the other hand, there are many people who know no other way of worshipping and a powerful charismatic/pentecostal movement competes with liturgy in the Anglican Church of Kenya. A dormant period followed the publications of 1989 and 1991 and a number of services remained in draft form. Now those drafts are under review and more liturgies are being prepared, with a view to publishing a new prayer book by the end of 2001 or early in 2002.

Joyce Karuri said ... she is working on the publication of a new hymnbook in Kiswahili, using authentic melodies from across the county. It will be written and harmonized in both staff and sofa notation. Modernizing worship in Africa calls for improved singing as well as revised liturgy ...

> it will be important to translate the prayer book into local vernacular languages ...

The new prayer book *Our Modern Services* (2002) has been produced and is a notable development of Anglican liturgy. Buchanan (2002, p. 2) comments that the whole book is 'a combination of inherited Anglican styles, genuine unfettered liturgical imagination, and African twenty-first century realism . . . It is a triumph for Africa'.

There have been a number of commentators on the rites (Tovey, 1988b; Morgan, 1997; and Kings & Morgan, 2001). As the latter includes a detailed commentary on the text, I do not intend to repeat that task. Rather an examination of some themes and method will be undertaken. The services that are being produced are the fruit of much work by a number of people. An extract from the service will give a flavour of the work. This is from the dialogue and preface of the eucharistic prayer:

> Is the father with us?
>
> **He is.**
> Is Christ among us?
>
> **He is.**
> Is the Spirit here?
>
> **He is.**
> This is our God.
>
> **Father, Son, and Holy Spirit.**
> We are his people.
>
> **We are redeemed.**
> Lift up your hearts.
>
> **We lift them to the Lord.**
> Let us give thanks to the Lord our God.
>
> **It is right to give him thanks and praise.**
> It is right and our delight to give you thanks and praise,
> great Father, living God, supreme over all the world, Creator, Provider, Saviour and Giver.
> From a wandering nomad you created your family;
> for a burdened people you raised up a leader;
> for a confused nation you chose a king;
> for a rebellious crowd you sent your prophets.
> In these last days you have sent your Son, your perfect image,
> Bringing your kingdom, revealing your will,
> Dying, rising, reigning,
> Remaking you people for yourself.
> Through him you have poured out your Holy Spirit,
> Filling us with light and life.
> Therefore with angels . . .

Kings (Kings & Morgan, 2001, p. 21) comments on this, 'The list of seven titles of God reflects African ways of praying'. He says that the focus on Old Testament salvation history resonates with contemporary Kenya, which had nomads, the leader raised up is Moses (but resonates with Kenyatta) and the king was Saul,

David and the kings of Israel, which resonates with the presidents of Kenya. Schineller (1990, p. 71) makes resonance an important category, as 'The moment ... when ... separate poles merge in mutual illumination ...'. This interpretation of the Kenya liturgy is of course Kings' interpretation, for on one level this is a rehearsal of the Old Testament story, but at another there is a resonance between this story and modern Kenya. This has been commented on before, not least that reading the Bible gave Kenyans hope of freedom from colonialism. This method has now been incorporated into the production of the liturgical text.

In creating this liturgy a number of influences can be seen. Firstly, there is the significant influence of the 1662 *Book of Common Prayer*. ACK was formed in the tradition of the *Book of Common Prayer*, which was translated into the vernacular along with the Bible. One of the problems of this early work, as Karuri reports above, is the quality of the translation. It is important for western people here to remember a number of points. Firstly, in translating the Prayer Book the missionaries did not use archaic language, thus at the point of translation they were in contemporary vernacular. Secondly, in some languages the Bible and Prayer Book were the first written documents. This has led to some of the translations now being out of date. Thirdly, in some languages types of words did not exist. Thus in Acholi, to take a biblical example, there was no word for gentle*ness* or good*ness*; each of these qualities was translated by a phrase. This resulted in the fruit of the Spirit in Galatians being a very long and almost incomprehensible paragraph. Likewise words such as 'baptism', 'eucharist' and 'confirmation' may well not have existed and loan words were used. Fourthly, vernacular languages may well have moved on since the original translation and so the language now seems odd. Finally, some of the translations were simply not very good pieces of work. Thus the only liturgy in ACK was the *Book of Common Prayer*, but not one reading as the great prose of Cranmer.

The Prayer Book had a deep influence in Kenya. It was the book provided by the missionaries and taken up by the elder Christians. It was natural for this to be the starting-point for revision as Kenya never went through an independent Liturgical Movement or ever adopted new eucharistic prayers from elsewhere, as could be seen in other Provinces in Africa. This makes ACK unique in its starting-point.

Secondly, a biblical theology is emerging. It is clear from the observations of the commentators that there has been a careful inclusion of biblical theology in the text. The evangelical Church Missionary Society (now Church Mission Society) helped found ACK. ACK has been known as a low-church evangelical Province. Some might suggest that it had tendencies towards biblical fundamentalism. However, a careful examination of these texts will show that there is the start in the euchology of a serious engagement with contextual issues (see Gitari, 1990; Kings & Morgan, 2001). In some ways this is radical and shows the emergence of an African biblical theology.

Thirdly, traditional sources are adapted. The commentators, Kings & Morgan

(2001), helpfully show that the service's inspiration at a number of points is from traditional prayers, e.g. the litany is based on a traditional Kikuyu prayer, and the blessing comes from a Turkana prayer. There has also been the inclusion of a phrase from the national anthem. It would seem that ACK has been able to 'purify' some African traditional prayers in a way the Roman Catholic Church has as yet found impossible.

It should also be noted that there appears to be an increase in responsorial style, e.g. in the preparation, first version of the Gloria, dialogue in the eucharistic prayer, responses before reception, and blessing. Again there are echoes of traditional African styles, which are more communal and interactive than individual and cerebral.

Fourthly, local creativity has been encouraged. The service includes a number of local compositions: the first version of the Gloria was written for the consecration of Embu cathedral; John Nyesi wrote the third post-communion prayer. While these are the only two examples of completely new compositions, there are other examples of reworking of Anglican traditional texts for Kenya. In part, creativity is the way beyond inculturation.

Fifthly, there is the underlying influence of the East African Revival. This is found not only in a few references in the text, e.g. 'that we may walk in the light', in the Kenya collect for purity (section 4) but in the leadership that has produced this service. Amusan (1994, p. 51) talks of the need to 'avoid imitation of foreign practice'. Kenya has certainly not done that. In part this is due to the revival. This has given East Africans their own distance from and distinct version of traditional Anglicanism. It has also been a crucible to provide leaders, of whom some have set their mind on liturgy. One of the key people in the process has been David Gitari, who became Archbishop of ACK.

It might be appropriate at this point to quote some of the words of Gitari (1990, p. 10), which show his intention in working on this service. 'We believe this new rite is both thoroughly biblical and authentically African, both faithful to Anglican tradition and contextually creative.' Also in the preface to the service he wrote, 'This is not a modern translation or even adaptation of the old, nor an importation of liturgical revision from the West, but a new liturgy which has grown out of recent developments in African Christian Theology and liturgical research.' Rather than draw conclusions about the Kenyan service at this point, we next go on to examine the Holy Communion from the Anglican Church of Congo and then do some comparison of the two services.

Kitabu Cha Sala Kwa Watu Wote (1998)

The Anglican Church of Congo began with the mission work of an African from Uganda, Apolo Kivebulaya, who crossed the mountains and began to preach the gospel in what is now western Congo. This is an area where Swahili is the language used for the writing of liturgy and the language used after local vernaculars.

Tarrant has made a study of liturgical reform in Congo (1999) and was himself the secretary of the Liturgical Commission. The previous books in Swahili were published in 1973 (reprinted in 1979) and in 1984. This latter book had incorporated features of the Church of England Series 3, including a translation of the eucharistic prayer. The 1998 book was to move out of imitation to incarnation.

Tarrant was able to draw on the insight of Kenya, the IALCs, and the Kanmai statement, being present at these various meetings. He himself says (1999, p. 42) that he was influenced by Talley (1994), some of the more radical ideas of Dublin IALC, and some of the work of the English Liturgical Commission. However, like Kenya, this is no mere borrowing from the west but shows distinctive African creativity, which is particularly clear in the eucharistic prayers. Eucharistic prayer B emphasizes creation in the preface:

> Indeed, it is our joy to thank you,
> O heavenly Father, for you created all things:
>   the stars, sun, moon, and this world;
>   hill and valley, forest and field, river and lake,
> and all that dwell in them.
> You created human beings,
> making them more intelligent and powerful than all the animals;
> and you chose one nation to know more of you.
> We give you thanks,
> because when your people rejected your will,
> you called them to return to your ways,
> by filling the prophets with your Holy Spirit,
> to be witnesses to your righteousness and power.
> With the words that the prophet Isaiah heard in the temple,
> we join with the angels and archangels,
> and all the host of heaven,
>   praising you forever, and saying, ...

Tarrant (1999, p. 42) comments on this:

> I wrote most of this prayer during the IALC at Dublin in 1995, and it had its first airing at the Centenary celebrations of the Anglican Church in Congo in 1996 – with a thanksgiving for the work of Apolo Kivebulaya in the final section. The retention of the conventional prompts and responses meant that it could easily be used with book-poor congregations. However, the theological structure was a new departure.

The phrases in the creation section also resonate with the Zaire Mass. Like Kenya, there is an emphasis on Old Testament salvation history, in this case bringing in nothing about the New Covenant prior to the *Sanctus*. In this it is similar to Prayer F in *Common Worship*, a prayer that has roots in the liturgy of St Basil, an ancient North African prayer.

Eucharistic prayer C has an 'unconventional ten-part structure'. It has a Trinitarian structure, each with three sections. An extract will illustrate this:

After two sections on the nature of God the prayer continues:
Presbyter Loving God, friend of sinners:
you seek to gather your lost children
    beneath your wings;
time and again you call us back to you.
All **We praise your holy name!**
Presbyter You sent your Son,
to be born of the Virgin Mary,
to be human like us, but without sin,
and you filled him with your Holy Spirit.
All **Thanks be to Jesus Christ, he came to save us!** . . .

After the epiclesis the prayer continues:
Presbyter Revive your church,
that it might be salt, yeast and light in the world,
bearing witness to your holiness and love,
while we wait for Christ's return in glory.
All **May your Holy Spirit be with us every day!**

Tarrant (p. 42) comments on this:

> I drafted this after the Dublin IALC, and was no doubt influenced by some of the more radical ideas there . . . However, I wanted to write something with a trinitarian structure, and something for which musical settings might be easy for musicians to create and easy for congregations to learn. I expected lively debate and large-scale editing at the Workshop, but the younger delegates enthused, and the others did not object, so the text was accepted with only minor changes.

This prayer is a collection of phrases from the Bible set in Trinitarian structure. Pastoral issues can be seen in making it welcome, easy to learn, easy to sing, and enthusiasm of the youth (it has to be remembered that in Africa these can be half the church).

The Congo Eucharist is based on Anglican tradition but also has shown growing local creativity, two of the eucharistic prayers were original compositions, and material has been borrowed from Kenya and from the Church of the Province of Southern Africa. This means that texts that have now been given another context and are beginning to operate in a pan-African way. Perhaps the texts speak of the confidence of independent Africa and to Churches finding identity in that climate.

Two Experimental Rites

This chapter so far has examined two authorized rites. There are, however, other experimental services in existence which are of some interest. One is an experimental rite from Uganda and the other is a children's service of Holy Communion. These are the result of a certain amount of local creativity.

An Experimental Liturgy for Archbishop Janai Luwum Theological College (1985) was authorized for use in the chapel of the college in Gulu, Northern

Uganda. It follows the pattern of the English *Alternative Service Book* (1980) with some significant changes, two of which are from the Zaire Mass. Firstly; there is an assertion of the presence of ancestors and saints:

> Brothers and sister, we who are living on earth are not the only followers of Christ; many have already left this world and are now with God. Together we make up one great family. Let us join ourselves with them . . .
> Apostles and evangelists (N), witnesses of the resurrection, you are with us as we celebrate this Holy Communion.
> **You're with us. You're with us. Praise the Lord.**
>
> *A similar assertion is made with saints and then martyrs and then:*
>
> And you, our ancestors in the faith (N), who have served God with a good conscience, you are with us as we celebrate this Holy Communion.
> **You're with us. You're with us. Praise the Lord.**

This is clearly based on Zaire but is an assertion of the presence of saints and ancestors rather than an invocation.

Secondly, the confession is turned into a *kyrie* litany. This includes phrases that were designed to resonate 'We have spoilt your name . . . our hearts are hard. We have been stubborn'. This is the language that people will use about themselves in conversation, more particularly about others when pointing out their shortcomings.

Thirdly, the eucharistic prayer follows a draft version of the Zaire rite. The preface is mostly word-for-word the same. The major addition in the preface is in the Christological section where it says 'He obeyed you, suffered, died on the cross, defeated Satan, conquered death, rose from the dead . . .'. The pre-narrative epiclesis, anamnesis and prayer for fruitful reception are based on English models. The doxology returns, however, to the Zaire Mass, having nine phrases which are responded to with 'Yes'.

This was a bold experiment, considering it was done in 1985. Perhaps Uganda was not as wedded to 1662 as some commentators had thought. The college was reduced to ashes in a later conflict. So this experiment is unlikely to have survived.

The second example is *Children's Service of Holy Communion*, Diocese of Kirinyaga. This is not dated, but as it is based on the Kenyan Holy Communion it must be post-1989. It was designed for use with children, in the context of schools. One feature of the whole thing is to make it more responsorial. Thus the confession is a series of short petitions with 'Lord Jesus forgive us' as the response. The creed is turned into a set of questions as in ASB baptism. There is a rubric saying 'testimonies and songs'. Testimony has a big place in revival spirituality. There is a new litany for intercession including 'bless our school, our Head Teacher, our teacher'. The preface has been shortened in the eucharistic prayer and three verses of a hymn are sung after each dominical word. The rest of the eucharistic prayer is then curtailed.

This clearly tries to deal with a particular context, that of school worship. It does show that there are all sorts of experiments happening, contextualizations of the worship of the Church. In some ways the service has lost some of the distinctive elements of the Kenyan rite, which we will discuss next. In other ways it has tried by its style and ethos to be a pastoral adaptation of the Kenya Communion.

Issues and Themes

Both of the authorized services that have been examined have built on their Anglican roots. Kenya had a stronger 1662 tradition while Congo has adopted the Liturgical Movement through the revision of the Church of England in Series 3. While this may be seen as a form of liturgical colonialism and neo-colonialism, this is only a part of the story. All traditions are based on previous traditions going back to the early Church and ultimately the Last Supper. This is shown in the eucharistic prayer itself. Chauvet has shown that there is a linguistic interruption in that prayer. One moment you are here giving thanks to God in your own cultural style, the next you are 'on the night that he was betrayed'. Ladrière (1973) argues that there is a perlocutionary force in the language that brings you into the events then, and out of normal existence. Thus eucharistic praying is about both being in your culture and then moving out of it into an ancient event. Tradition always arrives through a missionary, as in England with St Augustine, and may continue relatively unchanged; yet it does to some degree make itself at home. The inculturation discussion has developed in Africa because there is more to do to make the worship be authentically African. This, however, does not necessarily mean the wholesale rejection of received liturgical tradition. Chupungco says (1982, p. 73), 'The composition of new liturgical texts should not be taken to mean *creation ex nihilo*'. Even some of the African Independent Churches, as has been seen, shows some continuity with the body from which they separated.

Some draft proposed prayers from the Roman Catholic Church were a collection of adapted prayers from African traditional sources. Kenya had made a similar approach in a few instances. But more important is local creativity, thus some authors have begun to talk about 'beyond inculturation'. Both Kenya and Congo have locally-produced new texts, e.g. the eucharistic prayers. But creativity is more than that. It is also a question of the way the whole thing links together. Kenya is a distinctive variation on 1662. Congo shows an African agenda. They do this in different ways and that is to be expected in local theology (cf. Schreiter, 1985). One criticism of inculturation theologians has been to suggest that the approach is archaeological. Kenya shows that this is not so. A complex new web of Anglican culture is being built drawing on a number of traditions: 1662, Turkana tradition, Kikuyu tradition, theologies of the struggle for independence, and modern Kenya life. There are good pastoral reasons why this mix fits, not least that most people in Kenya or the Congo are influenced by a number of traditions, their own tribe, neighbouring tribes, the national context and global forces. These prayers show a reorientation of the Church to fit this newer, more complex, situation. In so doing it is an attempt to overcome cultural alienation and resonate with contemporary Africa.

A number of themes arise from the liturgies that show some important directions of African euchology and theology. Firstly, there is a stress on the created world. Many Africans are subsistence farmers. The failure of the rains means starvation. Thus the phrases in the litany 'May the flocks and herds prosper and the fish abound in our lakes ... May the fields be fertile and the harvest plentiful' are vital petitions. The second Congo prayer and Kenyan prayer have put more emphasis on creation than the western sources. In this area Africa may be recovering a neglected part of the Christian tradition.

Secondly, the Kenyan services made a particular approach to the place of ancestors. This theme can be seen to start in the introduction to the Creed, 'We stand together with Christians throughout the centuries ...'. It develops in the ending of the second intercession 'we heartily thank you for our faithful ancestors and all who have passed through death to the new life of joy'. This type of refrain is repeated in the introduction to the Sanctus 'with angels, archangels, faithful ancestors and all in heaven'. It completes in the third post-communion prayer 'O God of our ancestors, God of our People, before whose face the human generations pass away'. This does not answer all questions and seems to limit the scope to faithful ancestors, but it is a much-needed move in an incorporation of ancestors into the euchology of the Church.

Thirdly, there are important developments in Christology. The faces of Jesus in the world Church and Africa have been an ongoing discussion (cf. Schreiter, 1991). Kenya introduces Jesus as 'Light of the World'; while this is a biblical phrase it connects to walking in the light from the Revival. In the eucharistic prayer he is called 'Brother'. As this is in the context of his death there is a resonance with blood brother ceremonies. In the baptism service Christ is called 'Elder Brother'. These might be only small steps but the reflexive question might be about the choice of Christological titles in the west and the implicit hermeneutic thereof.

Finally, there is an elusive question of sacramentality. This can be seen in a critical incident in the revision of the blessing. The text of the first draft was to send all problems, difficulties and the devil's works to the setting sun. This was accompanied by the action of sweeping the hands to send these issues away (text in Tovey, 1988). This was changed to sending these things to the cross of Christ. The reason for this was because theologians from the western dioceses complained that all the problems of others were being sent to them (Kings & Morgan, 2001). On one level this could be seen as literalistic. But deeper reflection indicates an implicit sacramentality here. Kenya was evangelized by low-church CMS missionaries. The response of the theologians shows a belief in the effectiveness of sacramental actions, this time of the whole congregation and the priest in the context of the blessing. This might reflect a different grid / group and so a different style of sacramentality than the culture of expatriates.

The examination of various themes reveals that the Congo Communion is in some ways more conservative than Kenya. While it has developed a greater thanksgiving for creation and responsive form appreciated by the youth, it has not begun to take on the breadth of issues that are found in the Kenyan service. This might be in part to do with a variety of factors such as stability, resources and the evolution of the Church.

Anglican Struggles with Inculturation

Anglicans came later into the field of inculturation. Vatican 2 made inculturation an official part of the Roman Catholic agenda in 1963 with *Sacroscantam Concilium*. This document was only five years after the 1958 Lambeth Conference but the difference between the two is vast. Undoubtedly Vatican 2 has had an influence on the Anglican Communion. One big difference has been the commitment to Provincial autonomy that in theory allows a lot more flexibility. Lambeth 1988, the York statement (1989) and the Kanamai statement (1993) are the three high points of inculturation within Anglicanism. With dispersed authority it is difficult to monitor progress. In some ways the moral weight of the question is the impetus within the Anglican Communion.

To avoid colonial or neo-colonial approaches any study of inculturation ought to follow a complete hermeneutical circle. The cross-cultural traveller finds that they are distancing themselves from their own culture and at a distance from the new culture. This can be an aid in understanding, as in Ricoeur's (1981) concept of distanciation. However, critical evaluation is needed in both in living in the new culture and on return to one's own. This is a hermeneutical circle that leads to fuller understanding both of cultures and of self. Reading a cultural text is a key part of this circle. It has already been pointed out that the York discussions saw that there was scope for inculturation in the west. In England the discussion has been about worship in the city. This has become incorporated into the Church of England with the Service of the Word in *Common Worship*. While it might be hard to see the multicultural face of England in that book, there are plenty of examples of changes in hymnody, with standard hymnbooks including African hymns. Maybe there is a law in worship that it is easier to change hymns and songs than liturgical texts. There has also been a discussion about the use of language and *Common Worship* has adopted inclusive language. Attempts have been made at inculturation in England, not least in the eucharistic prayers for use with children, but this has yet to be resolved. Thus the examination of some examples from Africa and contrasts with England show that inculturation is not just an issue for Africans, nor is it imposed by missionaries, it is a common shared concern in the Anglican Communion.

CHAPTER 8

Inculturation and Liturgical Theology

This study of inculturation has looked at the cultural situation in the Church, particularly based on African experience and asking questions about the worship event. There has been a quest in this book for the theological and anthropological tools to analyse the issues, and some of these tools used have opened up the issues in greater depth. In this last chapter I want to put inculturation back into a theoretical context, moving away from the case studies that have been the focus of the last few chapters. The journey has tried to be inclusive and wide ranging. There has been a deliberate plan to look at Churches from African Independent, Orthodox, Roman Catholic and Anglican traditions. There has been no attempt to do an exhaustive examination of each. Rather a case studies approach has been taken, which does not claim to be exhaustive of each Church, rather a snapshot is given of the Church at a particular point, one which is appropriate for the issue of inculturation. As has been pointed out, many others have looked at one or other of these Churches (e.g. Lumbala, 1998; Kings & Morgan, 2001) but few bring all together (e.g. Hastings, 1999). One of the theses of this book is that a broad comparative method is required to see the depth of the issue. This necessarily entails a wide spectrum of methods, using both theological and anthropological approaches.

Alexander Schmemann (1966a) raised the question of liturgical theology. This has already been touched upon with reference to Kavanagh (1984) and the phrase *lex orandi lex credendi*. Liturgical theology has been of considerable interest in the last decades of the previous millennium. Wainwright (1980) made a seminal contribution. This, with the other two authors mentioned, has sparked a number of contributions: Fagerberg (1992), Lathrop (1993), Irwin (1994), Pickstock (1998), Crainshaw (2000), to name a few. A variety of approaches have been used including 'theology from worship', postmodernism, semiotics and wisdom. Stone & Duke (1996) in their introduction to thinking theologically make the distinction between 'first-order theology' and 'second-order theology'. 'First-order theology' is also called 'embedded theology' and is the implicit theology that Christians live out, which is based on formal and informal Christian education. 'Second-order theology' is also called 'deliberative theology' and comes after reflecting on implicit convictions. It entails a certain amount of space, reflection and translation into discourse. This type of distinction is also found in liturgical theology, and will be connected in this chapter to inculturation in that inculturation is asking questions about the cultural dimension of this imbedded theology. But first I want to put this discussion in a wider theoretical context by starting with liturgical theology, then looking at models of learning from experience, and finally linking this to theological reflection.

Liturgical Theology

Liturgical Theologians

In *On Liturgical Theology* (1984) Kavanagh distinguishes between *theologia prima* and *theologia secunda*. *Theologia prima* is about the adjustment of the assembly to 'its being brought regularly to the brink of chaos in the presence of the living God' (p. 74). He sees this as closer to liturgical theology than the *theologia secunda*, which is viewed as a 'theology of the liturgy'. He looks back to Schmemann for his support. He comments that theology on the primordial level is a dialectic between the thesis, 'the assembly as it enters the liturgical act', the antithesis, the changed condition of the assembly after its 'liturgical encounter with the living God', and the synthesis 'is the assembly's adjustment in faith and works to that encounter' (p. 76). This process will add up to a 'critical and reflective theology' (p. 76). He includes some value judgements to this distinction when he says (p. 77):

> the adjustment which the assembly undertakes in response to the God-induced change it suffers in its liturgical events is a dynamic, critical, reflective, and sustained act of theology in the first instance of the *theologia prima*. And I maintain that our fall from this into the *theologia secunda* has imperceptibly rendered us aphasic and inept in regard to it. For this reason, it is far easier for us to write and react to theologies *of* the liturgy than to perceive liturgical theology . . .

While not necessarily buying into all the values asserted here, I do want to hold on to the basic distinction of two categories of theology as important to liturgical theology.

Lathrop (1993) refines these distinctions. He talks of 'primary liturgical theology' as 'the communal meaning of the liturgy exercised by the gathering itself' (p. 5). This is expressed in the way the assembly uses words and symbols to speak of God. This symbolic action is more than a code to be translated into language and it requires participation to grasp the meaning. 'Secondary liturgical theology' is the 'written and spoken discourse that attempts to find words for the experience of the liturgy . . . intending to enable a more profound participation' (p. 6). As a written discipline it can intentionally share in the reflections that arise from the interactions of the assembly (p. 5). While maintaining a similar distinction to that of Kavanagh, Lathrop is more generous to the secondary level and sees both as valid forms of liturgical theology.

Crainshaw (2000) wants to put this in the context of the wisdom tradition of Judaeo-Christian tradition. She sees wisdom liturgical theology as having a 'journey of faith-from praxis to theory to praxis, from communal tradition or actions to critical reflection on those actions to renewed communal action' (p. 251). This journey has a goal which is 'to enable the faith community to enter into the tragic structure of human existence with a new understanding of what is ultimate . . . as the community encounters God in authentic liturgy, participants are enabled to look at the world and their existence in a new way' (p. 251). Like Kavanagh she stresses encounter with God, but by setting that encounter in the wisdom tradition this is given a positive anthropological dimension. Praxis – theory – praxis is a more processual model than the other two, having a transit motif in liturgical theology's relationship to the liturgical act. In this respect it links to liberation, but it is more primarily seen as growth in wisdom.

Correlations

The discussion so far in this chapter can be used to understand the liturgical movement. Fenwick & Spinks (1995) identify a number of its characteristic values, e.g. community, participation and vernacular. These were not arrived at by abstract theological discourse. Rather they were the result of a reflection on the praxis / experience of the liturgy of the time. This led to both a variety of experiments in change and also in a critical rediscovery of liturgical studies. It bore fruit in a programme of liturgical reform in both the Roman Catholic Church and many Churches of the Reformation. This connects with inculturation in that the reflection of many on the worship of different Churches in the world is that there is something inadequate at the cultural level. The imported or imposed liturgy leads to an experience of foreignness, or cultural change leads Churches to feeling shunted into a backwater. It is this reflection on liturgical praxis / experience that has led to this particular conclusion and reflection on the assembly in its cultural context is giving rise to new inculturated liturgies. God speaks in the assembly and while saying 'you are all one in Christ Jesus' there is an affirmation of diversity in that body, diversity that can include cultural difference. In one way this is a path that has been trod before. The patristic period saw the development of families of liturgies, e.g. Syrian, Byzantine, Coptic, Armenian, Roman. Maybe the same process is beginning today.

Some of the underlying assumptions in the three liturgical theologies discussed above, particularly the idea of meaning as arising from a reflection on experience, critically links with wider movements in the academy, in the Church and in society. In the world of education, both professional and theological, there has been a growing school of experiential learning. In theology the approach of theological reflection has come more to the fore. These all are following the same movement of experience – reflection – discourse and new praxis. Although there are a wide variety of approaches within the various disciplines, at root there is a similar methodology. I want to widen the theoretical base by looking at educational models of experiential learning and then go on to theological reflection before returning to liturgical theology and inculturation.

Learning from Experience

Introduction

Theories of experiential learning look back to Dewey, Lewin and Piaget. They have developed within a number of contexts: adult learning, e.g. Boud, Keogh & Walker (1985), Brookfield (1987) and Mezirow (1991); management studies, Kolb (1984); professional education, Schön (1983); and literacy, Freire (1970), to name a few.

Freire begins with concern about humanization. His interest is for the oppressed and their liberation. This leads to his view of praxis as 'reflection and action on the world to transform it' (p. 33). Here various values are paramount, e.g. humanization, liberation and the evil of oppression. The aim is transformative. The method is that of reflection on experience to lead to critical action.

Brookfield and Mezirow look to develop critical thinking in adult learners. Both are interested in people understanding their own frameworks of understanding or meaning perspectives. Both are interested in transformation of the world-view, i.e. going beyond the present way of thinking into new paradigms. This is done by reflection on the experiences of life and critical reassessment leading to a new way of thinking and action. They are not directly connecting themselves to any social transformation, but do say that the questioning involved in doing this is essential for a democracy. In some ways their work and the whole area of experiential learning theory has close links to world-view and thus to spiritual dimensions to life.

These theories are based on the idea of 'reflection on experience for learning' and it is in the work of Kolb; Boud, Keogh & Walker; and Schön that I want to examine this theme further.

The Process of Learning

Kolb sees learning as a process and looks upon this as having four structural dimensions. He turns this into a learning cycle that has been greatly used by other authors. This circular model is shown in Figure 8.1.

Thus, beginning with a concrete experience, one begins to reflect on the event, often by re-examining it. This leads to a conceptual statement about the experience, which in turn leads to a plan to experiment. When this is worked into action, it becomes a new experience.

The liturgical movement can be used to illustrate this theory. The experience at the beginning of the last century was of a passive laity in the Latin Mass. Reflecting on this observation, particularly asking if this was a true self-actualization of the liturgy as encounter with God, the conceptualization was that this experience was not as it should be, and that there was a failure in community and participation.

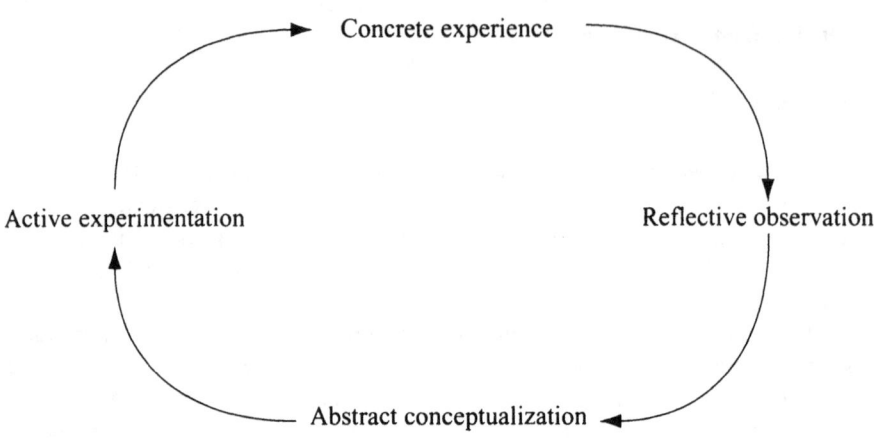

8.1 Kolb's learning cycle

Therefore, the plan was that a new set of values needed to be adopted and actions had to be taken to achieve this, e.g. through holding liturgical conferences. There were experiments in music, and participation was stressed. This has eventually led to the changes in the liturgies that we have seen in movements for liturgical reform. These are now forming the new situation of liturgical experience, building a new cycle.

A similar cycle can be seen on the cultural level in Africa. The eucharist was taken to Africa by a variety of mission organizations. European practices were transplanted with the elements to be used as in Europe. People began to question, for example, if the elements to be used have to be of Mediterranean provenance (reflective observation). A large discussion begins on the subject, becoming an object for debate in, say, Anglican dioceses and eventually on the inter-Provincial level (abstract conceptualization). Some people begin to experiment with local materials (active experimentation).

Kolb's theory has been widely used in adult education and in community development (e.g. Hope, Timmel & Hodzi, 1984). It has strong power in explaining a process of learning that is transformative and it is relatively simple to grasp. It is ambiguous about the nature of concrete experience, which is both a strength, in that it becomes adaptable, and a weakness, as it shows a lack of clarity.

Affective Dimensions

Boud, Keogh & Walker have, in one way, a more linear model than Kolb. It can be represented as in Figure 8.2:

Inculturation and Liturgical Theology 155

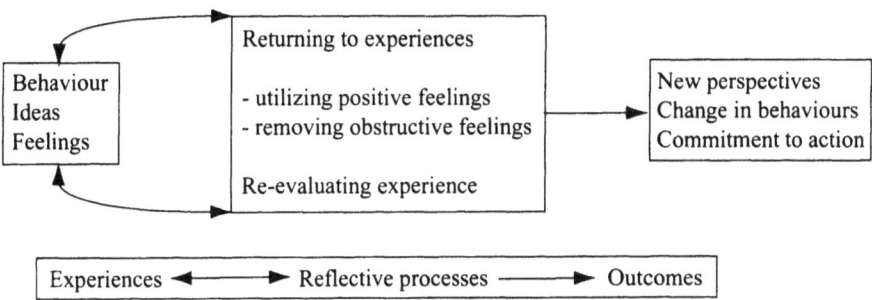

8.2 Boud, Keogh & Walker's learning cycle

In the reflective process their model particularly attends to the affective dimension. They note that previous experiences and learning have feelings attached and that these can harm or hinder learning. Re-examination of these feelings can help learning and lead to action in specific outcomes. This can be illustrated by a personal example. Asked to recite a poem before the class at age 13, I was interrupted by the teacher three times. This led me to believe I could not speak in public and I did not do so again until I was 21. This event coloured my thought about my skills and undermined my confidence. This is an example of a feeling (inadequacy) colouring a skill (public speaking). Reflecting on the experience led to new confidence.

This is a simple model. Like Kolb, these authors are interested in a process of change. They utilize a particular type of reflection for learning. It may seem that they are stressing the psychological but they would not see their process as one of counselling. Rather they acknowledge an affective dimension in learning and as such give an added dimension to Kolb. Our own experience of worship is coloured by pre-understandings. This might be warm memories from childhood (if we had them), or bad memories linked to a negative experience, e.g. being told you are sitting in someone's seat. These might need to be overcome in order to change and grow.

Thus reflection on the worship event may have important affective dimensions. Certainly encounter with God in the Scriptures was often met with awe. Cultural temperament also is a factor in an assembly. In Africa there can be the contrast between the more restrained worship taught by the missionaries and the more exuberant worship in an Independent Church or a revival fellowship. These will colour the experience and need to be included in reflection.

Reflective Practice

Schön (1983) has developed the concept of the Reflective Practitioner, which has become a paradigm for professional education in England and many other countries. This adds to the theory above by creating a distinction between two types of reflection:

1   Reflection-in-action
2   Reflection-on-action

These two different types of reflection were developed by observation of professional behaviour. The second, reflection-on-action, is probably the image that so far has been primarily drawn on in a discussion of reflection.

This distinction can be illustrated with the following scenarios. The worship event happens and then questions about something are raised in the church council, e.g. the appropriate nature of the hymns. This is reflection-on-action. Reflection-in-action is more immediate. Realizing that a prophet is moving to the front, do the leaders allow a prophecy or not? How do they handle the situation after the prophecy has been delivered but still in the worship event? Another example is of the preacher who changes the prepared text while preaching in order to respond to the needs of the congregation. These immediate reactions, reflection-in-action, might show more about the assembly's implicit liturgical theology and is closer to Kavanagh's more restricted definition. Reflection-on-action can be seen as more like Lathrop's secondary liturgical theology.

Correlations

Liturgical theology as found in Kavanagh, Lathrop and Crainshaw was pointing towards reflection on experience as one of the key elements in its methodology. The educational models that we have examined develop more the nature of the element 'reflection'. It is part of the process of learning, it includes affective dimensions, and it is complex in nature having at least two distinctive forms (one being almost instantaneous), and may be seen as coming from the collective unconscious. All of this enriches the discussion of the liturgical theologians who have previously neglected this wider perspective. However, so far this has not been a distinctively theological discussion and so looking at the theological reflection movement will develop the argument further.

Theological Reflection

Introduction

As in experiential learning theory, advocates of theological reflection come from a variety of different perspectives. Clearly one large field within this variety of diversity can be linked to liberation theology. Liberation theologians start from concrete experience, e.g. Del Valle (1980). This has influenced a whole set of theologies that take the same method. African theologians look at their context, e.g. Martey (1993), and this has similarities and differences with Black theology, e.g. Cone (1986, 1990). Much has been written from women's experience, e.g. Carr (1988). Some reflective theology has been written from gay liberation, e.g. Sweasy (1997). In a more tradition liberationist line, Holland & Henriot (1980, 1998) have emphasized the need for social analysis in reflection. These all fall more clearly in the liberationist perspective.

In pastoral studies theological reflection is also a key theory. The pastoral cycle had been developed in a number of ways. Green (1990) sees this as a community action. Kinast (1996) emphasizes the importance of reflection on pastoral experience. Chadwick & Tovey (2000) develop one method, critical incidents, for parish teams, and then (2001) apply the approach to the practice of preaching. Ballard & Pritchard (1996) see theological reflection as the method for practical theology. Finally Killen & De Beer (1994) come at the method with a prayerful spiritual approach that has links to some Jesuit traditions.

From this wide variety of uses of the model I want to look in more detail at two questions: firstly, what is the nature of the process of theological reflection? This will be illustrated by Green's work. Secondly, who reflects on what? Then we will begin to return to inculturation.

The Theological Cycle

Green, working in an inner city parish, has developed a method of theological reflection for the community based on a Kolbian cycle. He does this by adding a secondary cycle of theological reflection to the circular model of Kolb. Thus the whole process becomes one of going through a figure of eight, as is shown in Figure 8.3.

This model starts with an experience. This is explored and thus reflection on the experience can begin. It is at the point of reflection that a secondary cycle kicks in. Connections are made to Christian faith by an intuition, which leads to wider exploration of the resources of theology and history. This is based in part on Tillich's correlation theory. All of this gives new witness that can be taken into the reflection. The response moves the community on to a new situation. The bottom part of the figure of eight Green calls the secondary cycle of theological reflection. Thus he explicitly develops the Kolbian cycle to necessarily develop a theological dimension.

In the liturgical movement reflection on the experience of worship in many denominations led to the intuition that something was wrong. There was an intuition about the importance of community and participation. This led to a considerable amount of exploration in the Church. Liturgical studies was rescued from being about rubrics or a small subsection of systematic theology. Much work was done on historical texts, and comparative method linked to ecumenism led to a healthy cross-fertilization of effort. This secondary cycle was considerable. Issues

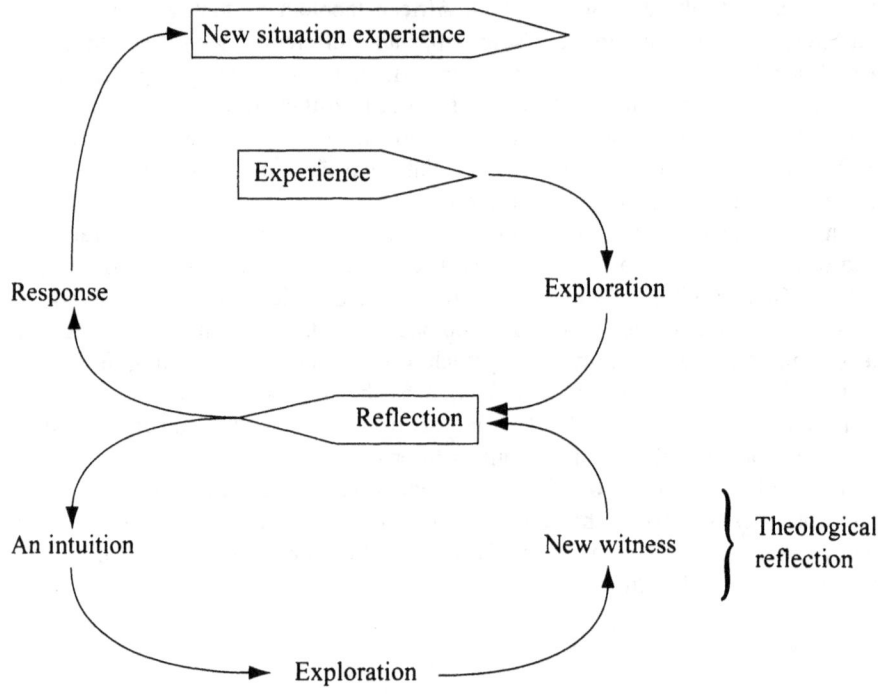

8.3 Green's model of theological reflection

to do with children and communion in the Anglican Church might further illustrate Green's method of theological reflection. Some questioned the traditional pattern of confirmation and then communion. Many church members explored this and the exploration included looking at the whole of Christian history to consider different attitudes, which led to more reflection, leading to policy documents in some Provinces and inter-Provincial documents.

So Green further clarifies the issues of reflection and brings a distinctive theological element to that by drawing on the whole resources of the Christian tradition. However, his method concentrates on reflection-on-experience. But there is a further question to ask: Who reflects on what?

Examining Experience?

Hellwig (1982) asks a crucial question: Whose experience counts in theological reflection? This is where focus is so crucial for the analysis of concrete experience. Liberationists have argued for a bias to the poor in their social analysis. Feminists would argue for women's experience to take a more central place.

Some African theologians would say that while there is an external authority in

Rome, Canterbury or Alexandria, for them there is a political control that can inhibit true creativity in Africa. Certainly it is hard to see how liturgical creativity will be able to flourish if it has to work within the 'substantial unity of the Roman Rite'. There is a cultural dimension here of how the Church orders herself within a multicultural world in the context of globalization. Postmodernism might point out that this is the increasing nature of our reality.

Kavanagh tried to answer this question in his work in relation to liturgical theology. He tried to avoid elitism seeing liturgical theology as proletarian, communitarian and quotidian (1984, p. 89). He wants to reject liturgical theology as something done by academics and keep the primary theology with the assembly. Whatever the validity of this, and there are some problems, for he is still raising the political question in reflection: Whose experience counts?

Starting with experience we have seen that there is a diversity of foci in different theologies. Many people major on one focus and thus produce a different theology, but the method remains the same, i.e. that of reflection on experience. Some of these foci in examining experience and their concomitant theologies are:

1 Social injustice, liberation theology
2 Gender issues, feminist theology
3 Racial oppression, black theology
4 Sexuality, queer theology
5 Religious experience, spiritual theology
6 Pastoral encounter, practical theology
7 Cultural context, incultural theology
8 Liturgical encounter, liturgical theology

The last category is part of the thesis of this chapter, i.e. that liturgical theology is not an esoteric subject but actually shares a similar methodology with many other forms of theology. It may look different in focus and interest, but the method is at root the same.

The Priority of Liturgical Theology

Many of those who have advocated liturgical theology have also advocated its priority in theological discourse. This can be seen in part as a reaction to a marginalizing attitude of the wider theological academe to liturgists and liturgical studies. Schmemann (1966a) argued that liturgical theology needed to take its place in relation to dogmatics in a similar way to that of biblical studies. He was particularly concerned to move away from a scholastic approach to liturgy, i.e. beginning with dogmatic sacramental theology in an approach to the eucharist: 'It is only right that liturgical theology should occupy a special, independent place in the general system of theological disciplines ... Without liturgical theology our understanding of the Church's faith and doctrine is bound to be incomplete' (p. 16).

Kavanagh (1984) continues the same line of argument, perhaps making liturgical theology even more important: 'Christian worship seems to be ... somehow primary and fundamental, rather than secondary and peripheral, to the whole theological enterprise' (pp. 21–2). Thus he looks forward to liturgical theology unifying theology. Irwin (1994) continues the same line, noting that some theologians argue for a doxological approach 'that relies on the liturgy ... for stimulus and corrective to an overly intellectual doctrinal theology' (p. x). While this argument has been going on for forty years there is little sign that these hopes are being fulfilled.

Rowan Williams (2000) sees theology as coming out of the life of the Christian community. This is at a number of levels, not least in the acting out of faith as much as in the conscious reflecting. He places Christian worship as one source of theology alongside other aspects of the life of the community. Clearly the worship experience is a high priority. One Sunday I hear 'the body of Christ'. This both nourishes faith and raises theological questions. But similar questions can be raised in personal prayer and Bible reading, and may be raised from an encounter with Christ in conversion or later in the faith journey. Thus liturgical theology has a key place in theological study but alongside other key disciplines. Like other aspects of theology the method is reflection on experience; however, the argument here is that experience is always in a cultural context.

Inculturation

The introductory chapter of the book told briefly my story of experience in Africa and reflection on that experience. My experience was widened with further visits to Africa and African Churches in England, and refined by further experiences in India and in Black Churches in the USA. The whole book is set in the context of action and reflection, with intuition coming from the field of theology and anthropology. This final chapter has tried to put inculturation in the context of liturgical theology and learning from experience.

Inculturation is an examination of a particular aspect of the wider issue of culture and worship, looking at the need for the cultural appropriateness of worship. The history of the Church in encountering new cultures and of culture change makes it a permanent item on the agenda of the Church. In order to look at inculturation this book has advocated a number of theses. Firstly, the importance of an interdisciplinary approach using the resources of both theology and social sciences. Secondly, the value of use of case studies in a wider comparative methodological framework. Thirdly, the conviction that the study of the inculturation is best helped by using the method of learning by reflection on experience, a method shared by other branches of theology and other disciplines. Thus the thesis advanced here has been that liturgical theology can be seen as a variant on theology that makes the worship experience a starting-point. It starts from the assembly at worship and develops in a secondary phase to producing written discussion of the issues. One dimension to the assembly is a cultural one. Inculturation takes seriously the cultural dimension of experience; it can do this both on a wider Church level and at the point of worship. This book has tried to look at particularly the worship dimension. Reflecting on experience and listening to the experience of others will continue to be a part of the ongoing life of the Church. This book, I hope, is a positive contribution to that discussion.

Works Cited

Abana, G.N. (1956), *The Key to Salvation*, Aba, Nigeria: Ideal Press.
—— (1972), *Advent of the Ark of the Covenant of our Lord and Saviour Jesus Christ*, place of publication and publisher unknown.
—— (n.d.), *Holy Communion Ordinance (Revised)*, Aba, Nigeria: Sacred Cherubim and Seraphim Church of Nigeria.
—— (n.d.), *Lenten Season and The Feast of Passover (Revised and Enlarged)*, Aba, Nigeria: Cherubim and Seraphim Churches of Nigeria.
Abega, P. (1978), 'Liturgical Adaptation' in Fasholé-Luke, E. W. et al. (eds.), *Christianity in Independent Africa*, London: Rex Collins.
Adam, D. (1996), *The Rhythm of Life: Celtic Daily Prayer*, London: Triangle.
Adejobi, E.O.A. (1950), *The Bible Speaks on the Church of the Lord*, Kamasi, Ghana: Central Printing Press.
—— (n. d.) *The Observances and Practices of the Church of the Lord (Aladura) in the Light of the Old Testament and the New Testament*, place of publication and publisher unknown.
Alvarez, F. (1881), *Narrative of the Portuguese Embassy to Abyssinia during the Years 1520-1527*, London: CUP for Hakluyt Society.
Amusan, S. (1994) 'Beginning the Response: A Nigerian Contribution', in Gitari, D. (ed.), *Anglican Liturgical Inculturation in Africa: The Kanamai Statement 'African Culture and Anglican Liturgy'*, JLS 28, Grove Books: Nottingham, pp. 49-52.
—— (1998), 'Sacrifice in African Traditional Religion as a Means of Understanding Eucharistic Theology', in Holeton, D.R. (1998), *Our Thanks and Praise*, Toronto: Anglican Book Centre, pp. 141-6.
Anglican Consultative Council (1990), *Mission in a Broken World*, London: ACC.
Arbuckle, G.A. (1990), *Earthing the Gospel*, New York: Orbis Books.
Arnold, J. (1971), 'Dancing Before the Lord', *Frontier*, **14**, 142-3.
Austin, J.L. (1962, 1975), *How to Do Things with Words*, Oxford: OUP.

Ballard, P. and Prichard, J. (1996), *Practical Theology in Action*, London: SPCK.
Barrett, D.B. (1968), *Schism and Renewal in Africa*, London: OUP.
Barrett, T. (1977), *Incarnating the Church in Turkana*, Spearhead 52, Eldoret: Gaba Publications.
Bell, C. (2002), 'Ritual Tensions: Tribal and Catholic', *Studia Liturgica*, **32**, 1, 15-28.
Berthier, J. (1982), *Music From Taizé*, London: Collins.
Bevan, E. (1938), *Symbolism and Belief*, London: Allen and Unwin.
Bevans, S.B. (1998), *Models of Contextual Theology*, New York: Orbis Press.
Bishop, E. (1909), 'Fear and Awe Attaching to the Eucharistic Service', in Connolly, R.H., *The Liturgical Homilies of Narsi Translated into English*, London: CUP, pp. 92-7.
Boud, D., Keogh, R. and Walker, D. (1985), *Reflection: Turning Experience into Learning*, London: Kogan Page.
Bourdillon, M.F.C. and Fortes, M. (eds.) (1980), *Sacrifice*, London: Academic Press.
Bouyer, L. (1968), *Eucharist: Theology and Spirituality of the Eucharistic Prayer*, Notre Dame and London: University of Notre Dame Press.
Brabant, F.H. (1932), 'Worship in General', in Lowther Clarke, W.K. (ed.), *Liturgy and Worship*, London: SPCK, pp. 12-37.
Bracken, J.A. (1995), 'Towards a New Philosophical Theology Based on Intersubjectivity', *Theological Studies*, **59**, 703-19.
Bridge, A. (1958), 'The Life and Death of Symbols', *Theology* **LXI**, January, 8-14.

Brookfield, S.D. (1987), *Developing Critical Thinkers*, San Francisco: Jossey-Bass.
Brown, L.W. (1965), *Relevant Liturgy*, London: SPCK.
Bruce, J. (1804), *Travels to Discover the Source of the Nile*, Edinburgh: publisher unknown.
Buchanan, C.O. (1968), *Modern Anglican Liturgies 1958–1968*, London, New York and Toronto: OUP.
—— (1975), *Further Anglican Liturgies 1968–1975*, Bramcote: Grove Books.
—— (1985a), *Latest Anglican Liturgies 1976–1984*, London: SPCK/Grove Books.
—— (1985b), *Anglican Eucharistic Liturgy 1975–1985*, Grove Liturgical Study 41, Bramcote: Grove Books.
—— (1989), *Lambeth and Liturgy*, W106, Bramcote: Grove Books.
—— (2002), 'Editorial', *News of Liturgy* 335, November, 1–2.
Budge, Sir E.A.W. (1922a), *Legends of our Lady Mary the Perpetual Virgin and her Mother Hanna*, London: Medici Society.
—— (1922b), *The Queen of Sheba and her Only Son Menyelek: A Translation of Kebra Negast*, London: Medici Society.
—— (1923), *One Hundred and Ten Miracles of our Lady Mary*, London: Medici Society.
—— (1928a) *The Book of the Saints of the Ethiopian Church: A Translation of the Ethiopic Synaxarium*, Cambridge: CUP.
—— (1930), *Amulets and Superstitions*, London: OUP.
Bujo, B. (1992), *African Theology in Its Social Context*, New York: Orbis Books.
Burmester, O.H.E. (1959/60), 'A Comparative Study of the Form of the Words of the Institution and the Epiclesis in the Anaphorae of the Ethiopian Church', *Eastern Churches Quarterly*, **13**, 13–42.
Buxton, D. (1970), *The Abyssinians*, London: Thames and Hudson.

Carr, A.E. (1988), *Transforming Grace*, New York: Continuum.
Chadwick, C. and Tovey, P. (2000), *Growing in Ministry: Using Critical Incident Analysis*, P 84, Cambridge: Grove Books.
—— (2001), *Developing Reflective Practice for Preachers*, W164, Cambridge: Grove Books.
Chapple, E.D. and Coon, C.S. (1942), *Principles of Anthropology*, New York: Henry Holt.
Chauvet, L.-M. (1987, ET 1995), *Symbol and Sacrament*, Collegeville: Liturgical Press.
—— (1992), 'What makes Liturgy Biblical? Texts', *Studia Liturgica*, **22**, 2, 121–33.
—— (1995a), 'Editorial: Liturgy and the Body', *Concilium*, vii–x.
—— (1995b), 'The Liturgy in its Symbolic Space', *Concilium*, 29–39.
—— (1997, ET 2001), *The Sacraments*, Collegeville: Liturgical Press.
Chima, A.B. (1984), 'Africanising the Liturgy – Where are we 20 Years after Vatican II?', *AFER*, **25**, 280–92.
Chrysostom, St. J. (1964), *6 Books on the Priesthood*, trans. G. Neville, London: SPCK.
Chupungco, A.J. (1979), 'Greco-Roman Culture and Liturgical Adaptation', *Notitae*, **15**, 202–18.
—— (1982), *Cultural Adaptation of the Liturgy*, New York: Paulist Press.
—— (1989), *Liturgies of the Future: The Process and Methods of Inculturation*, Mahwah: Paulist Press.
Church of England (1985), *Faith in the City*, London: CHP.
—— (1989, 1995), *Patterns for Worship*, London: CHP.
Church of the Lord (1958), *Hymn Book*, place of publication unknown: Thaminehin-Ola Press.
—— (n.d.), *Book of Rituals*, place of publication and publisher unknown.
Church, J.E. (1981), *Quest for the Highest: An Autobiographical Account of the East African Revival*, Exeter: Paternoster Press.
Clarke, S. (1985), *Let the Indian Church be Indian*, Madras: Christian Literature Society.
Collins, M. (1979), 'Critical Questions for Liturgical Theology', *Worship*, **53**, 302–17.
Cone, J.H. (1972, 1991), *The Spirituals and the Blues*, New York: Orbis Books.
—— (1986, 1990), *A Black Theology of Liberation*, New York: Orbis Books.

Congregatio pro Cultu Divino (1988), 'Le Missel Romain pour les Dioceses du Zaire', *Notitae*, **28**, 455–72.
Congregation for Divine Worship and the Discipline of the Sacraments (1994), *Instruction: Inculturation and the Roman Liturgy*, http://www.ewtn.com.library/curia/cdwinclt.htm (accessed 11/10/01).
Crainshaw, J.Y. (2000), *Wise and Discerning Hearts: An Introduction to Wisdom Liturgical Theology*, Collegeville: Liturgical Press.
Crane, W.H. (1970), 'The Kimbanguist Church and the Search for Authentic Christianity', *The Christian Century*, **87**, 691–5.
Crichton, J.D. (1980), 'Liturgical Adaptation', in Stevenson, K. (ed.), *Symbolism and the Liturgy 1*, Grove Liturgical Study 23, Nottingham: Grove Books.

Dallen, J. (1986), *The Reconciling Community: The Rite of Penance*, New York: Pueblo.
Daoud, M. (1959), *The Liturgy of the Ethiopian Church*, place of publication unknown: Egyptian Book Press.
Davies, J.G. (1970/71), 'The Introduction of the Numinous into the Liturgy: an Historical Note', *Studia Liturgica*, **8**, 216–23.
Del Valle, L.G. (1980), 'A Theological Outlook Starting from Concrete Events', in Gibelini, R. (ed.), *Frontiers of Theology in Latin America*, London: SCM Press.
Diagienda, K.J. (1974), *Liturgical Ceremonies of the Church of Jesus Christ Through the Prophet Simon Kimbangu*, Kinshasa: The Church.
—— (1980), 'Essence de la théologie Kimbanguist', in *Christian Theology and Strategy for Mission*, Geneva: Lutheran World Federation, pp. 224–50.
Diocese of Northern Uganda (1985), *An Experimental Liturgy for Archbishop Janani Luwum Theological College*, Gulu: Catholic Press.
Dirven, P.J. (1970), 'The Maria Legio: The Dynamics of a Breakaway Church among the Luo in East Africa', unpublished DD dissertation, University of Rome.
Donovan, V.J. (1978), *Christianity Rediscovered: An Epistle from the Masai*, London: SCM Press.
Douglas, M. (1970, 1973), *Natural Symbols: Explorations in Cosmology*, Harmondsworth: Penguin.
—— (ed.) (1970), *Witchcraft, Confession and Accusations*, London, New York, Sydney, Toronto and Wellington: Tavistock Publications.
Dourley, J.P. (1975), *Paul Tillich and Bonaventure: An Evaluation of Tillich's Claim to Stand in the Augustinian-Franciscan Tradition*, Leiden: E.J. Brill.
Dreisbach, D.F. (1979), 'Paul Tillich's Doctrine of Religious Symbols', *Encounter*, **37**, 326–43.
Drower, E.S. (1956), *Water into Wine*, London: John Murray.

Ecumenical Review (1967), The Kimbanguist Church in the Congo, **19**, January, 29–36.
Egbulem, N.C. (1996), *The Power of Africentric Celebrations: Inspirations from the Zairean Liturgy*, New York: Crossroad.
Ela, J.-M. (1980, 1986), *African Cry*, New York: Orbis Books.
Erickson, J.H. (1970), 'Leavened and Unleavened: Some Implications of the Schism of 1054', *St Vladimir's Theological Quarterly*, **14**, 155–76.

Fagerberg, D.W. (1992), *What is Liturgical Theology?* Collegeville: Liturgical Press.
Fasholé-Luke, E.W. (1974), 'Ancestor Veneration and the Communion of Saints', in Glasswell, M. K. and Fasholé-Luke, E. W. (eds.), *New Testament Christianity for Africa and the World: Essays in Honour of Harry Sawyerr*, London: SPCK.
Fenwick, J. and Spinks, B. (1995), *Worship in Transition*, Edinburgh: T&T Clark.
Flad, J.M. (1869), *The Falashas of Abyssinia*, London: William Macintosh.
Flannery, A. (1975), *Vatican Council II: The Conciliar and Post Conciliar Documents*, Leomister: Fowler Wright.

Francis, M.R. (2000), *Shape a Circle Ever Wider: Liturgical Inculturation in the United States*, Toronto: Liturgy Training Publications.
Freire, P. (1970, 1993), *Pedagogy of the Oppressed*, London: Penguin.
Furlong, P.J. (1983), 'Catholic Initiatives in the Africanization of Christianity', *Journal of Theology for Southern Africa*, **43**, June, 25–34.

Gallagher, P. (1997), *Clashing Symbols*, London: DLT.
Garrett, P. (1984), 'Fr Alexander Schmemann: A Chronological Bibliography (excluding Book Reviews)', *St Vladimir's Theological Quarterly*, **28**, 11–26.
Garrett, T.S. (1961), *Christian Worship*, London: OUP.
Geertz, C. (1973), *The Interpretation of Cultures*, New York: Basic Books.
Gibellini, R. (ed.), (1994), *Paths of African Theology*, New York: Orbis Books.
Gibson, P. (1999), 'International Anglican Liturgical Consultations: A Review', *Studia Liturgica*, **29** (2), 235–50.
Gibson, P. (2001), *International Anglican Liturgical Consultations: Minutes from Berkeley 2001*, http://www.anglicancommunion.org/documents/liturgy/ialc2001minutes.html#navmap (accessed 10/03/02).
Gitari, D. (1990), 'An Offering from Africa to Anglicanism', *Church Times*, 6 April, p. 10.
—— (ed.) (1994), *Anglican Liturgical Inculturation in Africa: The Kanamai Statement 'African Culture and Anglican Liturgy'*, JLS 28, Bramcote: Grove Books.
Goodwin, L. (1979b), 'Eucharist and Liminality', *AFER*, **21**, 348–52.
Green, L. (1990), *Let's Do Theology*, London: Mowbray.

Haile, G. (1981), 'The Letter of the Archbishops Mika'el and Gabre'el Concerning the Observance of Saturday', *Journal of Semitic Studies*, **26**, Spring, 73–8.
—— (1983), 'On the Identity of Silondis and the Composition of the Anaphora of Mary Ascribed to Heraqos of Benensa', *Orientalia Christiana Periodica*, **49**, 366–89.
Hammerschmidt, E. (1961), *Studies in the Ethiopic Anaphoras*, Berlin: Akademie-Verlag.
—— (1965), 'Jewish Elements in the Cult of the Ethiopian Church', *Journal of Ethiopian Studies*, **3**, 1–12.
Hansen, H.B. (1985), *Mission Church and State in a Colonial Setting: Uganda 1890–1925*, London, Ibadan and Nairobi: Heinemann.
Hastings, A. (1979), *A History of African Christianity, 1950–1975*, Cambridge: CUP.
Hearne, B. (1975), 'The Significance of the Zaire Mass', *AFER*, **17**, 212–20.
—— (1980), 'Christology and Inculturation', *AFER*, **22**.
Hellwig, M. (1982), *Whose Experience Counts in Theological Reflection?* Milwaukee: Marquette University Press.
Hemple, C. and Hammerschmidt, E. (1965), 'Position and Significance of the Sabbath in Ethiopia', *Mundus*, **1**, 305–6.
Hickey, R. (1980), *Africa: The Case for an Auxillary Priesthood*, London: Geoffrey Chapman.
Hillman, E. (1993), *Toward an African Christianity: Inculturation Applied*, Mahwah: Paulist Press.
Hoffman, L.A. (1987), *Beyond the Text: A Holistic Approach to Liturgy*, Bloomington: Indiana University Press.
Holeton, D.R. (ed.), (1990), *Liturgical Inculturation in the Anglican Communion*, JLS 15, Bramcote: Grove Books.
Holland, J. and Henriot, S.J. (1980, 1998), *Social Analysis*, New York: Orbis Books.
Holmes, U.T. (1977), 'Ritual and Social Drama', *Worship*, **51**, 197–213.
Hope, A., Timmel, S. and Hodzi, J. (1984), *Training for Transformation: A Handbook for Community Workers*, Vols. *1–3*, Gweru: Mambo Press.
Hubert, H. and Mauss, M. (1964), *Sacrifice: Its Nature and Function*, London: Cohen and West.

Idowu, E.B. (1965), *Towards an Indigenous Church*, London and Ibadan: OUP.
Iona Community (1988), *The Iona Community Worship Book*, Glasgow: Wild Goose Publications.
Irwin, K.W. (1994), *Context and Text: Method in Liturgical Theology*, Collegeville: Liturgical Press.
Isaac, E. (1968), *The Ethiopian Church*, Boston: Harry Sawyer.
—— (1972), 'An Obscure Component in Ethiopian Church History: An Examination of the Various Theories Pertaining to the Problem of the Origin and Nature of Ethiopian Christianity', *La Museon*, **85**.

John Paul II (1995), *Ecclesia in Africa*, http://www.afrikaworld.net/synod/exhortation.htm (accessed 10/3/02).
Johnson, C.V. (2001), 'The Children's Eucharistic Prayers: A Model of Liturgical Inculturation', *Worship*, **75** (3), May, 209–27.
Joint Liturgical Group (1992), *Confirmation and Re-affirmation of Baptismal Faith*, Norwich: Canterbury Press.
Jones, A.H.M. and Monroe, E. (1935), *A History of Abyssinia*, Oxford: Clarendon Press.
Jungmann, J.A. (1959), *The Early Liturgy*, London: DLT.
—— (1965), *The Place of Christ in Liturgical Prayer*, London and Dublin: Geoffrey Chapman.

Kanamai Statement (1993) in Gitari, D. (ed.) (1994), *Anglican Liturgical Inculturation in Africa: The Kanamai Statement 'African Culture and Anglican Liturgy'*, Bramcote: Grove Books, pp. 33–6.
Kane, M. (1984), 'African Liturgy and the Papal Visit to Zaire', *AFER*, **26**, 246–7.
Kavanagh, A. (1984), *On Liturgical Theology*, New York: Pueblo.
—— (1990), 'Liturgical Inculturation: Looking to the Future', *Studia Liturgica*, **20** (1), 95–107.
Kelfer, R.A. (1976), 'The Unity of the Roman Canon: An Examination of its Unique Structure', *Studia Liturgica*, **11**, 39–58.
Kelly, H.A. (1985), *The Devil at Baptism: Ritual, Theology and Drama*, Ithaca and London: Cornell University Press.
Killen, P. and De Beer, J. (1996), *The Art of Theological Reflection*, New York: Crossroad.
Kinast, R.L. (1996), *Let Ministry Teach*, Collegeville: Liturgical Press.
Kings, G. and Morgan, G. (2001), *Offerings from Kenya to Anglicanism: Liturgical Texts and Contexts including 'A Kenyan Service of Holy Communion'*, JLS 50, Cambridge: Grove Books.
Kolb, D.A. (1984), *Experiential Learning: Experience as the Source of Learning and Development*, New Jersey: Prentice-Hall.
Krow, S. (1961), *99 Questions and Answers on the Church of the Lord Doctrine*, Accra: publisher unknown.
Kunnie, J. (1994), *Models of Black Theology: Issues in Class, Culture, and Gender*, Valley Forge: TPI.

Ladrière, J. (1973), 'The Performativity of Liturgical Language', *Concilium*, **2**, 9, 50–62.
Lambeth Conference (1958), *The Lambeth Conference 1958*, London: SPCK & Seabury.
—— (1988), *The Truth Shall Make You Free*, London: ACC.
Langley, M.S. (1982), 'Charismatics and Liturgy', unpublished paper.
Lathrop, G. (1993), *Holy Things: A Liturgical Theology*, Minneapolis: Fortress Press.
Leach, E.R. (1961, 1966), *Rethinking Anthropology*, London School of Economics Monographs on Social Anthropology 22, University of London: Athlone Press.
Levine, D.N. (1965), *Wax and Gold: Tradition and Innovation in Ethiopian Culture*, Chicago and London: University of Chicago Press.
Lloyd, T. (1990), 'Liturgy for the Urban Deprived', *Studia Liturgica*, **20** (1), 81–94.
Lowther Clarke, W.K. and Harris, C. (1932), *Liturgy and Worship*, London: SPCK.
Lumbala, F. K. (1998), *Celebrating Jesus Christ in Africa: Liturgy and Inculturation*, New York: Orbis Books.

Malinowski, B. (1945), *The Dynamics of Social Change*, New Haven: Yale University Press.
Manicom, P. (1979), *Out of Africa – Kimbanguism*, place of publication unknown: CEM Student Theology Series.
Martey, E. (1993), *African Theology: Inculturation and Liberation*, New York: Orbis Books.
Martin, M.-L. (1971), 'Congolese Church Celebrates', *Pro Veritate*, **10**, January, 4–5.
—— (1974), 'Worship and Spirituality in the Kimbanguist Church', unpublished paper for a seminar at SOAS, 25 Sept 1974.
—— (1975), *Kimbangu: An African Prophet and his Church*, Oxford: Blackwell.
Mathew, G. (1991), 'Whose Culture and Why?' in Stevenson, K. and Spinks, B. (eds.), *The Identity of Anglican Worship*, London: Mowbray, pp. 144–55.
Maxwell, M.E. (1999), *The Rites of Christian Initiation*, New York: Pueblo.
Mbiti, J.S. (1969), *African Religions and Philosophy*, London, Ibadan, and Nairobi: Heinemann.
—— (1971), *New Testament Eschatology in an African Background*, London: OUP.
Mbonigaba, E.G. (1988), 'Indigenization of the Liturgy', in Talley, T.J. (ed.), *A Kingdom of Priests: Liturgical Formation and the People of God*, JLS 5, Grove Books: Nottingham, pp. 39–47.
—— (1994), 'The Indigenization of Liturgy', in Gitari, D. (ed.), *Anglican Liturgical Inculturation in Africa: The Kanamai Statement 'African Culture and Anglican Liturgy'*, JLS 28, Grove Books: Nottingham, pp. 20–32.
McKenna, J.H. (1999), 'Eucharistic Presence: An Invitation to Dialogue', Theological Studies, **60**, 294–317.
Meyers, R.A. (1998), 'One Bread, One Body: Ritual, Language, and Symbolism in the Eucharist', in Holeton, D. R. (ed.), *Our Thanks and Praise: The Eucharist in Anglicanism Today*, Toronto: Anglican Book Centre, pp. 82–98.
Mezirow, J. (1991), *Transformative Dimensions of Adult Learning*, San Francisco: Jossey-Bass.
Mitchell, N. (1994), 'The Amen Corner: Liturgy Encounters Culture – Again', *Worship*, **86** (4), July, 369–76.
Mondin, B. (1963), *The Principle of Analogy in Protestant and Catholic Theology*, The Hague: Martinus Nijhoff.
Morgan, J.G.S. (1997), 'An Analytical, Critical and Comparative Study of Anglican Mission in the Dioceses of Nakuru and Mount Kenya East, Kenya, from 1975', unpublished MPhil thesis, Open University.

Nalunnakkal, G.M. (1998), *New Beings and New Communities: Theological Reflections in a Postmodern Context*, Thiruvalla: KCC/EDTP.
Naussbaum, S. (1984), 'Rethinking Animal Sacrifice: A Response to some Sotho Independent Churches', *Missionalia*, **12**, August, 49–63.
Ndofunsu, D. (1978), 'Role of Prayer in the Kimbanguist Church', in Fasholé-Luke, E., *Christianity in Independent Africa*, London: Rex Collins, pp. 578–96.
Needham, R. (1980), *Reconnaissances*, Toronto, Buffalo and London: University of Toronto Press.
Niebuhr, H.R. (1952), *Christ and Culture*, London: Faber and Faber.

Okot, J. p'Bitek (1980a), *African Religions in Western Scholarship*, Kampala: Uganda Literature Bureau.
—— (1980b), *Religion of the Central Luo*, Kampala: Uganda Literature Bureau.
Ornstein, R.E. (1972), *The Psychology of Consciousness*, New York: Viking Press.
Otto, R. (1917, 1959), *The Idea of the Holy*, Harmondsworth: Pelican.

Pannenberg, W. (1985), *Anthropology in Theological Perspective*, trans. M.J. O'Connell, Philadelphia: Westminster Press.
Paul VI (1975), *Evangelii Nuntiandi*, London: Catholic Truth Society.

Pawlikowski, J.T. (1971-2), 'Judaic Spirit of the Ethiopian Orthodox Church: A Case Study in Religious Acculturation', *Journal of Religion in Africa*, **4**, 178-99.
Peel, J.D.Y. (1968), *Aladura: A Religious Movement among the Yoruba*, London: OUP.
Pickstock, C. (1998), *After Writing: On the Liturgical Consummation of Philosophy*, Oxford: Blackwell.
Pieris, A. (1988), *An Asian Theology of Liberation*, Edinburgh: T&T Clark.
Pitts, W.F. (1993), *Old Ship of Zion: The Afro-Baptist Ritual in the African Diaspora*, Oxford: OUP.
Pobee, J.S. (1976), *Religion in a Pluralistic Society*, Leiden: E.J. Brill.
—— (1983), 'African Spiritualtiy', in Wakefield, G. S. (ed.), *A Dictionary of Christian Spirituality*, London: SCM Press, pp. 5-8.
Power, D.N. (1984), *Unsearchable Riches: The Symbolic Nature of Liturgy*, New York: Pueblo.
—— (1992), 'Sacrament: Event Eventing', in Downey, M. and Fragomeni, R. (eds.), *A Promise of Presence*, Washington: Pastoral Press, pp. 271-99.
—— (1994), 'Postmodern Approaches', *Theological Studies*, **55**, 648-93.
Putnam, L.J. (1965), 'Tillich on the Sacraments', *Theology and Life*, **8**, 108-16.

Quevedo-Bosch, J. (1994), 'The Eucharistic Species and Inculturation', in Holeton, D.R. (ed.), *Revising the Eucharist: Groundwork for the Anglican Communion*, JLS 27, Nottingham: Grove Books, pp. 48-9.

Rahner, K. (1966), *Theological Investigations Vol. 4: More Recent Writings*, London: DLT.
Ricoeur, P. (1971, ET 1981), 'The Model of the Text: Meaningful Action Considered as Text', in Thompson, J.B. (ed. and trans.) *Paul Ricoeur: Hermeneutics and the Human Sciences*, Cambridge: CUP.
Roberts, A. and Donaldson, J. (eds.), (1957), *Writings of the Ante-Nicene Fathers Vol. 5*, Grand Rapids: Eerdmans.
Roberts, P. (1999), *Alternative Worship in the Church of England*, W155, Cambridge: Grove Books.
Robins, C.E. (1983), '"Tukutendereza": A Study of Social and Sectarian Withdrawal in the "Balokole" Revival of Uganda', Unpublished PhD, Xerox University Microfilms.
Rowbotham, A.H. (1942), *Missionary and Mandarin: The Jesuits at the Court of China*, Berkley and Los Angeles: University of California Press.
Rowe, W.L. (1968), *Religious Symbols and God: A Philosophical Study of Tillich's Theology*, Chicago and London: University of Chicago Press.
Russell, J.K. (1966), *Men without God? A Study of the Impact of the Christian Message in the North of Uganda*, London: Highway Press.

Sawyerr, H. (1968), *Creative Evangelism: Towards a New Christian Encounter with Africa*, London: Lutterworth Press.
Schineller, P. (1990), *A Handbook of Inculturation*, New York: Paulist Press.
—— (1992a), 'Inculturation and Syncretism: What is the Real Issue?' *International Bulletin of Missionary Research*, **16**, 50-53.
Schmemann, A. (1963), 'Theology and Liturgical Tradition', in Shepherd, M. H. (ed.), *Worship in Scripture and Tradition*, New York: OUP, pp. 165-78.
Schmemann, A. (1965), *The World as Sacrament*, London: DLT.
—— (1966a), *Introduction to Liturgical Theology*, Leighton Buzzard: Faith Press.
—— (1971), 'Theology or Ideology?', in Preston, R. H. (ed.), *Technology and Social Justice*, London: SCM Press, pp. 226-36.
—— (1972a), 'Liturgy and Theology', *Greek Orthodox Theological Review*, **17**, 86-100.
—— (1972b), 'Russian Theology: 1920-1972: An Introductory Survey, *St Vladimir's Theological Quarterly*, **16**, 172-94.
—— (1972c), 'Worship in a Secular Age', *St Vladimir's Theological Quarterly*, **16**, 3-16.

—— (1973a), *For the Life of the World: Sacraments and Orthodoxy*, Crestwood, NY: St Vladimir's Seminary Press.
—— (1973b), 'On the Question of Liturgical Practices', *St Vladimir's Theological Quarterly*, **17**, 227–38.
—— (1985), 'Liturgy and Eschatology', *Sobornost*, **7** (1), 6–14.
Schön, D.A. (1983), *The Reflective Practitioner*, London: Temple Smith.
Schreiter, R.J. (1985), *Constructing Local Theologies*, London: SCM Press.
—— (ed.), (1991), *Faces of Jesus in Africa*, London: SCM Press.
—— (1999), *The New Catholicity: Theology between the Global and the Local*, New York: Orbis Books.
—— (2000), *The New Catholicity*, New York: Orbis Books.
Shorter, A. (1970), 'An African Eucharistic Prayer', *AFER*, **12**, 143–8.
—— (1973a), *African Culture and the Christian Church*, London and Dublin: Geoffrey Chapman.
—— (1973b), 'Three more Eucharistic Prayers', *AFER*, **15**, 152–60.
—— (1975a), *African Christian Theology: Adaptation or Incarnation*, London: Geoffrey Chapman.
—— (1975b), *Prayer in the Religious Traditions of Africa*, Nairobi: OUP.
—— (1977), 'Liturgical Creativity in East Africa', *AFER*, **5**, 258–67.
—— (1988), *Toward a Theology of Inculturation*, London: Geoffrey Chapman.
Sperber, D. (1974, 1975), *Rethinking Symbolism*, Cambridge: CUP.
Stevenson, K. (1986), 'Lex Orandi and Lex Credendi – Strange Bed-fellows? Some Reflections on Worship and Doctrine', *Scottish Journal of Theology*, **39**, 225–41.
Stevenson, K. and Spinks, B. (eds.), (1991), *The Identity of Anglican Worship*, London: Mowbray.
Stone, H.W. and Duke, J.O. (1996), *How to Think Theologically*, Minneapolis: Fortress Press.
Stott, J.R.W. (1964), *Confess Your Sins: The Way of Reconciliation*, London: Hodder and Stoughton.
Stuart, E. (1992), *Daring to Speak Love's Name: A Gay and Lesbian Prayer Book*, London: Hamish Hamilton.
Sweasey, P. (1997), *From Queer to Eternity*, London and Washington: Cassell.

Taizé Community (1998), *Prayer for Each Day*, London: Cassell.
Talley, T.J. (1994), 'Eucharistic Prayers, Past, Present, and Future', in Holeton, D.R. (ed.), *Revising the Eucharist: Groundwork for the Anglican Communion*, JLS 27, Nottingham: Grove Books, pp. 6–19.
Tarrant, I. (1999), 'Anglican Liturgical Reform in Congo/Zaire', unpublished paper, Windsor: St George's House.
Taylor, J.V. (1963), *The Primal Vision*, London: SCM Press.
The Minority Rights Group (1989), *Uganda: Report No. 66*, London: The Minority Rights Group.
Thompson, P.E.S. (1974), 'The Anatomy of Sacrifice: A Preliminary Investigation', in Glasswell, M. K. and Fasholé-Luke E. W. (eds.), *New Testament Christianity for Africa and the World: Essays in Honour of Harry Sawyerr*, London: SPCK, pp. 19–35.
Thurian, M. and Wainwright, G. (1983), *Baptism and Eucharist: Ecumenical Convergence in Celebration*, Grand Rapids: Eerdmans; Geneva: WCC.
Tillich, P. (1951), *The Protestant Era*, London: Nisbet.
—— (1953), *Systematic Theology 1*, Welwyn: Nisbet.
—— (1955), 'Theology and Symbolism', in Johnson, F. E. (ed.), *Religious Symbolism*, New York and London: Harper Brothers.
—— (1957a), *Dynamics of Faith*, London: Allen and Unwin.
—— (1957b), *Systematic Theology 2*, London: SCM Press.
—— (1959), *Theology of Culture*, New York: OUP.
—— (1966), 'The Religious Symbol', in Dillistone, F. W. (ed.), *Myth and Symbol*, London: SPCK.
Toren, C. (1983), 'Thinking Symbols: A Critique of Sperber', *Man*, **18**, 260–68.
Tovey, P. (1988a), 'The Symbol of the Eucharist in the African Context', unpublished M Phil thesis, University of Nottingham.

—— (1988b), *Inculturation of the Eucharist in Africa*, JLS 7, Cambridge: Grove Books.
Turner, H.W. (1965), 'Pagan Features in West African Independent Churches', *Practical Anthropology*, 12, 145-51.
—— (1967a), *History of An African Independent Church Vol. 1: The Church of the Lord (Aladura)*, London: OUP.
—— (1967b), *History of An African Independent Church Vol. 2: The Life and Faith of the Church of the Lord (Aladura)*, London: OUP.
Turner, P. (1971), 'The Wisdom of the Fathers and the Gospel of Christ: Some Notes on Christian Adaptation in Africa', *Journal of Religion in Africa*, 1, 45-68.
Turner, V. (1967), *The Forest of Symbols: Aspects of Ndembu Ritual*, New York: Cornell University Press.
—— (1968), *The Drums of Affliction: A Study of Religious Processes among the Ndembu of Zambia*, Oxford: OUP.
—— (1969), *The Ritual Process: Structure and Anti-Structure*, New York: Cornell University Press.
—— (1972a), 'Passages, Margins and Poverty: Religious Symbols of Communitas', *Worship*, 46, 390-412.
—— (1972b), 'Passages, Margins and Poverty: Part 2', *Worship*, 46, 482-94.
—— (1976), 'Ritual, Tribal and Catholic', *Worship*, 50, 504-26.
—— and Turner, E. (1978), *Image and Pilgrimage in Christian Culture*, Oxford: Blackwell.

Udiodem, S.I., Makozi, A.O. and Thompson, D.B. (1996), *Pope John Paul on Inculturation*, Lanham: University Press of America.
Ullendorff, E. (1968), *Ethiopia and the Bible*, London: OUP.
Uzukwu, E.E. (1979), 'The "All-Africa Eucharistic Prayer" – a Critique', *AFER*, 21, 338-47.
—— (1980a), 'Igbo/Nigerian Eucharistic Prayer', *AFER*, 72, 17-22.
—— (1980b), 'Food and Drink in Africa and the Christian Eucharist', *AFER*, 72, 370-85.
—— (1982), *Liturgy, Truly Christian, Truly African*, Spearhead 74, Eldoret: Gaba Publications.
—— (1991), 'African Symbols and Christian Liturgical Celebration', *Worship*, 62 (2), March, 98-111.

Vagaggini, C. (1976), *Theological Dimensions of the Liturgy: A General Treatise on the Theology of the Liturgy*, Collegeville: Liturgical Press.
Van Gennep (1908, 1960), *The Rites of Passage*, London: Routhedge and Kegan Paul.
Vellian, J. (1975), *The Romanization Tendency*, Kottayam: KP Press.
Vundla, T.J. (1990), 'Example 2: African Ancestors', in Holeton, D.R. (ed.), *Liturgical Inculturation in the Anglican Communion*, JLS 15, Nottingham: Grove Books, pp. 32-6.

Wainwright, G. (1971), 'Theological Reflections on "The Catechism Concerning the Prophet Simon Kimbangu" of 1970', *Orita*, 5, 18-35.
—— (1980), *Doxology: The Praise of God in Worship, Doctrine and Life*, London: Epworth Press.
Walsh, C. (1980), 'Liturgy and Symbolism: A Map', in Stevenson, K.W. (ed.), *Symbolism and the Liturgy 1*, Grove Liturgical Study 23, Nottingham: Grove Books.
Warren, M.A.C. (1954), *Revival: An Enquiry*, London: publisher unknown.
Wigan, B. (1962), *The Liturgy in English*, London: OUP.
Wiles, M. (1967), *The Making of Christian Doctrine*, Cambridge: CUP.
Wilkinson, J. (1981, revised edn), *Egeria's Travels to the Holy Land*, Jerusalem and Warminster: Ariel Publishing House and Aris and Phillips.
Williams, R. (2000), *On Christian Theology*, Oxford: Blackwell.
Wilson, B.R. (1973), *Magic and the Millennium: A Sociological Study of Religious Movements of Protest among Tribal and Third World Peoples*, London: Heinemann.
Winslow, J.C. (ed.) (1920), *The Eucharist in India: A Plea for a Distinctive Liturgy for the Indian Church with a Suggested Form*, London: Longmans, Green.

Winter, M.T. (1987), *Woman Prayer Woman Song*, Oak Park: Meyer Stone Books.
Woolley, B.D. (1913), *The Bread of the Eucharist*, London: Mowbrays.

Yarnold, E. (1971), *The Awe Inspiring Rites of Initiation*, Slough: St Paul's Publications.

Zimmerman, J.A. (1999), *Liturgy and Hermeneutics*, Collegeville: Liturgical Press.

Name Index

Abana, G.N. 89, 90, 92, 93
Amusan, S. 53, 143
Arbuckle, G.A. 1, 34

Bevans, S.B. 2, 4, 5, 6
Bishop, E. 76, 88
Bowen, R. 41, 51
Brown, L. 2, 140
Buchanan, C.O. 41, 131, 132, 133, 139, 141
Budge, Sir E.A.W. 59, 60, 67

Calvin, J. 28, 31
Chauvet, L-M. 8, 15–22, 29, 30, 147
Chupungco, A. 1, 3, 5, 108–110, 147
Clarke, S. 3, 5
Cone, J. 5, 6, 157
Cranmer, T. 36, 88, 130, 142
Cyprian 44, 46, 100
Cyril of Jerusalem 69, 76, 77, 88

Daoud, M. 57, 60, 61, 65, 66, 67, 68, 70, 71, 76
Diagienda, K.J. 98–100
Douglas, M. 8, 18, 33–36, 41, 55, 75, 104–107, 116
Durkheim, E. 1, 63, 72, 75

Flannery, A. 113–115, 119
Furlong, P.J. 125, 126

Gallagher, P. 2, 115
Gibson, P. 47, 135, 138, 138, 140
Gitari, D. 3, 136, 140, 142

Hammerschmidt, E. 57, 58, 60, 63
Hearne, B. 47, 53, 54, 55, 126
Holeton, D. 135, 136
Holmes, U.T. 42, 43

Idowu, E.B. 47, 111

John Chrysostom 76, 77, 78
John Paul II 4, 5, 119
Jungmann, J.A. 77, 110

Kane, M. 128, 129
Kavanagh, A. 2, 25, 29, 31, 150, 151, 152, 156, 159, 160
Kimbangu, S. 13, 79, 80, 92, 96–103, 105, 106
Kings, G. 5, 50, 141, 142, 148, 150
Kolb, D. 153, 154–155, 157

Leach, E.R. 63, 72, 74, 75
Lumbala, F.K. 3, 47, 50, 124, 150

Martey, E. 6, 157
Martin, M-L. 96, 97, 100–102
Mbiti, J. 39, 46, 49, 51, 54, 74, 79, 88
Meyers, R. 47, 137
Morgan, G. 5, 50, 141, 142, 148, 150

Needham, R. 85, 100

Orimolade 81, 89, 90, 92
Otto, R. 56, 75, 77, 78

Pieris A. 2, 6
Pobee, J.S. 50, 52, 105
Rahner, K. 8, 17, 19, 23, 28, 50
Ricoeur, P. 17, 135, 149
Rowe, W.L. 2, 10, 11, 15

Sawyerr, H. 49, 50, 53, 74
Schineller, P. 123, 142
Schmemann, A. 8, 22–32, 150 151, 159
Schreiter, R.J. 112, 129, 135, 147, 148
Shorter, A. 2, 48, 49, 55, 117, 118, 125
Sperber, D. 34, 37, 39, 41–43, 56, 61, 110

Spinks, B. 133, 152
Stevenson, K. 25, 133

Tarrant, I. 5, 144, 145
Theodore of Mopsuestia 62, 69
Tillich, P. 1, 9–15, 23, 26, 29, 30, 46, 104, 136, 157
Tovey, P. 1, 2, 135, 140, 141, 148, 157
Tucker, Bp. 38, 45, 140
Turner, H.W. 5, 81–85, 91
Turner, V. 8, 10, 21, 33, 36, 37–41, 41, 43–55, 61, 63, 72, 74, 75, 105, 116, 117

Ullendorff, E. 51, 58, 59, 60
Uzukwu, E.E. 45, 47, 103, 117–120, 124, 127–129

Vagaggini, C. 111, 115

Van Gennep 40, 63, 72,

Winslow, J. 5, 139
Woolley, B.D. 69, 76

Yarnold, E. 69, 76

For Product Safety Concerns and Information please contact our EU
representative GPSR@taylorandfrancis.com
Taylor & Francis Verlag GmbH, Kaufingerstraße 24, 80331 München, Germany

www.ingramcontent.com/pod-product-compliance
Lightning Source LLC
Chambersburg PA
CBHW052125300426
44116CB00010B/1789